The Ultimate Microwave Cookbook

This 1986 edition published by WestWind Publishers Inc.
2285 Dunwin Drive, Suite 18
Mississauga, Ontario, Canada L5L 3S3

Photography by Ashley Barber
and Norman Nicholls.

Copyright © 1985 by Bay Books

Copyright © 1984 by Yvonne Webb (Microwave Cooking for One)

ISBN 0-373-15108-X

Printed in the U.S.A.

The Ultimate Microwave Cookbook

WestWind Publishers Inc.

Contents

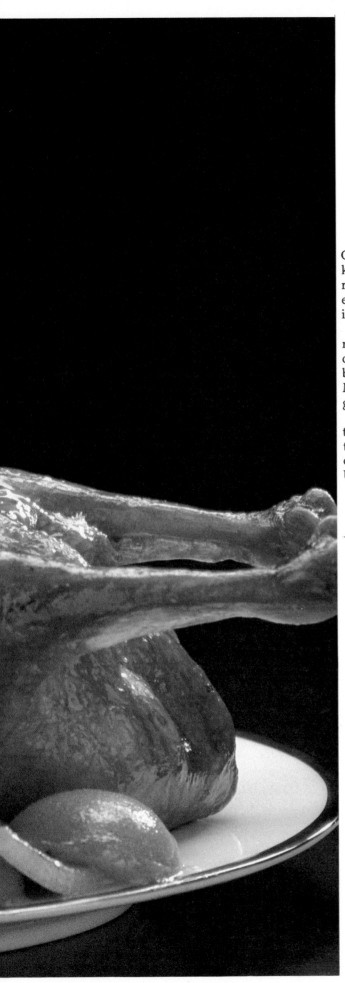

All about the Ultimate Microwave Cookbook

Over the last 25 years, microwave ovens have revolutionised kitchens in homes, restaurants and fastfood outlets. The reasons for the boom are obvious: microwave ovens are quick, efficient, compact, clean and above all, allow the cook to work in a cool and comfortable environment.

Today's microwave ovens are even more flexible. There are models to suit every kitchen, every requirement. We can choose from 500 to 750 watt units which boast variable power, browners, computer memories and convection cookers. Microwave ovens are even available with combination gas/electric or electric models. The options are enormous.

This book is for those cooks who want to make the most of their culinary skills using their microwave oven. Divided into three sections with over 350 recipes for all occasions, and over 150 color photographs and step-by-step recipes the Ultimate Microwave Cookbook is simply that.

Roast Apricot Duck

The Microwave Story

The microwave oven is here to stay. This modern appliance is revolutionizing kitchens and cooking as the sales figures show. It won't be too long before there's one in every home as we all discover how easy they are to use and just how naturally they fit into our busy lives. Microwave cooking is fast, efficient and economical. Microwave meals are delicious. In fact you can prepare any and every meal in your microwave — breakfast, lunch and dinner — as well as quick snacks, meals in moments and even elegant dinner parties.

This introductory section on microwave cooking has been prepared by the following home economists and microwave specialists: Jane Aspinwall, Mary-Lou Arnold, Douglas Marsland and Sheridan Rogers.

What are Microwaves?

A microwave is an electromagnetic wave within a particular frequency band. It is similar to electromagnetic waves found in radio, light and heatwaves. A microwave is generated by electricity passing through a special vacuum tube called a magnetron. Microwaves are short (hence the name 'micro'), high frequency waves which travel in virtually straight lines, and can be reflected, transmitted and absorbed. It is these special qualities which enable them to be used in ovens to cook food.

The Microwave Oven

Microwave ovens take advantage of microwave energy by trapping the waves which are then absorbed by the food. Once absorbed, the energy is converted into heat.

When you switch on the power, the electricity is converted to microwaves by a special tube called a **magnetron** — the heart of the microwave oven. (This only produces microwave when the oven is switched on, the door properly shut and the timer set.) A **wave guide** directs the microwaves into the ove cavity. Since the waves don't penetrate metal, they bounce of

How Microwaves Cook Food

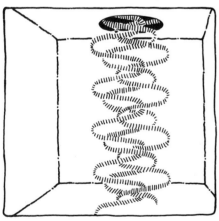

1. Microwaves are directed into the oven cavity by the wave guide.

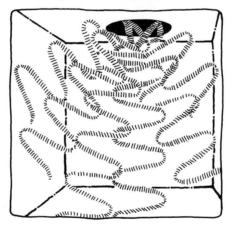

2. The stirrer fan distributes the waves. Some models also have a turntable to rotate food while cooking.

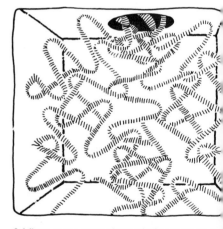

3. Microwaves cannot penetrate metal, so are randomly deflected off oven walls. This promotes even cooking.

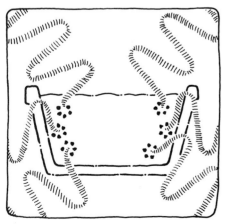

4. The waves penetrate the food to a depth of about 2 inches.

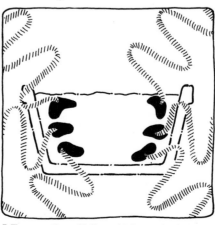

5. They produce friction which creates heat which cooks the food.

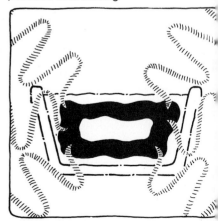

6. Heat spreads to the center by conduction. Stirring food or turning it encourages even cooking.

e metal of the interior walls and the fine mesh door screen
enetrating the food from all angles. With some models the
aves are distributed by a fan-like **stirrer**; others have a
rntable which rotates the food through either 180 or 360
egrees; some of the newer models have both.

Microwave cooking offers an exciting new approach to food
eparation. You can cook and serve meals in the same dish,
cook and eat off the one plate. China, paper, plastic and
eat-resistant glass can all be used for cooking or reheating in
e microwave oven. Recipes are a little different, too. Times
e shorter and less liquid is used.

In traditional conventional ovens the food slowly absorbs
e heat from the oven or element. The food gets hot and so
oes the kitchen and the cook. In microwave cookery, because
e heat is inside the food, the kitchen stays cool, likewise the
ook.

The microwaves penetrate the food from all angles causing
e water and fat molecules to vibrate. This produces friction
hich creates the heat which cooks the food. Because the heat
inside the food, it keeps cooking once you take it out of the
ren. In fact standing time is an important part of the
chnique of microwave cooking: it completes the cooking.

Microwaves are odorless and tasteless. No residue remains
the food at all. In fact microwaved meals can be especially
elicious and nutritious because the food is cooked quickly
ith all the flavor retained — not boiled or baked away.

Microwave breakfast with bacon, egg,
sausages, tomato and a hot cup of coffee

Microwave Safety

Microwave ovens are among the safest of household
ppliances if used in accordance with the manufacturers',
structions. They are manufactured to meet stringent safety
andards.

Manufacturers have gone to great lengths to make sure that
icrowaves stay inside the ovens. Safety devices, such as the
oor seal, are built-in to prevent any energy leakage. As soon
s the door is opened the microwave energy stops. The
llowing simple precautions are important.
Do not try to operate the oven with the door open.
Do not place any object between the front face of the oven
and the door or allow any dirt or cleanser residue to
build up.
Never try to operate the oven if it does not seem to be
working properly.

The Advantages of Microwave Cooking

Time   Microwave cooking can save time. Superb meals
or the family can be prepared in moments and that meat
ou forgot to take out of the freezer can be quickly
efrosted.

Economy   Microwave cooking uses less energy.
ecause the energy output is less, the oven uses less
ower. And of course foods cook faster and unless you are
sing the browning dish, there's no preheating. Savings in
nergy and time mean savings with the utility bill.

Convenience   Time, defrosting, reheating and shorter
ooking times make the microwave oven ideal for today's
busy lifestyle. Meals can be prepared, cooked, frozen and
reheated all in the same dish then served piping hot.

Nutrition   Microwave ovens don't boil all the goodness
away. The speed of cooking plus the small amount of
liquid required mean super-nutritious meals. Vegetables
retain their vitamins and minerals. In addition, the color
of cooked vegetables is excellent and food presentation is
thus enhanced. For many people the microwave is
worthwhile just for cooking vegetables.

Diet   Because nutritious, low calorie foods can be
ready in minutes, the temptation to reach for fattening
snacks 'while waiting for dinner' is greatly reduced.

Cool cooking   The microwave is particularly useful
during the hot summer months. No more slaving over that
hot stove or in a steam-filled kitchen. Microwave ovens do
not generate heat. All the energy produced is absorbed by
the food. The kitchen remains cool and comfortable.

Quick cleanups   Food does not stick or bake onto
casserole dishes in the microwave which makes cleaning
up much easier. And because fewer dishes are used (one
dish can go from freezer to oven to table) there's often less
washing up. The ovens themselves just need a quick
wipeoff to clean.

Which Microwave?

Buying a microwave is much the same as purchasing
another major household appliance. In making your
selection, whether buying your first or updating an earlier
model, consider your requirements and look carefully at all
the options.

What wattage?
Power output is all important. The small ovens with lower
wattage are popular but less versatile. They are light, easy
to move for cleaning, and suitable for small kitchens,

campers or even to take outdoors for pool parties or barbecues where food may need to be reheated. However, meals may take a little longer to cook and some of your larger casseroles or the useful microwave browning dish may not fit in the oven cavity.

In the higher powered ovens, food cooks quickly and the larger ovens will readily accommodate a range of casseroles including every size of browning dish.

Size

Oven capacity varies. Actual measurements can be deceptive as to the space available, especially if there is a turntable. Before investing, try out your favorite casserole dishes. Do they fit? Will they rotate on the turntable without touching the sides? An additional convenience with larger units is that you should be able simply to open the door and stir food without having to take the dish out.

Variable controls

Variable power controls allow you to prepare a wide range of foods very easily. Unfortunately, different manufacturers call the settings by different names, so you really need a basic guide as to the settings and their function. Check your instruction manual. In this book we use the following terms. We also include a basic guide to help you decide which setting on your microwave would be appropriate.

High	full power for quick cooking, vegetables, fish, meats, sauteing and preheating browning dish
Medium high	for roasting and reheating
Medium	for baking cakes, bread, soups and stews
Medium low	for slow cooking or braising tougher cuts of meat
Defrost	for thawing frozen foods without cooking
Low	for small amounts of food that must be cooked slowly
Warm	for keeping food warm

Turntables

Turntables rotate the dish to ensure even cooking. Although this feature saves having to open the door and turn food frequently, the turntable itself takes up space and limits the size of dish that will fit in the oven. With some ovens you cannot use a temperature probe with the turntable. On other models you can immobilize the turntable. Some turntables can be removed for ease of cleaning.

Temperature controls

Temperature probes are inserted into the meat to measure its internal temperature and 'tell' the oven when to switch off. Some probes are designed to swivel so that they can be used with turntables.

Sensor controls let you cook automatically without having to check anxiously for doneness. The device 'senses' the temperature and automatically switches the oven off when the food is cooked.

Timer

All models have a timer — time is the essence of microwave cookery — and a buzzer or bell to let you know when cooking time has finished.

Browning element

The built-in browning element is just like the conventional broiler. If you already have a good broiler and/or you are planning to buy a browning casserole or dish then this feature may simply mean you are doubling up unnecessarily.

Combination ovens

The appliance for those who need both microwave oven and a new oven! Combination ovens provide the speed and efficiency of microwave plus the traditional benefits of conventional cooking with the turn of a switch.

A Microwave in your Kitchen

If you are like most people with a new microwave oven, you rush to open the box, put the oven on the table, plug in and switch on. Don't. It is essential to carry out a thorough post-delivery check and to read the instructions carefully.

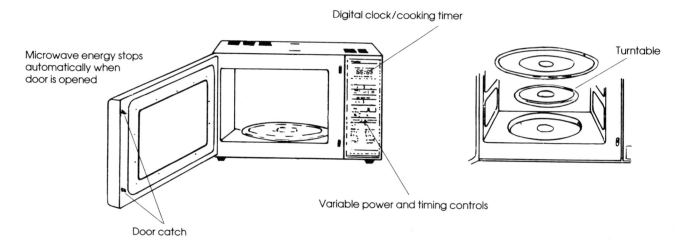

Digital clock/cooking timer

Turntable

Microwave energy stops automatically when door is opened

Variable power and timing controls

Door catch

and sit down to fill in the warranty card while you recover your equilibrium. Keep your instruction booklet nearby so that you can refer to it just as often as you need to.

Installing your microwave

Microwave ovens need no special installation as they simply operate off normal household power supply. Place the oven on a strong, stable, level countertop or table away from the sink and the gas or electric stove. For maximum operating efficiency, microwave ovens need breathing space. In general allow about 2 in above the oven and 4 to 6 in at the back and sides. Do not remove the feet or place books or other objects over the air vents (they must be kept clear). Microwave ovens can be built in, but remember that doors open to the left and observe the manufacturer's ventilation requirements.

Using your microwave for the first time

First use is something that the manufacturer will discuss in detail. The two most important steps, however, are:
1. Read the instruction book carefully.
2. Do not operate the oven empty.
The standard first-time test is boiling water. Having done this make a cup of tea or coffee (with your boiling water)

Grasshopper Torte *(see recipe)*
cooked in a heat-resistant glass pie dish

Which Dish?

Microwave-safe cookware

There's no need to rush out and buy special cookware for your microwave oven. The kitchen cupboard is probably full of bowls and casserole dishes which are ideal — Pyrex, Corningware, china bowls, plates and casseroles, for example. Even ordinary items such as paper or plastic plates, wooden or wicker baskets can be used if you just want to warm food. For cooking, utensils need to be tough enough, however, to withstand extremely hot food or boiling water: with microwave, the food heats the dish. If food cooks or reheats in less than 5 minutes, however, the cookware may keep quite cool.

Microwave-safe materials include heatproof glass, glass ceramic, earthenware, stoneware, china (without a metal trim) and even porcelain (but don't use your finest). If you have a browning element, utensils must be nonflammable.

Plastic food storage containers or supermarket packages are fine just for defrosting but tend to melt or distort once cooking temperatures are reached. Do not use plastic containers, like ice cream buckets and take-out food containers, in the microwave.

Paper plates are useful for heating dry foods, and paper napkins or paper towels for absorbing moisture.

Special microwave containers are available for freezer-to-table meals. You can mix, cook, freeze, defrost, reheat and serve all in the one dish.

Wooden or wicker baskets can be popped into the oven to heat up bread, but will crack if left in too long.

To find out whether or not a favorite dish is microwave safe, try this simple test. Place the dish in the oven on high with 5 fl oz of water for 2 minutes (china, pottery) or 20 seconds (glass, plastic). If the water heats but not the dish, then it is safe to use.

Shape is important in microwave cookery. Round dishes or ring dishes with straight (not bowl-shaped) sides give best results. If a recipe states a specific size or shape, use it. Cooking times can change when you use square or rectangular dishes and food can overcook at the corners with microwaves penetrating from both sides. Shallow dishes are best for foods like vegetables or portions of fish or meat. High-sided dishes are preferable for cooking rice, pasta, soups, stews and casseroles. Do not cook using a container with a restricted opening, such as a cordial or salad oil bottle.

What about metal?

Microwaves can't penetrate metal and metal can cause arcing if it comes in contact with the oven sides. Metal pots and pans and aluminum trays deeper than $1^3/_{16}$ inch form a barrier that microwaves can't pass through and reflect the energy back into the oven.

Decorative metallic trims can also cause arcing. Aluminum foil can be used to shield, reheat and even cook foods in a microwave oven. But certain rules must be followed. Check what the manufacturer recommends in your instruction book.

Basic Equipment for Successful Microwave Cooking

Item	Use
8 x 8 inch square dish	Cakes, whole corn cobs, confections, vegetables, lasagne.
Roasting dish and rack	Pork, beef, lamb, chicken, duck, turkey and all roasts.
Browning casserole dish	Broiling chops and steaks, stews and curries, baking biscuits, frying seafood, crumbed foods, eggs and small quantities of chips.
2½ quart casserole with lid	Soups, pasta, rice, casseroles, corned beef, vegetables, chowders.
Casserole lid	Pies, quiches, vegetables, omelets cheese cakes and for cooking small quantities of food.
Ring dish	Baked custards, breads, biscuit rings, cakes, whole potatoes.
Flan ring	Cheesecake, fruit flans, quiches, vegetables.
Loaf dish	Meat loaves, loaf cakes, breads.
Flat round platter	Fruit or savory pizzas, vegetable platters, sweet and savory cookies, fruit flambe.
Various sized mixing bowls 2 or 3½ pint glass measures	Melting, blanching, sauteing. Savory sauces, custards, reheating.
Souffle dish	Cakes, souffles, reheating soups, casseroles.

The browning dish

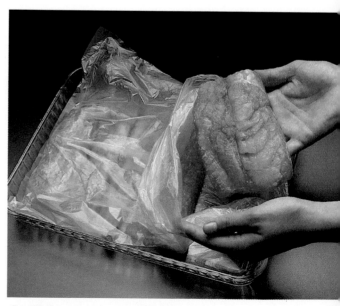

Cod fillets cooked in a plastic bag

Cover Story

Covering food with a lid or plastic wrap holds in steam keeping the food moist, tender and full of flavor. Loose coverings will also prevent splatters and small pieces of aluminum foil can be used to shield protruding angles or edges of roasts or poultry to prevent overcooking. You can also shield foods with a sauce to keep them moist.

Item	Use
Plastic wrap and plastic bags	Use recognized brand names for covering seafood, sauces and vegetables when no casserole lid is available. Lids are better if you need to turn or stir food during cooking. Plastic oven bags are microwave-safe so long as they are pierced. Tie bags with string — not metal ties. Plastic storage bags should be removed if you are heating food. Do not use plastic wrap and bags when cooking roasts or broiling as the plastic can melt. Do not completely seal cake and bread dishes with plastic wrap as condensation can result.
Wax and paper towels	Reheating dry foods such as cakes and breads. Lining dishes and covering food to prevent splatters. Absorbent paper allows steam to escape, stops fat splattering and absorbs excess moisture. Waxproof paper is less absorbent, provides a loose cover for preventing splatters and is useful as a lining.
Aluminum foil	When baking cakes. As long as the density of the food is greater than the amount of aluminum foil, it can be used on the edges of roasts, cakes and drumsticks. During standing time partially cover roasts so that heat is retained. Aluminum foil liners can also be used to prevent the sides of a fruit cake from drying out. Use aluminum foil to cover the cooked portion of a cake when the center is still moist.

Practical Microwave

Standing Time

If you study microwave recipes or timecharts you will notice that 'standing time' is as important as 'cooking time'. With microwave cookery you can't stop cooking simply by taking the food out of the oven because the heat is inside the food. Standing time finishes the cooking. The heat cooks the center of the food by conduction — a fuel saving bonus! Food can remain covered and left to stand in the oven on warm or on the counter.

With small items of food, standing time is a matter of minutes. Poultry or roasts of meat, however, require 15–20 minutes — or half the cooking time. These large items should be wrapped in aluminum foil for standing time to retain their heat. During this time the internal temperature will increase by 16–20°F, thus completing the cooking cycle. Standing time gives you time to cook vegetables and sauces.

Even Cooking

The following simple techniques for microwave cooking make sure that the food cooks evenly in the oven.

Arranging and spacing Place individual portions such as potatoes or chops an equal distance apart in the dish and in a single layer. Never stack foods for microwave cooking. With drumsticks, chops or similar portions, make sure that the thicker part faces the outside of the dish where it will receive the most microwave energy.

Stirring Stir food to spread and redistribute heat during cooking. As the outside will heat first, stir from the outside towards the center. Rotate foods which can't be stirred — cakes and breads, for example — to prevent one side or corner from overcooking.

Turning Many recipes tell you to turn foods — usually about half way through the cooking time. This makes sure that top and bottom cook evenly.

Arrange food in layers

Piercing

Do not bake potatoes, tomatoes or apples unless the skins have been pierced. Be sure that all foods with an outer skin or membrane (this includes eggs) are pierced to allow steam to escape during cooking. Similarly, do not cook vegetables in a plastic bag or airtight container unless the bag or container has been pierced.

Pierce vegetables to let out steam

Is It Cooked?

For the novice, it can sometimes be a little tricky to determine if the food is cooked or not because some look different (usually paler) from conventionally cooked foods. A wise rule of thumb is to always undercook, to be patient and let food stand. If the dish is not cooked to your liking after standing time, you can always return it for further cooking. Undercooking at least gives you a choice. Once overcooked, there is little you can do for most foods. They taste spoiled and are usually tough.

Personal preference affects the degree of readiness to a certain extent. Some people prefer their foods underdone, so cooking times have to be adjusted to taste.

Many of the tests for 'doneness' or 'readiness' are the standard ones. However, some microwave ovens offer special features to take away the guesswork and help you determine whether or not food is cooked.

Probes are inserted in the meat or poultry which is cooked until a preset temperature is reached. They are specially constructed for use in microwave ovens. For an accurate reading, insert probe into center of food away from fat or bone. (Do not use a regular meat thermometer in the oven while operating. Most meat thermometers contain metal. Special meat thermometers are available for use in microwave ovens.)

Electronic sensors inside the oven 'sense' the temperature. The oven switches off when the preset temperature is reached.

Recipe times and time charts   When you start using your microwave, it is wise to follow cooking and standing times. As most cooking times given are only approximate, use your eyes and nose — if you can smell the food, then it is wise to check, as this usually indicates that it is done or ready to be stirred. Remember, the denser the food, the longer it will take to cook: for example, a 2 lb roast will take longer to cook than 2 lb of diced meat in a casserole. Foods that can be stirred will cook more quickly than foods which are whole.

After a while you will become an expert in timing foods in your microwave oven and learn how to adapt your favorite recipes to this new way of cooking.

Testing for 'Doneness'
When testing for 'doneness', always allow for the recommended standing time.

Cakes leave the sides of the dish when cooked and any moist spots on the surface will dry during standing time.

Egg mixtures   Test quiche fillings and baked custard by inserting a knife one-third in from the edge. The knife should be clean when withdrawn. Stand cooked custard in cold water when cooking is complete to cool and to stop further cooking.

Seafood   Green scampi, lobster and crabs turn pink when cooked. Cooked fish will flake easily when tested with a fork. Scallops, oysters and mussels become firmer when cooked.

Meats are fork tender when done. Always allow standing time. A final test for doneness can be carried out with a meat thermometer.

Drumsticks will move freely and juices will run clear when poultry is cooked.

Vegetables are brightly colored when cooked. Overcooking discolors and dulls vegetables. Large vegetables like whole potatoes and beetroot and quartered pumpkin should be turned during cooking.

Baked potatoes, which still feel firm when removed from the oven, will keep cooking during standing time, so don't overcook them. They will also keep hot if wrapped in aluminum foil for 30–40 minutes after cooking.

Browning

For those not familiar with modern microwave cooking, anxiety about how food will look when it is cooked is common. Many of us have visions of pale cakes, grey meat and wishy-washy sauces.

The browning dish
Such anxiety was understandable back in the days when microwave ovens were first introduced, but microwave cooking has come a long way since then. One of the first major breakthroughs was the introduction of the browning dish (or skillet), making it possible to actually broil steaks and chops, make toasted sandwiches and cook bacon and sausages. These dishes, specially treated with a tin oxide coating, attract microwaves and become very hot. When food is put onto the hot surface, it sears or browns rapidly. Pizzas, sausage rolls, pies and other pastries can also be placed onto the dish to give a crisper base.

A great variety of shapes and sizes in browning dishes is now available including casserole-type browners, grill-type, sizzlers and minuettes (a small round casserole type browning dish with long handle and clear glass lid).

Use sauces to mask and enhance.
Beef Olives *(see recipe)*

Although such browning dishes are not essential, they certainly help to make foods which are normally broiled or fried look more attractive.

The browning element
Another breakthrough has been the introduction of the browner, a browning element or hot air blower in the top of the oven. This lets a limited amount of dry heat into the oven, enough to brown and crisp the outer surface of foods like cauliflower cheese, but not strong enough to cook a souffle.

The combination oven
Probably the most miraculous breakthrough has been the combination oven. This is a basic microwave oven combined with a convection oven. It includes all the cooking, baking and broiling features of a conventional oven, plus microwave cooking features which can be used separately or in combination with baking or grilling heat. This results in a new kind of flexibility for microwave cooking and meal preparation. With roasts, for example, microwave energy and dry heat combine to give a perfect result. Sponges and pastries, never a great success in the microwave alone, can be cooked and browned to perfection using the convection oven.

Microwave Browning Tricks
If you don't have a browning dish, a browner or a combination oven, there are still a number of ways you can enhance microwaved food. If you use a little imagination, there are any number of things you can do to help brown food in microwave cooking. See what delicious and attractive ideas you can invent.

Meat and poultry
Meat and poultry due to longer cooking times will brown in their own fat, but not to the same extent as in a conventional or combination oven. However, if you brush with melted unsalted butter and sprinkle with paprika

before cooking, this will help. Food can be coated with butter or Worcestershire, barbecue or soy sauce, which not only add to the appearance but provide added flavor.

Chicken brushed with honey, brown sugar and soy sauce is delicious — and looks good too.

- To enhance the color of chicken pieces dip the chicken in dried breadcrumbs or coating mixes.
- When roasting, use roasting bags (pierced) to increase color.
- Cook sausages, chops and steaks in the microwave then complete browning under the conventional broiler.
- Sear steak on the barbecue, freeze and defrost and finish cooking in the microwave when required.
- Ham and poultry can be brushed with jellies, preserves, glazes or marmalades after half the cooking time has elapsed.
- Soy, teriyaki and barbecue sauce are excellent brushed over hamburgers and other meats and poultry. Onion soup and gravy mix are also very good for color.
- Small amounts of dried herbs or spices mixed in with melted unsalted butter or oil can also be used to give added color.
- Dry poultry and meat with kitchen paper towels before cooking as this will aid browning.
- Casseroles can be made more interesting if sprinkled with breadcrumbs, Parmesan cheese, crushed corn chips or potato chips before serving.

Braised Lemon Chicken (see recipe)

Cakes, Bread and Pastry
- To color cake tops sprinkle a mixture of cinnamon and sugar or cinnamon and coconut over the surface before serving.
- Cake recipes which contain coloring agents like chocolate, coffee, carrot, dates, or banana are always best in a microwave.
- Grease your cake or loaf container and sprinkle it with chopped nuts and brown sugar, toasted coconut or cookie crumbs before pouring in the cake mixture.

- Before cooking savory pastry brush it with a mixture of 1 egg yolk and 1 tablespoon soy sauce; for sweet pastry use molasses, maple syrup or a mixture of vanilla extract and beaten egg.
- Bread and bread rolls respond well to being brushed wit beaten egg or milk and sprinkled with poppy seeds or toasted sesame seeds before cooking.

Carrot Cake (see recipe)

Micro/conversion

Converting conventional recipes is easy too, especially when you become familiar with your new appliance. Generally, microwave time will be one-quarter to one-third of conventional time. It is always best to undercook overcooking cannot be corrected.

Only choose conventional recipes that will make, at most, 6–8 servings. Recipes yielding large quantities will not effectively use the convenience of flat microwave cooking. Select recipes which use ingredients with high natural moisture levels such as poultry, minced meats, vegetables, fruits and sauces. When you have found a recipe you wish to convert, find a similar microwave reci and use it as a guide.

Basic Steps
Preparation Always cut meat and vegetables into piec the same size for casseroles and for steaming in the microwave.

Liquids Reduce liquid by one-third to one-half when converting recipes for microwave preparation as liquid attracts microwave energy and slows the cooking of other ingredients. If necessary add extra liquid towards the end cooking. Reduce liquids in cakes by 2½ tablespoons and replace with an extra egg. Thin liquids such as water, meat and fruit juices, stock and wine can be heated on high.

Fats and oils   Reduce those fats and oils which have been included in conventional cooking to prevent sticking. Add fats and oils only for their flavor qualities.

Delicate ingredients   Add delicate ingredients such as seafood, cheese, canned and fine cooked foods near the end of cooking to prevent toughening and overcooking.

Seasonings   Reduce salt by two-thirds for microwave cooking and adjust other seasonings before serving. Microwave cooking enhances the natural flavor of foods therefore conventional recipes can be over-seasoned.

Sauces   Sauces which contain cream, sour cream, yoghurt or moist cheese are cooked and then reheated on medium when other ingredients are added.

Major ingredients   Major ingredients like poultry, whole fish fillets and minced or cubed meats can be microwaved on high. Stir microwave-cooked foods that are stirred in conventional cookery. Soups, casseroles and roasts are best started on high for the first 5 minutes and finished on medium.

Cakes   Cakes are best cooked on medium and finished on high for the last 2–3 minutes. Foods that cannot be stirred should be cooked on medium and the dish rotated four times during cooking.

During standing time make sauces and toss salads. Allow 8–12 minutes to cook vegetable dishes. Reheat any pre-prepared foods just before serving.
- Take advantage of the space in your conventional oven to hold hot microwave food. Set oven at 200°F.
- Heat plates by placing a microwave casserole, soup or vegetable dish on top of them during standing time.
- Reheat desserts if necessary while clearing the table after the main meal.

Cooking Times

All cooking times given are approximate. However, the recipes in this book were prepared and tested in an average sized microwave oven and the times given are based on this. If you have a more powerful oven, you will need to reduce times by a minute or two; if yours is a smaller oven, add a minute or two. Remember, undercooking can be easily rectified, overcooking can't.

Beets with Orange Sauce *(see recipe)*

Oysters Kilpatrick *(see recipe)*

Menu Planning

Prepare desserts, soups, rice, casseroles and sauces early in the day as these dishes can be reheated in just minutes.
Wash and dry salad ingredients and place in plastic bags or wrap in foil and chill.
One hour before serving assemble seafood dishes, meat and poultry. Cook baked potatoes, remove from oven, then wrap in aluminum to retain heat; then cook main course.

Power Level Designations

The following guide is based upon the majority of American microwave ovens.

Power Level	%
Low	20%
Defrost	30%
Medium	50%
Medium High	70%
High	100%

Making the Most of Your Microwave

The delicious, mouthwatering recipes in this section have been selected so that microwave cooks — the novice and the experienced — can use their ovens and their skills to the fullest to make the most of their microwave. The delicious recipes and helpful hints reveal the secrets of perfect and exciting microwave cooking.

Coconut Shrimp Cutlets

Breakfast

Breakfast is often a time when there is simply not much time. So, why not microwave that traditional cooked breakfast? The nourishing, economical egg is even more convenient when cooked in the microwave. Scrambled eggs are especially tasty. With a little butter, lots of whisking and careful timing they are extra light and fluffy. Some recipe books suggest that you cannot cook eggs in their shells in the microwave but this is not true. Just follow the directions for a perfect, no fuss, 3½ minute egg. Because egg whites and yolks cook at differe speeds, pierce the yolk carefully with a toothpick if frying in the microwave.

Try some other delicious breakfast and brunch ideas by turning to the Eggs and Cheese and Snacks chapters.

Scrambled Eggs for 2

4 × 2 oz eggs at room
temperature
¼ cup milk or cream
½ teaspoon salt
1½ tablespoons butter

Time: 4 minutes. Serves 2

Combine eggs, milk, salt, in a bowl. Melt butter in a glass bowl for 30 seconds. Pour in egg mixture and cover with plastic food wrap. Cook 2 minutes, stir well and cook another 1½ minutes stirring 2 or 3 times. Remove eggs when softer than required and let stand 1 minute.

With Cheese

Add 1 tablespoon grated cheese to beaten eggs and milk. Add a few seconds to total cooking time.

With Bacon and Chives

Chop 1–2 slices of bacon, cook 1–2 minutes. Cook eggs 1 minute, add bacon with 2 teaspoons chopped chives, stir well, continue cooking.

Fried Egg

1 × 2 oz egg at room
temperature
½ teaspoon butter

Time: 55 seconds. Serves 1

Melt butter on a plate for 25 seconds. Add egg, prick yolk 2–3 times with a toothpick. Cook 30 seconds.

HINT: FRIED EGGS
Allow the following times for frying eggs.
2 eggs—1 minute 5 seconds.
3 eggs—1 minute 35 seconds.
4 eggs—2 minutes.

Boiled Egg

1 × 2 oz egg at room
temperature
1 teaspoon salt
water to cover egg

Time: 3½ minut

Boil water in small glass measure or bowl. Add 1 teaspoo salt, then the egg. Cook on defrost for 3½–4 minutes.

Grilled Grapefruit for 2

1 grapefruit
2 teaspoons brown sugar
2 teaspoons sherry

Time: 2 minut

Cut grapefruit in half and segment. Place on plate a sprinkle with brown sugar and sherry. Cook on high 1½ minutes for 2 halves.

Oatmeal for 1

¼ cup quick cooking oats
½ cup water, at room
temperature
⅛ teaspoon salt

Time: 1½ minut

Place oatmeal, water and salt into a serving bowl. Coo 1 minute 30 seconds on high, stir, cover, and let stand f a few minutes before serving.

Note: May be cooked in advance and reheated.

Scrambled Eggs with Bacon an
Pineapple Satay and Savory Biscu
Rin

Grilling

Sausages

Heat browning dish for 8 minutes on high. Lightly grease dish. Place up to 6 sausages in the dish and cook 3 minutes on each side on high.

Note: Prick sausages well before grilling and allow 2–3 minutes standing time.

Bacon

Place bacon on several layers of paper towels on a flat dish with one layer of paper covering the bacon. Cook bacon for about 1 minute per slice on high.

Sliced Tomatoes

Heat browning dish for 6 minutes on high. Grease lightly with butter. Add 9 thick slices of tomato. Coat with buttered herbed crumbs. Cook 1 minute, turn slices and cook another 1–1½ minutes on high.

Note: Use 3 tomatoes cut into 3 thick slices each, cutting off top and bottom so that slices lie flat.

Pineapple and Bananas

Heat browning dish 5 minutes, lightly butter slices of fresh pineapple and cook 4 minutes on one side and 1–1½ minutes on the other. Reheat browning dish as above; using 3 bananas split lengthwise, cook 1–1¼ minutes on one side only.

Bacon and Pineapple Satay

Remove rind from thin slice of bacon. Cut into 3 or 4 pieces. Roll up and place onto bamboo sate stick. Place wedge of pineapple between bacon curls. Cook 3–4 minutes between paper towels on high.

Note: Button mushrooms or cherry tomatoes could be used instead of pineapple wedges.

Microwave Grilling Plate Vegetables

8 oz button mushrooms
4–6 tomato halves
parsley, finely chopped

Time: 12 minutes. Serves 2–3

Preheat grilling plate on high 5 minutes. Lightly butter plate and microwave mushrooms on high 2–3 minutes.

Preheat grilling plate on high 5 minutes. Top tomatoes with parsley.

Whole Mushrooms with French or Garlic Dressing

6 medium mushrooms
French dressing or garlic
    dressing

Time: 2 minute

Arrange mushrooms in a circle on a plate and sprinkle eac with ½ teaspoon of your favorite dressing and coo covered, for 2 minutes on high.

Sliced Mushrooms

8 oz mushrooms, thinly sliced
1 tablespoon lemon juice
1 tablespoon chopped parsley
2 oz butter

Time: 2 minute

Arrange mushrooms in a shallow dish. Sprinkle wit lemon juice and parsley. Dot with butter and cook covere for 2 minutes on high.

Stuffed Mushrooms

6 medium mushrooms, whole
2 slices ham
4 oz cream cheese
1 tablespoon chives

Time: 3 minute

Remove stalks from mushrooms. Chop ham finely an combine with cheese and chives. Spread mixture into ca ity of mushrooms and cook, covered, 3 minutes on hig

Stuffed Mushroom

22

Scones

2 cups self-rising flour
1 tablespoon sugar
½ teaspoon salt
1½ tablespoons butter
¾ cup milk

Time: 10 minutes

Sift flour into mixing bowl, add sugar and salt. Cut butter into small cubes, rub into flour. Add milk, blend mixture with a tableknife. Turn onto floured board. Cut into rounds. Heat browning dish 8 minutes on high. Cook scones 1 minute on each side on high. 8 scones.

Chive and Ham Scones

Add 1 tablespoon cut chives and 1 tablespoon diced ham to mixture. Delete sugar.

Savory Scone Ring

2 tablespoons butter
2 tablespoons sugar
1 cup pumpkin, mashed
1 small onion finely cut
2 tablespoons chopped parsley
1 egg
½ cup milk
2½ cups self-rising flour
½ teaspoon salt

Time: 7 minutes

Cream butter and sugar. Add pumpkin, onion and parsley. Add well-beaten egg. Add milk slowly. Cut in sifted flour and salt. Place into a well-greased microwave baking ring. Cook 7–8 minutes, remove and let stand for 4 minutes.

Golden Corn Bread

2 tablespoons butter or
   vegetable oil
2 tablespoons sugar
1½ cups all purpose flour
4 teaspoons baking powder
1 cup cornmeal
¼ teaspoon salt
¼ teaspoon chili powder
2 eggs, beaten
¾ cup milk
4 oz cream style corn
¼ cup red pepper, diced

Time: 7 minut

Cream butter and sugar. Add sifted flour and baking pow der. Add cornmeal, salt and chili powder. Stir in eggs, mi and beat until smooth. Fold in corn and pepper. Pla into a well-greased microwave baking ring and cook 7 minutes on high. Remove and let stand 4 minutes.

Tea, Coffee or Cups of Soup

Fill cups or coffee mugs with cold water. Heat uncovere in the oven on high.
1 cup—approximately 2½ minutes, depending on size cup.
2 cups—approximately 4½ minutes.
Then add your instant coffee, tea bag, or your single serv ing of instant soup mix.
   Note: Milk may be heated for coffee or tea, also fc oatmeal.

HINT: HOT DRINKS
Hot drinks are quick and easy in a microwave. They can usually be drunk from the container in which they were heated. When making more than two cups always place them in a ring leaving the middle empty. Do not overfill or they will spill. Also ensure liquid has been stirred before heating.

Eggs and Cheese

gs cooked in a microwave will always be successful if you low these rules. When poaching or frying cook the egg until e yolk is just how you like, then remove the egg from the crowave and allow standing time. During the standing time e white of the egg will continue to cook. To prevent the yolk m breaking during cooking, pierce it with a toothpick 2 or imes. Poached eggs are best cooked on the defrost setting pre-boiled water. Allow 4 minutes cooking time for 2 eggs. Boiled eggs should also be cooked on the defrost (4–6 nutes for 2 eggs) setting in pre-boiled salted water. Should e egg be uncooked when the shell is cut, prick the yolk then turn it to the oven to cook for a few seconds more. To keep e eggs upright during continued cooking, put them into egg ps. Fried eggs can be cooked on a lightly buttered plate. Set e microwave on high and cook for only 65–70 seconds for ggs.

For the complete egg and bacon breakfast use a preheated browning dish and cook the prepared bacon slices on high for 2 minutes. Remove the slices and break 2 eggs into the browning dish. Prick the yolks before cooking and baste with bacon fat. Cook covered for 30 seconds and allow the eggs to stand for 2 minutes until set.

Cheese melts rapidly in a microwave oven, but because of its high protein content, cheese will toughen and become stringy if overheated. Always grate or crumble cheese before adding to sauces, soups and casseroles.

The true flavor of cheese is brought out if cheese is warmed before serving. To save effort cheese can be microwaved directly on a dry wooden board.

Asparagus Omelet

cups roughly chopped, peeled, fresh asparagus
ablespoons water
cup grated Swiss cheese
ggs, separated
cup chopped onion
cup chopped green peppers
cup milk
easpoon all-purpose flour
teaspoon salt
teaspoon white pepper
ablespoon butter

Time: 14 minutes. Serves 4

ace asparagus and water in a 2 pint casserole dish. Cover d cook on high 6 minutes, or until tender. Stir after 3 min- es. Drain, stir in cheese, cover and let stand.
Combine egg yolks, onion, peppers, milk, flour and season- gs. Set aside. In a bowl beat egg whites until stiff, then fold to yolk mixture.
Melt butter in a pie plate on high 1 minute or until melted. lt dish to coat. Pour egg mixture into buttered dish and cook medium 7–10 minutes or until set, lifting edges every 2 inutes with a spatula so uncooked portion spreads evenly. Top with asparagus and cut into wedges to serve.

Eggs Benedict

4 crumpets
4 slices leg ham
4 poached eggs
butter

Toast and butter crumpets. Top each with a thin slice of leg ham and cook on high 3 minutes. Place a poached egg on top of ham and spoon over Hollandaise Sauce.

Hollandaise Sauce

2 egg yolks
⅓ cup butter
2 tablespoons lemon juice, strained
¼ teaspoon salt

Time: 1 minute 45 seconds. Serves 2–4

Place butter in a small bowl and cook on high 45 seconds. Stir in lemon juice, egg yolks and whisk until well blended. Cook on high 1 minute, whisking every 15 seconds. Stir in salt half way through.

> **HINT: MELTING BUTTER**
> 1 tablespoon butter:
>   30–45 seconds on high
> ½ cup butter:
>   1 minute on high
> 1 cup butter:
>   1–2 minutes on high

sparagus Omelet

Shrimp Omelet

4 × 2 oz eggs
5 oz shrimp meat
8 oz fresh mushrooms, sliced
⅓ cup finely chopped scallions
1 cup bean sprouts
⅛ teaspoon white pepper
2 tablespoons oil
1½ teaspoons cornstarch
2 teaspoons soy sauce
2 teaspoons oyster sauce
¼ cup chicken stock
1 teaspoon sugar

Time: 13 minutes. Serves 5

In a medium-sized bowl, beat eggs well. Fold in mushrooms, scallions, bean sprouts, pepper and shrimp meat. Cook on high 4 minutes, stirring 3–4 times until soft set.

Preheat browning dish on high for 5 minutes then add oil. Using a half-cup measure, pour mixture into dish to make 5 omelets. When sizzling stops turn omelets over and cook on high 1½ minutes until firm and set. Cover and set aside.

In a bowl combine cornstarch, soy sauce, oyster sauce, chicken stock and sugar. Cook on high 2–3 minutes or until thickened, stirring during cooking.

Pour sauce over omelets to serve.

Step 1 Shrimp Omelet. Add vegetables and shrimps to beaten eggs

Poached Eggs

4 × 2 oz eggs, at room
  temperature

Time: 11 minutes. Serves 2–4

Pour 16 fl oz water in a 2 pint dish. Cover and cook on high 6 minutes or until boiling. Break in eggs and cover. Cook on defrost 5 minutes or until set.

Step 2 Pour half-cup measures of mixture into dish

Egg and Bacon Rounds

4 × 2 oz eggs, at room
  temperature
2 extra long slices bacon
1 microwave muffin pan
¼ teaspoon paprika
½ teaspoon chopped parsley

Time: 2 minutes. Serves 2–4

Cut each slice of bacon in half. Place each around the outer edge of 4 muffin rings. One shelled egg to each ring. Prick each yolk 3–4 times with cocktail stick or thin skewer. Sprinkle with paprika and parsley. Cook on high 2 minutes. Serve each on a round of buttered toast.

Step 3 Cook omelets on both sides until firm

Cheese Souffle

6 eggs, separated
2 tablespoons butter
2 tablespoons all-purpose flour
¾ teaspoon salt
⅛ teaspoon cayenne pepper
½ teaspoon dry mustard
1½ cups evaporated milk
1½ cups grated tasty cheese
¼ cup finely chopped chives or
    parsley
1 teaspoon cream of tartar

Time: 24 minutes. Serves 6

Place butter in a Pyrex bowl and cook on high 1 minute. Stir in flour, salt, cayenne pepper and mustard. Cook 1 minute. Stir in evaporated milk and cook 4 minutes, stirring every minute. Stir in cheese.

Beat egg yolks and fold in 2 tablespoons of the cheese sauce. Stir yolks into remaining sauce and add chives.

Beat egg whites with cream of tartar until stiff peaks form. Fold whites into cheese mixture using a metal spoon.

Pour into an ungreased souffle dish. Cook on low 18–20 minutes until top is firm.

HINT: WARMING, SOFTENING AND MELTING CHEESE

Warming cheese before serving brings out its full flavor. Here is a guide to warming some of our favorite cheeses:
Block Cheese (tasty or mild)
To warm: place 8 oz block cheese on a plate. Cook on medium-low 45 seconds. Let stand for 5 minutes before serving. To melt: cut 8 oz block cheese in ½ inch cubes. Place in bowl and cook on medium 2–3 minutes.
Camembert, Brie
To warm: place 8 oz cheese on plate. Cook on medium-low 30–40 seconds. Let stand 5 minutes before serving.
Cream Cheese
To warm: Remove aluminum foil wrapper from 8 oz cream cheese and cut into quarters. Place in bowl and cook on medium 45 seconds. To melt: Remove aluminum foil wrapper from 8 oz cream cheese and cut into eighths. Place in bowl and cook on medium 1–1½ minutes.

Cheese Fondue

8 oz tasty cheese, cut into cubes
½ cup milk
1 teaspoon dry mustard
2 teaspoons Worcestershire
    sauce
1 teaspoon onion salt
2 tablespoons dry sherry or
    beer

Time: 8 minutes. Serve

In a large bowl combine all ingredients except dry she Cook on medium-low 8–10 minutes or until hot smooth, stirring three times during cooking. Blend sherry.

Serve with crusty bread cubes or blanched vegetab

Welsh Rarebit

1 oz butter
3 teaspoons all-purpose flour
5 fl oz milk
8 oz cheddar cheese, grated
1 egg yolk, beaten
4 tablespoons beer
½ teaspoon Worcestershire
    sauce
pinch salt
pinch cayenne pepper
pinch dry mustard

Time: 9 minutes. Serve

Place butter in bowl and cook on high 1 minute. Stir flour and cook on high 1 minute. Blend in milk and c on high 1½ minutes, stirring twice during cooking.

Add grated cheese and cook on medium 4–5 minute melt, stirring twice during cooking. Whisk egg yolk quic into cheese sauce.

Place beer into small jug. Cook on high until reduced 2 teaspoons. Add to cheese mixture with seasonings. Se with triangles of buttered toast.

HINT: WARMING CHEESE

As cheese contains a high proportion of protein it will become tough and stringy if heated for too long or at too high a temperature.

Hors d'oeuvres

Most hors d'oeuvres ingredients can be prepared in advance and frozen until required. Melba Toast (see recipe), savory butters and toppings, and meat and seafood balls can be stored carefully in the freezer and refrigerator and all that is needed to make you the perfect host is the microwave at the ready. And even those hors d'oeuvres which are at their best when freshly prepared will take only minutes to cook or heat in the microwave.

There are no set rules nowadays as to what should be served at cocktail parties or with pre-dinner drinks but the following selection of quick and exciting dips and finger foods have become firm party favorites.

Spicy Shrimp Rolls

*6 large green shrimps, shells and
   veins removed*
6 thin slices bacon
6 pieces green pepper
   1 × 2 inches

Sauce

2 tablespoons light soy sauce
2 tablespoons dry sherry
1 tablespoon chili sauce
2 tablespoons plum sauce

Time: 4 minutes. Serves 3–6

Arrange bacon slices between double sheets of paper towel on a plate and cook on high 4 minutes.

Remove bacon rind. Wrap one prepared shrimp and a piece of pepper in each strip of bacon and fasten with a cocktail stick. Place in a bowl.

Combine sauce ingredients and spoon over shrimp rolls. Allow to marinate 30 minutes. Cook on high 4 minutes or until shrimp are cooked.

Bacon Puffs, Cheese Canapes,
Spicy Shrimp Rolls, Crab Stuffed Zucchini

HINT: COOKING BACON
Cook bacon slices between sheets of white paper towel as this will absorb the fat, prevent splattering and keep oven walls clean.

Caraway Crisps

½ cup all-purpose flour
½ cup rye flour
½ teaspoon salt
1 teaspoon caraway seeds
3 tablespoons butter
1½–2 tablespoons cold water

Time: 3–6 minutes. Makes 24

Combine flours, salt and seeds in a mixing bowl and rub in butter to resemble breadcrumbs. Add water and blend together to form a dough.

Roll dough out thinly to form a rectangle on a floured board and cut into 1 inch squares. Arrange close together in circles on a large plate.

Cook on high 3–6 minutes or until dry and crisp. Remove carefully to a wire rack to cool.

Step 1 Caraway Crisps. Rub butter into dry ingredients

Hot Pizza Dip

7 oz bacon
¼ cup chopped onion and
   peppers
1 cup grated tasty cheese
¼ cup sliced stuffed olives
½ teaspoon chili sauce

Time: 8 minutes. Serves 6

Cut bacon into ½ inch dice and place in a Pyrex bowl. Cook on high 3 minutes. Drain off fat.

Stir in onion and peppers and cook on high 2 minutes. Add cheese, olives and chili sauce. Cook on medium 3 minutes or until cheese has melted. Serve hot with crackers or crisps.

Step 2 Use a knife to mix water into flour

Mushrooms with Pineapple Chicken Stuffing

6 large mushrooms, stalks
   removed
6 oz canned crushed pineapple,
   drained
6 oz cooked chicken, finely
   chopped
3 tablespoons mayonnaise
½ teaspoon lemon juice
pecan halves

Time: 7–8 minutes. Serves 6

Combine pineapple, chicken, mayonnaise and lemon juice. Spoon into mushroom caps and top each with a pecan nut.

Cook on high 2 minutes then reduce to medium and cook 5–6 minutes. Rearrange mushrooms during cooking to ensure that all heat evenly.

Step 3 Cut pastry into 1 inch squares

Spinach Balls

1 packet frozen spinach, about 9 oz
¾ cup grated tasty cheese
¼ cup dry breadcrumbs
2 tablespoons Parmesan cheese
1 tablespoon finely chopped
    scallions
½ teaspoon salt
¼ teaspoon pepper
1 egg, beaten

Time: 12–13 minutes. Serves 6–

Cook spinach in packet on high 5 minutes or until d
frosted. Drain all excess liquid. Combine chopped spinac
with remaining ingredients and shape into balls ¾ inch
diameter.

Place on baking tray lined with paper towel and coc
on high 2 minutes then on medium 5–6 minutes, until ho
Rearrange balls during cooking to ensure that all he
evenly.

Crab Stuffed Zucchini

1 lb even-sized zucchinis, cut
    into 1 inch rings
12 oz crabmeat
¾ cup finely chopped
    mushrooms
3 tablespoons butter
2 tablespoons all-purpose flour
¾ cup milk, warm
½ cup finely chopped scallions
¼ teaspoon paprika
¼ teaspoon salt
⅛ teaspoon pepper
2 tablespoons white wine

Time: 13–14 minutes. Serves 8–1

Cook mushrooms and butter in a bowl on high 2 minute
Stir in flour and cook on high 1 minute.

Blend in warm milk and add scallions, seasonings ar
wine. Cook on high 3–4 minutes or until thickened, stirrir
twice during cooking. Blend in crabmeat.

Hollow out half the center of each piece of zucchi
using a teaspoon.

Spoon crab mixture into zucchini cases and then place c
a plate lined with paper towel. Cook on high 2 minute
reduce to medium and cook 5 minutes or until hot. R
arrange during cooking.

> **HINT: WARMING MILK**
> Warm milk before
> blending into roux-based
> sauces. This avoids
> lumps and forms the
> sauce quickly. The sauce
> should always boil before
> serving.

Spinach Balls

Bacon Puffs

oz bacon, finely chopped
small squares bread,
  buttered on one side
egg white
cup grated tasty cheese
cup finely chopped green peppers
teaspoon chopped parsley
teaspoon salt
nch pepper

Time: 15 minutes. Serves 5

eat egg white until stiff. Fold in cheese, peppers, parsley,
lt and pepper. Spoon mixture onto unbuttered side of
read. Sprinkle tops with bacon. Preheat grilling plate for
minutes. Arrange canapes and cook, 10 at a time, on high
r 10 minutes.

Step 1 Bacon Puffs. Add peppers, cheese and parsley to beaten
egg white

Cheese Canapes

prepared canape bread
  bases
oz cream cheese
scallion, finely chopped
teaspoon horseradish relish
small smoked oysters

Time: 7½ minutes. Serves 4

ook cream cheese in a bowl 30 seconds on high. Stir in
allion and horseradish relish and spread onto prepared
nape bases. Top each with a smoked oyster. Preheat
illing plate on high for 5 minutes. Arrange canapes on
eheated griller a few at a time and cook on high 2 min-
es.

Step 2 Spoon mixture onto bread squares

Devils on Horseback

long bacon slices
prunes, pitted
toasted almonds
cocktail sticks

Time: 4 minutes. Serves 3–4

erind bacon slices and cut each slice into 3 strips. Place
almond inside each prune to replace the seed. Then
rap each prune in a strip of bacon. Secure with cocktail
ick.
Arrange rolls on a plate in a circle and cover with a paper
wel. Cook on high 4 minutes.

HINT: CANAPE BASES
Most types of bread are
suitable for microwave
canapes. First remove
crusts then cut the slices
of bread into squares,
rounds or rectangles.
Butter on one side.

Step 3 Sprinkle tops with chopped bacon.

Snacks

The microwave oven is ideal for preparing snacks, either to welcome those surprise visitors or to delight at simple family meals. For quick lunches, appetizing nibbles and snacks can be made in advance, frozen and simply reheated or defrosted when needed for a meal in a moment.

Anchovy Bread

loaf French bread
small can anchovy fillets
finely chopped parsley
oz butter

Time: 1½ minutes

Mash anchovies with butter and parsley. Cut bread into slices through the loaf. Spread slices with butter. As the loaf will be too long for the microwave oven, cut into four sections. Cook each section 1½ minutes on high. Serve hot.

Creamy Smoked Ham Vol-au-vents

oz sour cream
tablespoon chopped parsley
freshly ground black pepper to
  taste
egg yolks, beaten
dash nutmeg
oz smoked ham, diced
2 mini vol-au-vent cases

Time: 9 minutes. Serves 4–6

Combine sour cream, parsley, pepper, egg yolks and nutmeg in mixing bowl. Cook on medium high for 5–7 minutes, or until thickened, stir occasionally. Add ham. Cook –2 minutes on medium high.
Fill vol-au-vent cases and serve immediately.

Optional Fillings

As well as diced ham, the following ingredients make tasty fillings for vol-au-vent cases.

oz smoked oysters
¼ cup chopped mushrooms
  and ¼ cup chopped
  asparagus
¼ cup crumbled blue vein
  cheese
½ cup chopped cooked chicken

Party Pizzas

Lebanese bread

Sauce

8 oz can tomato paste
1 teaspoon sugar
½ teaspoon oregano
½ teaspoon freshly ground black
  pepper
½ teaspoon basil

Topping Suggestions

fresh mushrooms, sliced
onion rings
mozzarella cheese slices
pepper rings
rolled or flat anchovies
ham, cut in strips
sliced continental salami
black or green stuffed olives
Parmesan cheese, cayenne,
  paprika
grated tasty cheese
parsley

Time: 6 minutes

Prepare sauce by combining ingredients. Arrange the toppings on a serving platter for guests to make their own selection.
Spread sauce over each bread round, add toppings and cook 6 minutes on high. Cut into wedges.

Tuna or Salmon Mornay

2 cups canned tuna or salmon
2 cups Basic White Sauce (see
  recipe)
4 oz tasty cheese, grated
lemon wedges, parsley and
  paprika for garnish

Time: 10 minutes. Serves 4

Layer half tuna, half sauce, and half cheese in an 8 × 8 inch baking dish. Repeat second layer. Cook 10 minutes on high. Garnish with parsley, paprika and lemon wedges.

Chinese Chicken Savories

2 double chicken breasts
1 tablespoon oil
1 oz butter
1 tablespoon finely chopped
    ginger
2–3 cloves garlic, crushed
2 tablespoons soy sauce

Time: 9 minutes. Serves 4

Remove chicken from bone. Cut into ¾ inch pieces. Melt butter and oil in a pie dish. Add the ginger and garlic. Cook on high 1 minute. Add chicken pieces and soy sauce. Cover with plastic food wrap. Cook for 8 minutes. Stir halfway through cooking period. Do not overcook as chicken will toughen.

Macaroni and Cheese

1 cup macaroni, uncooked
2 pints hot water
½ teaspoon salt
2 cups cheese, grated
2 eggs
1 cup milk
½ teaspoon prepared mustard
dash of salt
dash of Worcestershire sauce
dash of paprika

Time: 18 minutes. Serves 4

Place macaroni into a 3½ pint casserole with water and salt. Cook in oven 10 minutes on high or until macaroni is tender. Stir after 5 minutes. Drain, rinse in hot water.

Place a layer of macaroni in a baking dish and sprinkle with grated cheese. Repeat, alternating macaroni and cheese, ending with cheese. Beat eggs lightly in a bowl. Add milk, mustard, salt and Worcestershire sauce. Stir well. Drizzle mixture on macaroni. Sprinkle with paprika. Cook, covered, on high 8 minutes, stirring after 4 minutes.

Spicy Frankfurters

2 lb cocktail frankfurters
1 cup chili sauce
¼ cup dry sherry
1 clove garlic, finely chopped
grated rind ½ lemon

Time: 7 minutes. Serves 6–8

Combine chili sauce, sherry, garlic and lemon rind. Place frankfurters in shallow baking dish and coat with chili sauce mix. Cover and cook on high 5 minutes. Stir once.

Stand covered to marinate 1–2 hours. Reheat uncovered on high 2 minutes and serve immediately.

Tuna-stuffed Peppers

1 lb large peppers
1 lb canned tuna
1 cup soft breadcrumbs
½ cup finely diced celery
⅓ cup mayonnaise
1 egg
2 tablespoons lemon juice
2 tablespoons prepared
    mustard
2 tablespoons soft butter
1 tablespoon finely chopped
    onion
¼ teaspoon salt
⅛ teaspoon tabasco sauce
2 slices cheese

Time: 18 minutes. Serves

Cut a slice from the upper third of each pepper. Dice strip that have been cut off. Remove seeds and membrane from inside of pepper. Parboil pepper in oven for 5 minutes on high. Drain. Mix diced pepper with remaining ingredients Fill peppers and stand them in a casserole dish. Cook covered on high 12 minutes.

Top with cheese strips in form of cross. Cook 1 minute on high.

Tuna Italian Style

1 (16 oz) can tuna, drained
2 tablespoons butter
2 tablespoons all-purpose flour
½ cup cream
½ cup milk
1 cup fish stock
2 tablespoons dry vermouth
½ teaspoon onion salt
¾ cup grated tasty cheese
2 scallions, finely chopped
6 medium mushrooms, sliced
2 cups cook spaghetti or
    macaroni
2 tablespoons chopped Italian
    parsley

Time: 11 minutes. Serves

Place butter in a 3½ pint casserole dish and cook on high 1 minute. Stir in flour and cook on high 1 minute. Blend in cream, milk, fish stock, vermouth and onion salt and cook on high 5 minutes, stirring twice during cooking.

Fold in cheese, scallions, mushrooms, tuna and cooked spaghetti. Cover and cook on high 4 minutes or until hot stirring mixture during heating.

Serve garnished with chopped parsley.

Tuna-Stuffed Pepper

Cabbage Rolls

2 cabbage leaves, medium size
lb ground beef
oz ground pork
oz chopped onion
cup cooked rice
teaspoon cumin powder
egg
teaspoon thyme
tablespoon chopped parsley
clove garlic, chopped
tablespoon salt
teaspoon pepper
½ cups fresh tomato sauce (see recipe)
cup butter

Time: 28 minutes. Serves 6

lace cabbage leaves in 2 tablespoons water in a casserole
ish. Cook covered on high for 8 minutes or until soft.
ombine ground beef, pork, onion, rice, cumin, egg,
hyme, parsley, garlic, salt, pepper, and ½ cup of tomato
auce.

Place two tablespoons stuffing on each cabbage leaf and
rap leaves around mixture firmly. Place cabbage rolls in
casserole dish. Spread butter on top of rolls and remain-
g ketchup. Cook, covered, 20 minutes on high, or until
eat is cooked and rolls are tender. Let stand, covered, 10
inutes.

Seafood Crepes

Crepes

oz all-purpose flour
fl oz milk
lt and pepper
arsley, finely chopped
egg
oz butter, melted
oz shortening, to grease crepe pan

illing

oz cooked crabmeat, frozen
or canned
oz cooked shrimp
oz cooked scallops
cups cheese sauce (see recipe)
tablespoons finely cut chives
–2 tablespoons finely chopped parsley
mon wedges for garnish

Time: 5 minutes. Serves 6

Mix all crepe ingredients except shortening to make a bat-
er. Grease crepe pan with shortening. Heat on range top.
dd 1½–2 tablespoons of mixture. Cook until mixture
ubbles, turn over and cook a further minute until lightly
rown.

Combine all filling ingredients. Place 2 tablespoons mix-
ure onto each crepe. Roll up and place side by side into
casserole dish and cook for 5 minutes on medium. Serve
ith lemon wedges.

Quiche Lorraine

Pastry

1¼ cups all-purpose flour
¼ teaspoon baking powder
pinch of salt
⅓ cup margarine
2 tablespoons water
squeeze of lemon juice
1 egg yolk

Filling

3 eggs
1 cup cream
1 cup milk
pinch of nutmeg, sugar,
   cayenne pepper and white
   pepper
6 slices bacon, chopped
1 cup tasty cheese, grated
parsley for garnish

Time: 18 minutes. Serves 4–6

Sift dry ingredients for pastry into bowl. Rub in margarine
using fingertips until mixture resembles fine breadcrumbs.
Combine remaining pastry ingredients. Make a well in the
center of dry ingredients, gradually add liquid, mixing to
form a dry dough. Turn onto a lightly floured surface, roll
out to fit a deep 9 inch glass pie plate. Cook 6 minutes on
high.

For filling, whisk eggs, cream, milk, and spices in mixing
bowl. Lightly fry bacon. Sprinkle bacon and cheese over
cooked pastry shell. Pour liquid mixture carefully into
pastry shell. Cook, uncovered in microwave oven for 12
minutes on medium. Allow to stand 5 minutes before serving. Garnish with parsley and serve.

Lamb Pilaf

1½ cups cooked lamb cut in
   ¾' inch dice
1 medium onion, chopped
1 stalk celery, cut in ½ in
   pieces
1 medium green pepper, cut in
   ½ inch dice
1 tablespoon oil
1½ cups quick cooking rice
1 cup tomato puree

¾ cup beef consomme or stock
4 oz mushrooms, cut in ½ inch
   pieces
2 teaspoons brown sugar
½ teaspoon basil
½ teaspoon salt
⅛ teaspoon pepper
1 bay leaf
⅛ teaspoon thyme
⅛ teaspoon cayenne pepper

Time: 13 minutes. Serves 4

In a 3½ pint casserole combine onion, celery, green peppers and oil. Cover and cook on high 3 minutes. Stir in
remaining ingredients, cover and cook on high 5 minutes.
Stir and re-cover.

Reduce power to medium. Cook 5–8 minutes until rice
is tender and liquid absorbed.

Lasagne with Ground Beef

8 oz lasagna noodles
8 cups boiling water
1 tablespoon salt
1 tablespoon oil
1 tablespoon butter, softened
1 cup onion, sliced
¼ cup sliced mushrooms
1 lb ground beef
1 clove chopped garlic
1 (8 oz) can tomato puree
1 (6 oz) can tomato paste
1½ cups beef stock
½ teaspoon sugar
½ teaspoon salt
dash of pepper
1 teaspoon basil
1 lb cottage cheese
8 oz mozzarella cheese slices
½ cup grated Parmesan cheese

Time: 48 minutes. Serves 6

Place lasagne noodles in a casserole. Pour over boiling water. Add salt. Cook 16 minutes on high until tender. Drain and mix with a little oil. Set aside.

Melt butter in casserole 30 seconds. Saute onion in butter 3 minutes. Add mushrooms. Cook 3 minutes. Remove from casserole. Cook ground beef and garlic in casserole 6 minutes, stirring every 2 minutes. Add onion and mushroom mixture, tomato puree, tomato sauce, stock, sugar, salt, pepper and basil. Stir well. Cook, covered, 10 minutes, stirring every 3 minutes to make meat sauce.

Layer meat sauce, noodles, cottage cheese and mozzarella cheese in a deep casserole dish. Repeat layers 3 times, ending with meat sauce. Sprinkle Parmesan cheese on top. Cook on high 10 minutes.

Moussaka

3 eggplants
4 tablespoons olive oil
1 lb ground beef
1 small can tomato paste
salt, cayenne and oregano
2 medium onions, sliced

1 egg
1 cup sour cream
1½ cups buttered breadcrumbs
tomato for garnish
parsley for garnish

Time: 30 minutes. Serves 6

Cut unpeeled eggplant into ½ inch slices. Sprinkle with salt and leave to stand for 30 minutes. Drain off liquid. Heat browning skillet 8 minutes, add oil and heat a further 3 minutes. Cook eggplant on each side 2 minutes on high. Combine meat, tomato paste and seasonings.

Place layers of eggplant, meat mixture and sliced onion in a greased casserole. Combine beaten egg with sour cream. Spread over mixture. Sprinkle thickly with buttered crumbs and cook 15 minutes on high. Serve hot garnished with tomato and parsley.

Spinach Pie

1 lb precooked spinach leaves
  (see Vegetables)
1 onion, finely chopped
3 eggs
4 oz feta cheese
1 cup cottage cheese
2 tablespoons Parmesan cheese
¼ cup chopped parsley
salt and pepper
¼ teaspoon nutmeg
1 packet filo pastry
½ cup butter, melted

Time: 15 minutes. Serves

Combine spinach, onion, eggs, cheese, parsley and seasonings in a bowl. Brush an oblong casserole dish with melted butter. Place 1 sheet filo pastry in dish so that it comes up to the top edges. Brush with melted butter and repeat until the base has 6–8 layers. Cook on high 2 minutes. Add filling to pastry, spreading evenly. Top with more layers of buttered pastry. Trim edges. Cut into squares through the first four layers of pastry. Cook uncovered in oven 13 minutes. Cut into squares and serve warm.

Optional: Brown top of pie under heated grill for 2 minutes.

Crustless Ricotta Cheese Pie

1½ cups ricotta cheese
1 × 10 oz package frozen,
  chopped spinach
½ cup finely chopped onion
2 eggs
¼ teaspoon salt
¼ teaspoon pepper
¼ teaspoon nutmeg
2 teaspoons flour
1 finely chopped scallion
⅛ teaspoon paprika

Time: 15 minutes. Serves

Combine spinach and onion in a 2 pint casserole dish. Cover and cook on high 5 minutes, stirring after 2 minutes. Drain well.

Beat eggs with a fork in a medium-sized bowl. Stir in ricotta cheese, salt, pepper, nutmeg and flour. Blend in spinach and scallion.

Spread mixture on a 9 inch pie plate. Sprinkle with paprika and cook on high 4 minutes. Reduce to medium and cook 6 minutes or until center is set. Let stand 5 minutes before serving.

Lasagne with Topside Mince

44

Chili con Carne

½ tablespoon butter
1 lb ground beef
1 small onion, diced
½ teaspoon garlic salt
1 tablespoon chili powder
½ teaspoon dry mustard
salt and pepper
½ can tomatoes
1 x 8 oz can kidney beans
1 x 8 oz can baked beans
1 x 8 oz can sliced mushrooms
2 stalks celery, diced
2 tablespoons tomato paste
1 teaspoon paprika
½ teaspoon oregano

Time: 13 minutes. Serves 6

Put butter, beef, diced onions and garlic salt into a 3½ pint casserole dish. Cook on high 3 minutes until brown. Add chili powder, mustard, salt, pepper and remaining ingredients. Cook for 10 minutes stirring after the first 5 minutes. Serve with rice or buttered toast.

Pork and Shrimp Rolls

4 oz ground pork
4 oz shrimp, shelled and finely
   chopped
3 sheets pie dough
1 oz butter
2 oz mushrooms, finely
   chopped
1 tablespoon dry sherry
2 scallions, finely chopped
1 hard-boiled egg, chopped
½ cup grated carrot
egg to glaze

Time: 14 minutes. Serves 8

Place butter and pork in a bowl and cook on high 4 minutes. Drain. Add mushrooms and scallions and cook on high 2 minutes. Fold in remaining ingredients.
   Cut each sheet of pie dough into thirds and brush each sheet with beaten egg. Arrange filling along the strips and roll up carefully. Brush tops of rolls with egg and cut into 1½ inch lengths.
   Heat browning grill on high 5 minutes. Place rolls on broiling plate and cook on high 1 minute on each side.

Ham Relish Finger Rolls

7 oz ham, chopped
2 tablespoons gherkin relish
¼ cup mayonnaise
2 teaspoons finely chopped
   scallion
6 slices whole wheat bread
¼ cup butter
1 egg, beaten
1 cup poppy seeds

Time: 4 minutes. Serves

Combine ham, relish, mayonnaise and scallion in a sma bowl.
   Remove crusts from bread. Roll each slice out thin with a rolling pin and spread thinly with ham mixture. Ro up and secure with two cocktail sticks.
   Place butter in bowl and heat on high 1 minute. Blen in beaten egg.
   Roll each sandwich in butter mixture, then coat gene ously with poppy seeds.
   Chill for 15 minutes. Cut each roll into 4 pieces ar arrange pieces 12 at a time on outer edge of a plate ar cook on high 3 minutes.

Bread Cases

6 thin slices of brown or white
   bread
butter
1 micromuffin pan

Filling Suggestions

1 cup cheese sauce and add
   either:
1 cup of cream style corn
1 cup flaked salmon
1 cup assorted seafood
   (shrimp, crabmeat, oysters)
1 cup chopped green asparagus

Time: 4 minut

Remove crusts from bread. Place bread in oven and co 1 minute to refresh. Butter bread. Place butter side dow in muffin pan, so that the corners form four peaks. Pla into oven and cook on high 2–3 minutes. Remove case which should be firm and crisp.

Rice and Pasta

Rice is available in many grades and varieties — local and imported, white and brown, short and long grain — but whatever variety, rice cooks far quicker in a microwave than it does on the conventional hot plate. It takes only 8 minutes to cook one cup of rice

Always use a large lidded casserole and it is a good idea to place a plain dinner plate under the casserole to catch any liquid that may boil over. Allow standing time for rice and before serving fork up grains.

To add zest to rice dishes add whole or ground spices, curry powder, chopped fruit, nuts, vegetable juices, stock, wine or dressings to the rice before cooking.

Dried pasta, unlike rice, does not cook quicker in a microwave. Always choose a large casserole or Pyrex bowl that can hold at least 6–8 cups of salted water. If you are using fresh pasta reduce cooking time a little.

Cooking White Rice

1 cup long grain rice, washed
1¾ cups boiling water
1 tablespoon butter
½ teaspoon salt

Time: 8 minutes. Serves 6

Place all ingredients in a 2 pint casserole dish. Cover and cook on high 8 minutes. Let stand 4 minutes before serving.

Cooking Brown Rice

1 cup brown rice, washed
2 cups water
1 tablespoon butter
⅛ teaspoon salt

Time: 22 minutes. Serves 6

Place all ingredients in a 3½ pint casserole dish. Cook on high 22 minutes. Let stand 5 minutes before serving.

> ### HINT: KEEPING RICE HOT
> Cooked rice will remain hot in a covered casserole dish for 30 minutes at room temperature. Take advantage of this time to cook or reheat accompanying food.

Fried Rice with Vegetables

Fried Rice with Vegetables

2 cups cooked rice
⅓ cup thinly sliced celery
⅓ cup chopped green pepper
⅓ cup chopped scallions
1 small carrot finely chopped
1 × 8 oz can sliced bamboo
　shoots, drained
1 tablespoon vegetable oil
1 teaspoon chopped parsley
⅛ teaspoon salt
⅛ teaspoon pepper
1½ tablespoons soy sauce
2 eggs, beaten

Time: 9 minutes. Serves 6

Combine vegetables, oil and seasonings in a bowl. Preheat browning dish on high for 3 minutes. Spoon in vegetable mixture and sauce, stir and cover. Cook on high for 3 minutes or until crisp but still tender. Set aside.

Place eggs into small bowl and cook on high for 1 minute, stirring every 20 seconds. Stir rice and eggs into vegetable mixture. Cook on high 2 minutes to reheat, stirring after 1 minute.

Wild Rice with Vegetables

1½ cups wild rice, washed
5 cups hot water
½ cup chopped onion
½ cup chopped celery
2 tablespoons butter
8 oz fresh mushrooms, sliced
2 chicken stock cubes

Time: 40 minutes. Serves 6–8

Combine rice and hot water in a 5 pint casserole dish. Cover and cook on high 30 minutes or until rice is tender, stirring every 10 minutes. Let rice stand uncovered 15 minutes.

In a 3½ pint casserole dish combine onion, celery and butter. Cover and cook on high 3 minutes. Add mushrooms and crumbled stock cubes and cook on high 3 minutes.

Drain and rinse rice with boiling water. Mix with vegetables, cover and cook on high 3–4 minutes until heated through.

HINT: REHEATING RICE
Cold cooked rice can be reheated on high. Add 1 tablespoon of warm water to rice, cover and heat for 2–3 minutes.

Step 1 Parsley Rice Ring. Add onion, parsley, rice and egg yolks to melted butter

Parsley Rice Ring

3 cups cooked rice
½ cup butter
2 tablespoons finely chopped
　onion
1 cup finely chopped parsley
3 × 2 oz eggs, separated

Time: 6 minutes. Serve

Place butter into 3½ pint bowl and cook on high 2 minut
Add onion, parsley, rice and egg yolks and blend togeth

Fold in stiffly beaten egg whites and pour mixture i
a greased ring dish. Level top of mixture with a spoon a
cook on high for 4 minutes. Unmold onto round plat
to serve. Center may be filled with various fillings.

Lemon Rice

1 cup white rice, washed
1 tablespoon butter
⅛ teaspoon cumin seeds
⅛ teaspoon coriander seeds
¼ teaspoon salt
½ teaspoon turmeric
1¾ cups boiling water
1 lemon, juiced
fresh coriander, chopped

Time: 10 minutes. Serve

Place butter in a 3½ pint casserole dish and cook on high
1 minute. Add rice, cumin, coriander seeds, salt and t
meric and cook on high 1 minute. Stir in boiling water a
cook on high 8 minutes. Let stand 4 minutes. Add strair
lemon juice, forking in lightly. Sprinkle with coriande

Step 2 Fold egg whites into rice mixture

Step 3 Spoon mixture into greased ring dish

Parsley Rice Ring

51

Fried Rice

slices bacon
oz fresh mushrooms
small onion
scallions
oz shelled shrimp
eggs
cups cold cooked rice, cooked
with 1 chicken cube
tablespoon dark soy sauce

Time: 11 minutes. Serves 4

ice bacon, mushrooms, onions, scallions and shrimp. lace bacon on glass dish, cover with paper towels and ook 3 minutes on high. Remove from dish, add onion, ushrooms and cook 2 minutes.

Fold lightly beaten eggs into rice, and add to dish. Cook n high 2 minutes, then stir, add bacon, soy sauce and stir ixture again. Cook 2 minutes. Stir in scallions and rimp. Cook 2 minutes to reheat. Season.

Saffron Rice

oz butter
small onion, chopped
teaspoon powdered saffron
or turmeric
cup washed rice
oz currants or raisins
cups boiling chicken stock
(can use stock cube)
oz almond slivers, toasted

Time: 11 minutes. Serves 4

lace butter into 2 pint casserole dish and cook 15 seconds. dd onion, saffron and cook on high 3 minutes. Add rice, urrants and boiling stock. Cook covered 8 minutes. Allow o stand 10 minutes. Sprinkle with almonds before serving.

Ginger Saffron Rice

cup washed rice
inch of salt
tablespoons diced red
pepper or crystallized ginger
teaspoon powdered saffron
at of butter
cups boiling water

Time: 8 minutes. Serves 4

lace rice into a 2 pint casserole, add salt, pepper or ginger, affron, butter and boiling water. Cook on high 8 minutes. llow to stand 10 minutes before serving. Can be molded nd turned out on serving plate.

Tomato Rice

1 cup washed rice
½ teaspoon sugar
pinch oregano
pinch onion salt
pat of butter
1 cup tomato juice
1 cup chicken stock
chopped parsley

Time: 8 minutes. Serves 4

Bring tomato juice and chicken stock to boil. Place rice into a 2 pint casserole dish, add sugar, spices, butter and tomato juice and stock. Cook covered on high 8 minutes. Allow to stand 10 minutes. Sprinkle with chopped parsley. Serve with chicken dishes or casseroles.

Basic Rice Pilaf

2 oz butter
1 small onion, chopped finely
1 cup long grain rice, washed
2 cups boiling chicken stock
salt and pepper

Time: 14 minutes. Serves 4

Place 1 oz butter and the onion into a casserole dish. Cook 3 minutes on high, stir in rice. Cook a further 3 minutes on high. Add stock, seasonings, cover with a lid and cook 8 minutes. Mix in remaining butter, allow to stand 5 minutes before serving.

Mushroom Pilaf

4 oz sliced fresh mushrooms can be added to the rice and cooked as above.

Vegetable Pilaf

1 oz cooked peas
1 oz diced peppers
1 oz diced tomato
2 oz grated cheese

Prepare Rice Pilaf as above. After cooking, fold all Vegetable Pilaf ingredients into rice with remaining butter and allow to stand 5 minutes before serving to heat through.

Ginger Saffron Rice

Vegetarian Rice

Vegetarian Rice

2 tablespoons butter
1 carrot, diced
2 large mushrooms, finely
  minced
1 onion
½ red pepper
½ green pepper
1 cup corn kernels
1 cup peas
3 cups cooked rice
salt and pepper
1 clove garlic, finely ground
1 slice ginger, finely ground
2 tablespoons chopped parsley
hard-boiled eggs

Time: 9 minutes. Serves 4–6

Dice all vegetables to the size of the corn. Wash and drain. Place butter into a 3½ pint casserole. Cook 15 seconds. Add all the vegetables and cook on high covered 4 minutes. Fold in rice and add salt, pepper, garlic, ginger and parsley. Cook 5 minutes, covered. Garnish with diced, hard-boiled eggs.

Paella

3 tablespoons oil
1 cup onion, sliced
1 clove garlic, minced
1 cup uncooked rice, washed
2 cups boiling chicken stock
1½ teaspoons salt
¼ teaspoon saffron
⅛ teaspoon pepper
1 can (4 oz) shrimp, drained
1½ cups cooked chicken, ¾
  inch cubes
6 mussels, in the shell
1 cup peas
½ cup stuffed olives, sliced

Time 13 minutes. Serves 4–

Heat oil in a 3½ pint casserole for 3 minutes. Add onion garlic and heat a further 2 minutes. Add rice, chicke stock, salt, saffron, pepper and cook for 3 minutes. Stir Fold in shrimp, chicken, mussels and peas and cook further 5 minutes, stirring after 2½ minutes. Add olives Remove from oven and allow to stand 10 minutes befor serving.

Note: Keep casserole covered while cooking.

Cooking Pasta

Pasta should be cooked in a large casserole dish with a lid. Place casserole onto a large plate during cooking to catch any spillover.

6–8 cups water
8 oz pasta
2 teaspoons salt
cooking oil

Serves 4–6

Place water and salt in casserole. Allow 2½ minutes cooking time on high for each cup of water. When water is boiling add pasta and cover. Cook on high for 16 minutes or until tender.

Drain, rinse well in hot water, drain again and stir in 1–2 teaspoons cooking oil. This keeps the pasta separate.

Macaroni with Tomato Sauce

8 oz large macaroni shells
2 oz grated cheese
2 oz butter
1½ cups tomato sauce (see recipe Tomato Sauce)

1 cup Tomato Concassee (see recipe)

Time: 26 minutes. Serves 4–6

Cook macaroni in boiling salted water until tender. Drain well and return to casserole dish. Mix in butter and tomato sauce. Correct seasoning. Add Tomato Concassee and cook on high 4 minutes to reheat. Serve grated cheese separately.

Tomato Concassee

1 oz chopped onion
1 oz butter
8 oz tomatoes, peeled and chopped
salt
freshly ground black pepper

Time: 6 minutes

Place onion and butter in a bowl and cook on high 2 minutes. Add chopped tomatoes and cook on high 4 minutes. Season with salt and pepper.

Tomato Sauce

½ oz butter
½ clove garlic, chopped
½ oz flour
12 fl oz stock
1 oz tomato paste
salt and pepper
½ oz bacon pieces
2 oz onion, chopped
2 oz carrot, chopped
1 oz celery, chopped
½ teaspoon dried basil

Time: 21 minutes

Place butter in casserole. Cook on high 45 seconds the add bacon pieces, onion, carrot, celery and basil. Cove and cook on high 5 minutes, stirring after 2 minutes. Blen in flour and cook on high 1 minute. Add tomato past stock, garlic and seasonings and cook on high 4–5 minute until boiling.

Reduce power to medium and cook 10 minutes. Pure sauce. Serve with pasta, eggs, fish or meat.

Fettuccine Carbonara

8 oz fettuccine, cooked (still hot)
6 slices bacon
5 fl oz cream
2 eggs
½ cup fresh Parmesan, grated
parsley

Time: 4 minutes. Serves

Cook bacon between sheets of paper toweling on high minutes. Place pasta in bowl, add beaten eggs, cream cheese and chopped bacon. Toss through pasta. Garnis with finely cut parsley and serve immediately.

Soups

Perfect soups can be cooked in the microwave oven in minutes and the variety is endless. Everything from clear consommes to chowders and rich cream soups can be prepared in a flash by using a food processor alongside your microwave.

Because vegetables retain their color, flavor and goodness when cooked in a microwave, vegetable soups always look great and taste delicious. Soups can be made in advance and frozen and by taking advantage of the defrost cycle, a hot snack will only be minutes away.

Shrimp Bisque

1 lb shrimp meat, chopped
2 tablespoons butter
1 onion, chopped
1 stalk celery, diced
2 tablespoons all-purpose flour
3 cups milk
½ teaspoon salt
pinch white pepper
½ cup fish stock (see recipe
    Quick Fish Stock)

Time: 16½ minutes. Serves 6–8

Place butter, onion and celery in a 3½ pint casserole dish. Cover and cook on high 4 minutes. Stir in flour and cook on high 2 minutes.

Stir in milk, salt and pepper. Cook on high 7½ minutes, stirring every 2 minutes to make a white sauce.

Blend in fish stock and shrimp. Cook on medium 3–4 minutes. Garnish with sliced pimiento and parsley to serve.

Minestrone

1 medium-sized onion, chopped
1 clove garlic, finely chopped
½ cup chopped celery
¼ cup diced green pepper
1 tablespoon cooking oil
1 × 14 oz can kidney beans
1 × 14 oz can tomato pieces
1 medium-sized zucchini, diced
¼ cup white rice
3 cups beef stock or consomme
¼ cup red wine
1 tablespoon chopped parsley
pinch dried oregano
½ teaspoon sugar
¼ teaspoon white pepper
¼ cup grated Parmesan cheese

Time: 26 minutes. Serves

Place onion, garlic, celery, pepper and oil in a 5 pint cassero dish. Cover and cook on high 6 minutes.

Add remaining ingredients except Parmesan cheese. R cover and cook on high 20 minutes, stirring 3 times durir cooking.

Sprinkle with extra parsley and serve with Parmesa cheese.

HINT: TO CHANGE YIELD

To increase or decrease the yield of a microwave recipe follow these hints:

Decreasing yield by half — use only ½ the specified quantity of ingredients and reduce cooking time by ⅓.

Doubling yield — double quantity of solid ingredients, increase liquids by 1⅔ to 1¾ and increase cooking time by about ½ to ⅔.

HINT: INDIVIDUAL INSTANT SOUPS

Pour cold water or stock into cup until ¾ full. Microwave on high 1½–2 minutes, until boiling. Add contents of individual soup packet. Microwave on medium for 1–2 minutes to infuse.

Borscht

8 oz beetroot, grated
2 medium-sized carrots, thinly
    sliced
1 large onion, shredded
1 medium-sized potato, cut in
    ½ inch cubes
1½ cups shredded green
    cabbage
1 clove garlic, finely chopped
½ teaspoon salt
¼ teaspoon marjoram
⅛ teaspoon white pepper
1 large bay leaf
2½ cups water
1 × 14 oz can beef consomme
sour cream
freshly cut dill

Time: 27 minutes. Serves 6–8

Step 1 Borscht. Prepare vegetables

Place beetroot, carrots, onion, potato, cabbage, garlic, seasoning and ½ cup water into a 5 pint casserole dish. Cover and cook on high 17 minutes or until vegetables are tender.

Add remaining water and beef consomme, cover and cook on high 20 minutes. Stir twice during cooking.

Remove bay leaf. Top individual servings with sour cream and dill before serving.

Quick Fish Stock

3½ oz white fish fillets
1 tablespoon chopped onion
1 bay leaf
1 teaspoon lemon juice
4 parsley stalks
3 peppercorns
2 cups water

Time: 11 minutes. Makes 3 cups

Step 2 Place vegetables in casserole

Place all ingredients in a 3½ pint casserole dish. Cover and cook on high 6 minutes. Stir. Cook on medium 5 minutes, then strain. Correct seasonings before using.

HINT: DON'T OVERCOOK THESE FOODS
When using ingredients like asparagus, mushrooms, cheese, strawberries or shellfish it is always best to add them to the mixture toward the end of the microwaving process so that these fairly sensitive foods are not overcooked.

Step 3 When vegetables are tender, add beef consomme

scht

Cheese and Almond Soup

oz butter
cup finely chopped onion
cup grated carrot
ablespoons chopped
blanched almonds
cup flour
teaspoon white pepper
teaspoon salt
cups milk
fl oz canned Cream of
Chicken soup
ups grated tasty cheese

Time: 17 minutes. Serves 4–6

ce butter, onion, carrot and almonds in a 3½ pint casser-
dish. Cook on high 4 minutes, stirring every minute.
r in flour, pepper and salt and then stir in milk and
cken soup.

Cook on high 8 minutes, stirring every 2 minutes. Add
eese, stir until melted. Cook on medium 5 minutes.

Mulligatawny Soup

2 oz butter
4 oz onions, chopped
1 clove garlic, finely chopped
2 oz flour
2 teaspoons curry powder
1 tablespoon tomato paste
2 pints brown stock or consomme
1 oz peeled, chopped apple
2 teaspoons fruit chutney
salt to taste
1 oz cooked rice
1 tablespoon chopped parsley

Time: 36 minutes. Serves 6–8

Place butter, onion and garlic in a 3½ pint casserole dish.
Cook on high 6 minutes. Blend in flour and curry powder.
Cook a further minute.

Add tomato paste and stock and cook on high 15 minutes
or until boiling. Stir in apple, chutney and salt. Cook on
medium 10 minutes.

Puree ingredients in a food processor. Correct seasonings. Cook on reheat 5 minutes. Fold in rice and parsley.

Chilled Strawberry Soup

3 cups sliced strawberries
1 cup sugar
½ cup water
2 teaspoons arrowroot
2 tablespoons cold water
1 cup red wine
1 cup orange juice
1½ cups sour cream
strawberries for garnish

Time: 14 minutes. Serves 8

Place strawberries, sugar and water in a 3½ pint casserole dish. Cover and cook on high 3 minutes or until boiling. Cook 5 minutes on medium.

Blend arrowroot with water, then blend with wine and orange juice into strawberry mixture. Cook on high 6 minutes or until boiling. Chill mixture.

Puree in food processor. Stir in cream and serve chilled, garnished with sliced strawberries.

Step 1 Strawberry Soup. Place strawberries, sugar and water in casserole

Step 2 Pour arrowroot, wine and orange juice over strawberries

Cream of Asparagus Soup

8 oz asparagus, fresh or canned
2 oz butter
2 oz onion, chopped
2 oz celery, cut in ½ inch pieces
2 oz all-purpose flour
2 pints white stock
1 bouquet garni
½ teaspoon salt
¼ teaspoon white pepper
5 fl oz cream or milk

Time: 35 minutes. Serves 6–8

Place butter, onion and celery into a 3½ pint casserole dish. Cook on high 6 minutes.

Stir in flour, cook a further minute on high. Stir in stock, cook on high 15 minutes or until boiling.

Add roughly chopped asparagus, bouquet garni and seasoning. Cook on medium 10 minutes. Remove bouquet garni. Puree ingredients in food processor. Add cream or milk. Cook on reheat 5 minutes. Serve with croutons.

Bouquet Garni

10 × 2 inch parsley stalks
3 large bay leaves
2 × 2 inch pieces celery

Place parsley stems and bay leaves into the hollow of one piece of celery. Place second piece of celery on top. Secure with elastic band or string. Use to flavor soups, stocks and casseroles.

Step 3 Puree in food processor

Crab and Sweet Corn Soup

6 cups chicken stock
1 cup crabmeat
1 cup cream style corn
1 tablespoon cornstarch, water
1 tablespoon sherry (dry)
½ teaspoon salt
½ teaspoon oil
½ teaspoon sesame oil
2 eggs, beaten
½ cup scallions, finely chopped

Time: 20 minutes. Serves 6

Place stock into a large casserole dish and cook 15 minutes or until boiling on high. Add crabmeat and corn and cook a further 2 minutes. Add blended cornstarch, sherry, salt and oils and bring to the boil, approximately 3 minutes. Remove from oven and add egg slowly to form egg flower. Add scallions. Serve hot.

Cream of Mushroom Soup

4 oz mushrooms
4 tablespoons butter
4 tablespoons all-purpose flour
1½ cups milk
1½ cups chicken stock
1 cup cream
salt and pepper
chopped chives

Time: 17 minutes. Serves

Slice and dice mushrooms. Place butter into a 3½ pint casserole dish and cook 1 minute to melt. Add mushroom and cook on high covered 3 minutes. Stir in flour, cook further 2 minutes. Blend in milk and stock. Cook 9 minut on high. Add cream and cook 2 minutes to reheat. Seaso with salt and pepper. Add a few chopped chives befo serving.

Clam Chowder

5 slices rindless bacon,
    diced ½ inch
¼ cup finely chopped onion
¼ cup finely chopped celery
¼ cup finely chopped carrot
¼ cup diced ½ inch potato
3 tablespoons flour
1 cup clam juice
2¾ cups milk
1 (8 oz) can clams
½ teaspoon thyme
1 bay leaf
1 teaspoon salt
½ teaspoon pepper
¼ cup cream
1 tablespoon finely chopped
    parsley

Time: 20 minutes. Serves 6

Sprinkle bacon into 3½ pint casserole dish, cook 2 minutes. Add vegetables and cook 1 minute. Blend in flour, add clam juice and milk, stir to blend. Add clams and cook on high 5 minutes. Add thyme, bay leaf, salt and pepper. Cook 12 minutes, stirring after every 3 minutes. Let stand covered 5 minutes. Remove bay leaf, stir in cream, correct seasoning, sprinkle with parsley and serve.

Vegetables

When cooking vegetables in the microwave always use the freshest vegetables available so that your cooked vegetables remain moist and succulent. Microwave vegetables on high and use as little water (or whatever liquid you are using in which to cook the vegetables) and salt as possible.

If you are using pre-cooked canned vegetables simply reheat the vegetables in 2 tablespoons of their own liquid on a medium setting. Stir vegetables twice during reheating. For frozen packaged vegetables, snip off the corner of the plastic bag (this will prevent the bag from splitting) before placing in the microwave oven.

Pumpkin Cheese Ring

½ cup chopped scallions
2 tablespoons butter
2 cups cooked, mashed pumpkin
½ teaspoon salt
¼ teaspoon cayenne pepper
¼ teaspoon nutmeg
1 cup freshly grated Parmesan
  cheese
4 × 2 oz eggs

Time: 19 minutes. Serves 6–8

Place scallions and butter in a medium-sized bowl. Cook on high 1 minute. Stir in remaining ingredients.

Pour into a greased 9 inch ring mold. Cook on high 18 minutes or until set. Let stand 8 minutes before turning out.

Jerusalem Artichokes

1 lb artichokes
1 teaspoon lemon juice

Time: 8–9 minutes. Serves 4

Scrub artichokes thoroughly with a brush under running water. Peel if desired and cut into ½ inch slices. Cover with cold water and a squeeze of lemon juice to prevent discoloring. Drain.

Place into a 3½ pint casserole on dish with ¼ cup water and lemon juice. Cover. Cook on high 8–9 minutes, until fork tender. Let stand 4 minutes.

Serve with Hollandaise Sauce (see recipe Eggs Benedict), melted butter, salt and pepper or Parmesan cheese.

Mushroom and Artichoke Casserole

2 cups sliced fresh mushrooms
½ cup chopped onion
½ cup chopped celery
2 tablespoons butter
1½ cups seasoned breadcrumbs
¼ cup hot water
6 slices bacon, cooked and
  crumbled
⅛ teaspoon salt
2 cans artichoke hearts, drained
  and quartered
3 tablespoons Parmesan cheese

Time: 10 minutes. Serves 6–8

Combine mushrooms, onions, celery and butter in a bowl. Cover and cook on high 3 minutes, stirring after 2 minutes.

Stir in seasoned breadcrumbs, hot water, half the bacon and salt. In a casserole dish, layer half the mushroom mixture, artichokes and cheese. Repeat layers.

Cover and cook on high 6 minutes. Sprinkle with remaining bacon and cook, uncovered, on high 1 minute.

> **HINT: CUTTING VEGETABLES**
> When preparing vegetables for casseroles bear in mind that smaller, evenly cut pieces microwave faster than large, irregularly cut vegetables.

Pumpkin Cheese Ring

Vegetable Lasagne

8 oz ricotta cheese
4 oz mozzarella cheese, grated
2 teaspoons chopped parsley
3 long zucchinis
2 large ripe tomatoes, sliced
8 fl oz Tomato Sauce (see recipe
   Macaroni with Tomato Sauce)
3 tablespoons grated Parmesan
   cheese

Time: 24 minutes. Serves 6

Combine ricotta, mozzarella cheese and parsley. Cut ends from zucchini and slice lengthwise into ¼ inch strips. Arrange strips in an 8 inch square dish. Cover with plastic wrap and cook on high 6 minutes. Rearrange strips during cooking. Drain well and cool slightly.

Place a layer of sliced zucchini on the bottom of the dish and spread ricotta mixture over. Cover with tomato slices and spread half Tomato Sauce over sliced tomatoes. Top with remaining zucchini strips. Pour over remaining sauce and sprinkle with Parmesan cheese.

Cook uncovered on medium for 20 minutes. Let stand 5 minutes before serving.

Step 1 Vegetable Lasagne. Combine ricotta, mozzarella and parsley

Vegetable Lasagne

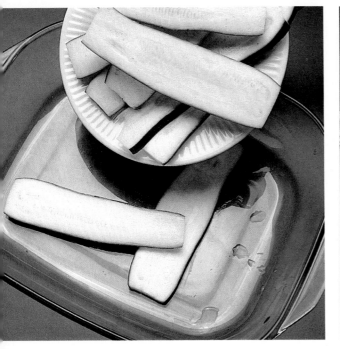

ep 2 Place a layer of sliced zucchinis in dish

Step 3 Cover cheese mixture with sliced tomato

Cauliflower Snow

-3 cups cauliflower florets
oz butter
onion, chopped
medium-sized tomatoes,
 chopped
oz flour
) fl oz milk
 teaspoon salt
 teaspoon white pepper
 teaspoon cayenne pepper
 teaspoon dry mustard
oz cheese, grated
eggs, separated
oz extra cheese
opped parsley

Time: 20 minutes. Serves 6–8

ace cauliflower in casserole with water and cook on high
r 6 minutes. Drain off liquid.
 Combine 1 oz butter and onion in bowl and cover with
astic wrap. Cook on high 3 minutes then add tomatoes.
ook 2 minutes and set aside. Melt remaining butter in
other bowl on high for 1 minute. Stir in flour and cook
minute. Blend in milk, salt, pepper, cayenne and mus-
rd. Cook on high 2½–3 minutes until thick and boiling.
old in cheese.
 Arrange cauliflower in casserole dish. Spoon over onion
ixture and coat with cheese sauce. Beat egg whites until
iff and spread over sauce. Make 4 indents into egg whites
ith a soup spoon and carefully place 1 yolk into each
ollow. Prick yolks 3–4 times and sprinkle with extra
heese. Cook on medium 4 minutes. Garnish with parsley.

Parsnips with Pineapple

1 lb parsnips, peeled and cut
 into Julienne strips
2 tablespoons butter
½ cup water
2 tablespoons brown sugar
2 teaspoons cornstarch
8 oz canned crushed pineapple
1 teaspoon orange zest
⅛ teaspoon salt

Time: 10 minutes. Serves 4–6

In a 3 pint casserole dish combine parsnips, butter and ¼
cup water. Cover and cook on high 7 minutes.
 In a medium-sized bowl combine brown sugar and
cornstarch. Stir in remaining water, pineapple, orange zest
and salt and cook on high 3–4 minutes, stirring after 2
minutes. Drain parsnips and add to pineapple mixture.

> **HINT: ARRANGING
> VEGETABLES FOR
> COOKING**
> Arrangement is the
> secret of microwave
> cooking many foods with
> different cooking times.
> Place larger items around
> the edge of the plate.
> Make a second ring of
> vegetables with medium
> cooking time inside these
> and place quicker
> cooking vegetables in the
> center.

69

Brussels Sprouts with Lemon Butter

1 lb fresh, even-sized Brussels
   sprouts
¼ cup water
1 tablespoon butter
1 tablespoon honey
1–2 tablespoons lemon juice

Time: 9 minutes. Serves 4–6

Wash sprouts, remove loose leaves and trim stems. Cut a cross into stem end for even cooking. Place into casserole dish, add water, cover and cook on high 8 minutes. Let stand 3 minutes and drain.

Heat butter and honey in small bowl on high 1 minute. Add strained lemon juice. Pour mixture over sprouts and toss to coat.

Baked Potato with Chicken Topping

4 medium-sized baking
   potatoes
¼ cup chopped peppers
¼ cup chopped celery
¼ cup chopped scallion
¼ cup grated carrot
8 oz mushrooms, sliced
½ chicken stock cube
2 tablespoons flour
¼ cup hot water
¾ cup milk
1 tablespoon white wine
1 teaspoon curry powder
¼ teaspoon salt
¼ teaspoon pepper
2 cups cooked, diced chicken
chopped parsley

Time: 22 minutes. Serves 4

Cook potatoes on high for 12 minutes, turning halfway through cooking. In a 2 pint casserole dish combine peppers, celery, scallion, carrot and mushrooms and pour over hot water. Cover and cook on high 4 minutes. Drain off liquid.

In a medium-sized bowl, combine chicken cube, flour and water. Blend in milk and cook on high 2 minutes until thickened, stirring during cooking. Stir in wine and seasonings. Add sauce to chicken and vegetables and cook on high 4 minutes.

Halve each potato lengthwise and using a fork coarsely break up the center. Spoon topping over. Serve garnished with parsley.

Beets with Dill Sauce

1 lb fresh beets
½ cup water
½ teaspoon salt

Time: 26 minutes. Serves 4–

Wash beets and cut off stalks 1½ in above the bulb. Plac evenly apart in a 3½ pint casserole. Stir salt into water an pour over beets. Cover and cook on high 15–20 minute turning beets over halfway through cooking. Let stand covered, 5 minutes.

Remove tips, skin and root ends and cut each bulb int quarters. Arrange in casserole dish and serve with Di Sauce. (See recipe following.) Cook on medium 2–3 min utes to reheat.

Dill Sauce

1 tablespoon butter
1 tablespoon flour
½ teaspoon onion salt
dash pepper
¼ teaspoon sugar
¾ cup milk
2 teaspoons chopped fresh dill

Heat butter in a small bowl on high 1 minute. Stir in flou seasonings and sugar. Blend in milk. Cook on high 2 min utes or until thickened. Stir in chopped dill.

Sweet Potato and Pineapple Bake

2 lb orange sweet potatoes
½ cup brown sugar
6 slices bacon, diced into ¾
   inch pieces
6 pineapple rings, diced into ¾
   inch cubes
¼ cup pineapple juice
2 tablespoons butter
chopped parsley
¼ cup brown sugar

Time: 20 minutes. Serves 6–

Peel potatoes and cut into even-sized dice. Place in a but tered casserole dish.

Arrange alternate layers of bacon, pineapple and brow sugar in the dish. Dot with butter and extra brown sugar Pour over pineapple juice, cover and cook on high 20 min utes or until potato is fork tender.

Sprinkle with chopped parsley to serve.

Vegetable Platter

oz cauliflower
oz broccoli
medium-sized carrots
oz small new potatoes
cup peas, beans or zucchini
  rings

Time: 12–14 minutes. Serves 6

'ash vegetables and cut into serving size. Prick potatoes
ith a skewer. Arrange cauliflower, broccoli, carrots and
otatoes around edge of plate. Place peas in center. Add 2
blespoons cold water and season lightly.
  Cover with lid or a double thickness of plastic wrap.
ook on high 12–14 minutes. Serve with butter or Hollan-
ise Sauce (see recipe Eggs Benedict).

Kohlrabi

lb kohlrabi bulbs

Time: 15–20 minutes. Serves 6–8

rim roots and stems from even-sized bulbs. (The leaves
ay be cooked like spinach leaves.) Peel and scrub bulbs
nd cut into slices. Place in casserole with ¼ cup water to
over.
  Cook on high 12–15 minutes, or until tender, stirring
very 4 minutes. Drain and serve with Dill Sauce (see
cipe Beet with Dill Sauce), Cheese and Caraway sauce
ee recipe following) or sour cream and chives.

Cheese and Caraway Sauce

tablespoons butter
tablespoons all-purpose flour
inch salt
 teaspoon dried mustard
 teaspoon cayenne pepper
cups milk
 teaspoon caraway seeds
 cup grated tasty cheese

Time: 6 minutes. Serves 6–8

Melt butter in a glass bowl and cook on high 1 minute. Stir
 flour, salt, mustard powder, cayenne pepper and cook
or 1 minute on medium heat. Blend in milk and cook on
igh 4 minutes, stirring every minute or until sauce
hickens. Stir in cheese and caraway seeds.

Peas French Style

1 cup shelled peas
⅓ cup thinly sliced celery
2 tablespoons water
3 cups shredded lettuce
1 tablespoon butter
1 tablespoon flour
½ teaspoon sugar
¼ teaspoon salt
dash lemon pepper
¼ cup sour cream

Time: 9 minutes. Serves 6

In a 3 pint casserole dish combine peas, celery and water.
Cover and cook on high 6–7½ minutes, or until tender. Stir
in lettuce, re-cover and cook on high 2 minutes, stirring
after 1 minute. Set aside.
  In a small bowl, combine butter, flour, sugar, salt and
pepper. Blend in cream and cook on high 1 minute or until
thick. Drain vegetables and fold in sauce to coat.

Baked Stuffed Potato

4 large potatoes
4 tablespoons butter
6 tablespoons sour cream
salt
pepper
4 tablespoons grated tasty
  cheese
2 slices bacon, cooked and
  diced
chopped chives

Time: 16 minutes. Serves 4

Pierce potatoes several times with a metal skewer. Arrange
potatoes 1 inch apart in a pie plate to enable microwaves to
penetrate from all sides. Cook on high 12 minutes, turning
potatoes over half way through cooking.
  Slice the top off each potato and scoop out center. Set
shells aside. Mash potato centers with butter and sour
cream. Season, add cheese and bacon pieces and spoon into
shells.
  Reheat on high 4 minutes. Serve with chopped chives.

> **HINT: WRAP COOKED POTATOES IN ALUMINUM FOIL**
> Wrap cooked skin potatoes in aluminum after cooking. They will retain their heat for 30 minutes and leave the microwave oven free for other cooking.

Vegetable Platter

Baby Squash Provencal

1 lb baby squash, even-sized
2 oz chopped onion
1 clove garlic, chopped
⅛ teaspoon salt
⅛ teaspoon pepper
2 oz butter
½ teaspoon basil
1 lb tomatoes, chopped
chopped parsley

Time: 10 minutes. Serves 6–8

Pierce each squash 5 times with a skewer. If large, cut into quarters. Heat butter, onion and garlic on high 4 minutes in medium-sized bowl. Add chopped tomatoes, basil, salt, pepper and squash.

Cover and cook on high 5–6 minutes until squash is fork tender. Sprinkle with chopped parsley to serve.

Step 1 Baby Squash Provencal. Pierce each squash 5 times with a skewer

Carrot Curls with Honey Sauce

4 large carrots, peeled
2 tablespoons water
1 tablespoon butter
2 tablespoons corn syrup
2 tablespoons vinegar
2 tablespoons orange or
    pineapple juice
2 teaspoons arrowroot
toasted sesame seeds

Time: 12 minutes. Serves 6–8

Using a vegetable peeler, cut carrots lengthwise into long thin strips. Place into cold water to form curls. Transfer carrots to casserole dish with 2 tablespoons water. Cover and cook on high 6–8 minutes. Drain.

Blend butter, syrup, vinegar, juice and arrowroot together in medium-sized bowl. Cook on high 1 minute, stirring after 30 seconds. Pour over carrot curls.

Cook on medium 2–3 minutes to reheat. Sprinkle with toasted sesame seeds to serve.

Step 2 Heat butter, onion and garlic

HINT: PRICKING VEGETABLES
Certain vegetables such as tomatoes, zucchini, baby squash and potatoes should be pierced with a skewer before cooking. This enables steam to escape during cooking and prevents the vegetables from splitting.

Step 3 Add squash, tomatoes, basil and seasoning

74

Cabbage

1 lb shredded cabbage, washed
    and drained
2 cloves garlic, chopped finely
1 tablespoon butter
2 large peeled tomatoes,
    roughly chopped
salt to taste

Time: 7 minutes. Serves 4–6

Place all ingredients in a small casserole dish or an oven
bag lightly tied with string or an elastic band. Prick bag
once or twice near opening. Cook 7 minutes on high, turning once during cooking.

Leaf Spinach

1 lb spinach leaves, no stalks,
    washed and drained
1 tablespoon butter
1 small onion, finely chopped
¼ teaspoon nutmeg
2 oz peanuts, roughly chopped

Time: 7 minutes. Serves 4

Place spinach, butter, onion, and nutmeg into an oven bag.
Fasten with an elastic band. Prick twice near opening.
Cook 7 minutes on high, turning once during cooking. Top
with roughly chopped peanuts.

Vegetable Medley

8 oz cauliflower florets
4 oz carrots, sliced crosswise
8 oz Chinese cabbage, sliced
4 oz sliced mushrooms
1 small can asparagus spears
2 slices ham, diced
chopped parsley

Sauce

2 tablespoons butter
2 tablespoons flour
1 cup chicken stock
2 cups milk

Time: 20 minutes. Serves 4–6

Place cauliflower and carrots into a casserole dish. Add 2
tablespoons water and cook covered 6 minutes on high.
Place carrots and cauliflower into a larger casserole, cover
with cabbage, mushrooms and asparagus spears. Spoon
sauce over, top with ham and parsley. Cook covered 6 minutes.
  Cook butter for sauce to melt 20 seconds. Stir in flour
and cook 2 minutes on high. Stir in stock and milk. Cook
6 minutes until thick and boiling. Stir during cooking.

Beets with Orange Sauce

4 precooked beets (see Cooking
    Chart)
2 tablespoons brown sugar
1 cup orange juice
2 tablespoons tarragon vinegar
1 tablespoon butter
1 tablespoon cornstarch

Time: 17 minutes. Serves

Use a melon baller and scoop out balls of beet from cooke
beets. Combine sugar, juice, vinegar, butter and cornstar
in a bowl. Cook 3 minutes on high, stir and cook un
boiling. Add beets, cook further 2 minutes and serve.

Parsley Potato Balls

1½ lb potatoes
water
2 tablespoons butter
2 tablespoons finely chopped
    parsley
salt to taste

Time: 12 minutes. Serves 4

Cut potatoes into balls using a melon baller. Place into ca
serole with water. Cook covered on high for 12 minute
stirring twice during cooking. Cook butter 20 seconds
melt. Add parsley and salt. Pour over drained potatoes. S
to coat.
  Note: Chopped mint may be used in place of parsley

Cauliflower au Gratin

2 tablespoons butter
1 lb cauliflower florets
¼ teaspoon garlic salt
pepper
2 large peeled tomatoes sliced
1 cup cheese sauce (see Sauces
    and Jams)
chopped parsley
paprika

Time: 9 minutes. Serves 4

Cook butter in casserole 20 seconds to melt. Ad
cauliflower, garlic salt, pepper and cook covered for 6 mi
utes. Top with sliced tomatoes, cheese sauce and parsle
Cook 3 minutes on high. Dust lightly with paprika befo
serving.

Parsley Potato Balls and Glaze
Carro

76

Glazed Carrots

1 lb carrots, cut into strips

Honey Sauce

1 tablespoon butter
2 tablespoons honey
2 tablespoons vinegar
2 tablespoons orange juice
salt
2 teaspoons cornstarch

Time: 10½ minutes. Serves 4

Place carrots in casserole dish with 1 tablespoon water. Cook covered 7–8 minutes on high, stir twice during cooking, drain.

Combine all sauce ingredients, place into glass dish and cook 1 minute on high. Stir after 30 seconds. Pour over carrots, cook 2 minutes to reheat.

Carrots with Marsala

1 lb carrots, sliced crosswise
1 onion, finely chopped
1 tablespoon brown sugar
2½ fl oz Marsala
1 tablespoon butter

Time: 8 minutes. Serves 4–6

Combine all ingredients and place in casserole dish just large enough to hold all ingredients. Cook 7–8 minutes on high, stirring twice during cooking.

Scalloped Sweet Potatoes

1½ lb orange sweet potatoes,
* sliced thinly*
2 slices of bacon, diced and
* precooked*
2 tablespoons flour
1 teaspoon salt
½ cup scallions, finely cut
2 cups milk
1 cup tasty cheese,
* grated nutmeg and paprika*
chopped parsley

Time: 15 minutes. Serves

Combine all ingredients in a greased casserole dish. Cov and cook 15 minutes on high, stirring every 4 minute Sprinkle with extra nutmeg, paprika and chopped parsle

Sweet Potato Parmesan

1 medium sweet potato
1 medium parsnip
1 bacon slice, chopped
½ cup grated Parmesan cheese
2 tablespoons water
1 small onion, chopped

Time: 8 minut

Wash, peel and cut sweet potato and parsnips into round Place in large glass bowl or casserole and add bacon, oni and water on high. Cover with lid or paper towel and co 6 minutes.

Top with Parmesan cheese. Cook for 2 minutes or un cheese begins to melt. Garnish with snipped chives.

Served with extra Parmesan cheese and a glass of whi wine this dish is a meal in itself.

Variation: For extra color and flavor add some dic peppers to the mixture before cooking.

Sweet Potato Parmesan

Step 1 Wash and peel sweet potato and parsnip and cut into rounds

Step 2 Place vegetables in bowl and add chopped bacon and onion

Step 3 Top with Parmesan cheese and cook for 2 minutes

Scalloped Sweet Potato

Braised Red Cabbage

½ head sliced red cabbage
2 tablespoons butter
2 green apples, peeled and
    sliced
1 small onion, chopped
½ teaspoon salt
¼ teaspoon pepper
2 cloves
1 bay leaf
2 tablespoons tarragon vinegar
1 cup dry red wine
1–2 tablespoons brown sugar

Time: 12 minutes. Serves 6

Combine all ingredients in casserole. Cook covered 12 minutes on high, stirring every 4 minutes.

Vegetable Kebabs

Time: 6 minutes. Serves 4

Spear a variety of vegetables onto bamboo satay sticks: cherry tomatoes, mushroom caps, chunks of red and green peppers, canned mini corn, small onions, and zucchini. Layer in dish and cook 6 minutes on high, turning every minute and basting with a mixture of melted butter and lemon juice.

Herbed Baked Potatoes

4 even-sized potatoes, unpeeled
peanut oil
4 tablespoons sour cream
2 slices bacon, diced,
    precooked
chopped chives
herb butter

Time: 11 minutes. Serves 4

Prick potatoes, brush with oil and wrap in plastic food wrap. Place in a circle on oven tray and cook 5 minutes on high. Turn over and cook a further 6 minutes. Remove wrap and cut a cross on top of each potato. Squeeze firmly so that the center will pop up. Top with herb butter, sour cream, bacon and chives.

Zucchini Special

1 lb unpeeled zucchini, sliced
1 tablespoon butter
onion or garlic salt
1 teaspoon fresh chopped dill
1 large peeled tomato, seeds
    removed, roughly chopped

Time: 8 minutes. Serves

Place all ingredients into a small casserole. Cover and cook 8 minutes on high

Fresh Broccoli Hollandaise

1 lb fresh broccoli
1 tablespoon water
2 tablespoons butter
onion salt

Time: 8 minutes. Serves

Cut broccoli into even lengths, remove skin from stalk and split ends with a knife. Place into a covered casserole dish or oven bag, with water, butter and onion salt. Cook minutes on high. Arrange onto serving dish and mask with Hollandaise Sauce (see recipe).

Cooking Chart for Fresh Vegetables

ITEM	QUANTITY	DIRECTIONS	SUGGESTED COOKING TIME IN MINUTES
Asparagus	1 lb	¼ cup water, ⅓ teaspoon salt in covered casserole	5–6
Beans	1½ lb	⅓ cup water, ¼ teaspoon salt in covered casserole	12–14
Beets	4 whole medium	Wrap each bulb in plastic wrap	12–16
Broccoli	1 small bunch	Cut away stalk, ½ cup water, 1 teaspoon salt in covered casserole	8–11
Brussels sprouts	1 lb		
Cabbage	1½ lb chopped	3 tablespoons water, ¼ teaspoon salt in covered casserole	8–10
Carrots	4 medium sliced	¼ cup water, ¼ teaspoon salt in covered casserole	8–10
Cauliflower	1½ lb	⅓ cup water, ⅛ teaspoon salt in covered casserole	10–12
Celery	6 cups	¼ cup water, ¼ teaspoon salt in covered casserole	10–12
Corn	3 ears	Remove silk, leave husk on and tie with elastic band	12
Corn kernels	3 cups	⅓ cup water, ¼ teaspoon salt in covered casserole	8
Aubergine	1 medium	¼ cup water, ¼ teaspoon salt in covered casserole	8–10
Onion	2 large (cut in quarters)	½ cup water, ¼ teaspoon salt in covered casserole	8–10
Parsnips	4 medium (cut in quarters)	½ cup water, ¼ teaspoon salt in covered casserole	8–10
Peas	1 lb	⅓ cup water, ¼ teaspoon salt in covered casserole	6–8
Potatoes	1 medium 2 medium 3 medium 4 medium 5 medium 6 medium 7 medium 8 medium	Scrub potatoes, and place on paper towel leaving a 1 in space between potatoes. Note: Prick potatoes before placing in oven	5 7 9 12 14 16 20 22
Potatoes	4 medium (thinly sliced)	2 tablespoons butter in casserole, sprinkle with salt and dot with butter. Cover	11
Sweet Potatoes	2 medium	Place on paper towel, leaving 1 in space between potatoes	7–8
Spinach	1 lb	Put in casserole with water to cling to leaves, ⅓ teaspoon salt and cover	6–7

Meat

mb is one of the all-time favorites for roasts, casseroles and ls. Legs and shoulders (boned and rolled) can be cooked covered on a roasting rack, and a sheet of paper towel can placed on top to absorb any fat splatters.

To avoid meat drying, cover the thin shank end of the leg th a 2 inch wide strip of aluminum foil. The aluminum foil ould be removed after half the cooking time has elapsed and fore the roast is turned. On completion of cooking, place a eet of aluminium foil over the roast, leaving the ends covered, and allow 10–15 minutes standing time before ving.

Lamb chops, stews and curries cook well in a preheated owning casserole dish. To cook 4 lamb chops (chops can be rinated in lemon juice, oil and garlic), cook on one side on h for 1 minute, then turn and cook the other side, also on h, for 3–4 minutes.

Seal lamb for casseroles and curries in a browning dish with mall amount of oil or ghee. Add remaining ingredients and ok on high for the first 3–5 minutes and finish cooking on dium. Cook covered and stir.

Tender cuts of beef are dry roasted on a roasting rack and uminum foil can be used to prevent meat from drying. As t draws out liquids and can cause drying it is best to season th garlic and fresh or dried herbs.

To defrost large pieces of beef, place on a roasting rack and ok on medium for 5–8 minutes for each 1 lb. Defrosting aks and chops takes only 3–4 minutes for each 1 lb but ould the meat start to brown while the center is still frozen, ver the cooked sections with aluminum foil.

Steaks and chops and burgers are cooked in a preheated owning dish but less tender cuts are best pot roasted, braised stewed and the cooking technique is the same as for nventional range-top cooking.

Roast pork will dry if overcooked and all care should be ken to monitor the internal temperature. When the mperature reaches 340°F remove the pork from the icrowave and allow it to stand for 5–10 minutes before rving. During the standing time the temperature will crease to 345°F. To cook, place fat side down on roasting ck in roasting dish and cook on high for the first 5 minutes. mplete cooking on medium and turn the roast half way rough cooking. Allow 12–16 minutes cooking time for ch 1 lb.

It is up to you whether you remove the rind but should you ant crackling, score the rind with a sharp knife and rub in l and salt before cooking.

Hams are available canned, boned, rolled, on the bone, cooked and uncooked and your microwave oven can successfully enhance the flavor of any ham. The flavor of canned or boneless rolled cooked ham is increased when heated. Allow 5–8 minutes for each 1 lb and cook on medium. Shoulders and pieces of leg ham can be heated if you allow 15 minutes for each 1 lb. In this instance, cook for the first 5 minutes on high, then set the microwave to medium.

For raw picnic hams and leg hams allow 16–18 minutes cooking time for each 1 lb. Cook on high for the first 5 minutes and complete cooking on medium.

Veal is the most tender of all meats and extra care should be taken to make sure that this very lean meat does not dry due to overcooking. When cooking thin steaks of coated veal for schnitzels preheat the browning dish for 6–8 minutes before adding a cup of oil. Heat on high for a further 3 minutes and add a slice of green ginger. When the ginger is brown the oil is the correct temperature for frying. Cook steaks 3–4 minutes on each side on high.

Grilled cutlets should be cooked on high in a preheated browning dish for 1 minute each side. Cook each side for further 5 minutes on medium.

When roasting veal allow 13–17 minutes for each 1 lb. Commence cooking on high for the first 5 minutes and complete on medium. Turn the roast half way through cooking and remove roast from the oven when the internal temperature reaches 325°F. During standing time the internal temperature of the veal will increase by 10–15°F. For cubes or slivers of veal, cook on medium for 10–15 minutes for each 1 lb.

Cooking Times for Beef Fillet Roasts

7½–9½ minutes per 1 lb : rare
8–10 minutes per 1 lb : medium rare
9½–11½ minutes per 1 lb : medium

If beef is under 2 lb cook on high for first 3 minutes; finish on medium. If beef is over 2 lb, cook on high for first 5 minutes; finish on medium. Test for readiness with meat thermometer: on standing the internal temperature will rise 40° for rare or medium rare, 30° for medium, 20° for well done.

vory Beef Roll, Lemon Lamb Satay

Step 1 Fillet of Beef Wellington. Turn beef 4 times while cooking

Step 2 Pour warmed brandy over beef

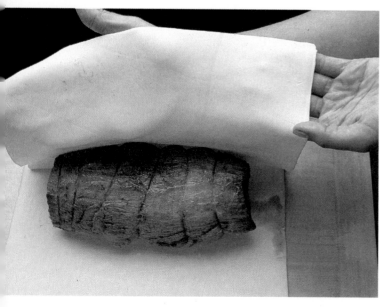

Step 3 Cover beef with puff pastry

Fillet of Beef Wellington

Fillet of Beef Wellington

3 lb middle cut fillet in one
    piece
2 cloves garlic, peeled
¼ cup brandy
2 tablespoons oil
2 tablespoons French mustard
2 sheets pie dough
1 egg, beaten

Time: 45–47 minutes. Serves 6–

ut each clove of garlic in four. Make 4 small cuts in each
de of beef and insert garlic. Tie roast at 2 inch intervals
ith kitchen string. This holds the beef in shape while
owning. Cook in browning casserole on high 6 minutes.
Remove beef, add oil and cook on high 2 minutes. Re-
rn beef to casserole and cook on high 4 minutes, turning
let four times during cooking for even browning. Cook
medium 20 minutes. Remove string.
Place brandy in jug and cook on high 15–20 seconds to

warm. Ignite with flaming taper. Pour over fillet and let
stand 5 minutes, turning beef twice.

Place beef onto sheet of pie dough. Spread top and sides
with French mustard. Brush edges of dough with beaten
egg and shape second sheet of dough over beef. Seal edges
and cut off excess dough. Brush dough with beaten egg and
decorate with excess dough.

Bake in convection microwave 400°F until dough is well
risen and golden. Serve with demi-glace sauce.

Savory Beef Roll

1½ lb lean ground beef
2 eggs
¼ cup dry breadcrumbs
1 tablespoon barbecue sauce
1 teaspoon beef seasoning
¾ cup chopped green peppers
¾ cup chopped red peppers
1 onion, chopped
1 cup grated cheese

Time: 32 minutes. Serves 4–6

Combine beef, eggs, breadcrumbs, sauce and seasoning. On a sheet of plastic wrap pat out to a rectangle ¾ thick.
Cook peppers and onion on high 2 minutes. Cool. Place onto meat leaving 1 inch border on all sides. Roll up and press edges together to seal. Place in baking dish seam side down.
Cook on high 5 minutes, then on medium 25–30 minutes. During the last 10 minutes of cooking time sprinkle with grated cheese.

Beef Bourguignonne

2 lb sirloin steak, cut into thin
    strips
4 slices bacon, cut into ¾ inch
    pieces
⅓ cup all-purpose flour
8 oz mushrooms, sliced
4 medium-sized onions, cut into
    sixths
1 medium carrot, sliced
1 clove garlic, finely chopped
1 cup dry red wine
½ cup beef consomme or stock
1 tablespoon chopped parsley
1 teaspoon salt
½ teaspoon thyme
¼ teaspoon pepper
2 bay leaves

Time: 48 minutes. Serves 6–8

Place bacon in 5 pint casserole. Cover and cook on high 3 minutes. Drain, leaving 1 tablespoon of dripping. Stir in beef strips, sprinkle with flour and toss to coat evenly.
Mix in remaining ingredients. Cover and cook on high 5 minutes. Stir. Cook on medium 40 minutes or until fork tender, stirring during cooking to thicken sauce evenly. Let stand 10 minutes before serving. Serve with buttered noodles or rice.
Note: For long slow cooking, microwave on low 60–75 minutes.

Filet Mignon

4 × 6 oz filet mignon
1 tablespoon butter

Time: 15 minutes. Serve

Preheat grilling plate on high 9 minutes. Butter one side each mignon and place buttered side down on prehea grilling plate. Cook on high 3 minutes. Brush tops w butter and turn mignons over. Cook on high 3 minutes rare. Serve with Mushroom Sauce.

Mushroom Sauce

4 oz mushrooms
1 tablespoon butter
1 tablespoon all-purpose flour
10 fl oz canned beef consomme
1 egg yolk
2 tablespoons cream
⅛ teaspoon salt
⅛ teaspoon pepper

Time: 6–8 minutes. Yield 10 fl

Place butter in jug and heat on high 1 minute. Add mus rooms and cook 1 minute. Blend in flour. Cook a furth minute on high. Stir in consomme and cook on high 3 minutes, stirring after 2 minutes.
Combine egg and cream in bowl. Add 2 tablespoons sauce and blend well. Fold into remaining sauce. Seaso Pour over mignons or other grilled meat.

Stroganoff

1 quantity basic beef mix
    thawed (see recipe Basic
    Beef Mix)
4 oz mushrooms, chopped
½ cup beef consomme
1½ tablespoons seasoned flour
1 teaspoon Worcestershire
    sauce
⅔ cup sour cream

Time: 8 minutes. Serves 4

In a 3½ pint casserole combine beef mixture, mushroom consomme, flour and sauce. Blend well and cook on hi 6 minutes, stirring twice during cooking.
Blend in sour cream and reheat on high 1–2 minute Serve with rice or pasta.

HINT:
Cut meat into slices parallel to the grain for tenderness and even cooking. Meat is easier to slice when partially frozen. Fully defrost before cooking.

Basic Beef Mix

2½ lb lean ground beef
2 onions, sliced
2 cloves garlic, chopped
2 tablespoons peanut oil
1 tablespoon chili sauce
1½ tablespoons onion soup mix
1½ tablespoons gravy powder

Time: 16 minutes. Serves 8–12

Combine onion, garlic and oil in a 3½ pint casserole. Cook on high 3 minutes. Crumble in beef and cook on high 7–8 minutes. Stir in remaining ingredients and cook on high 6 minutes, stirring twice during cooking. Cool.

The mixture can now be placed in a plastic container and frozen until ready to use for savory beef dishes such as lasagne or Bolognese sauce, or for stuffing vegetables.

Beef Roulades with Brazil Nut Stuffing

1 lb rump steak, thinly sliced
1 small onion, finely chopped
½ cup celery, thinly sliced
2 tablespoons butter
⅓ cup beef consomme or stock
½ cup chopped Brazil nuts
1 cup prepared stuffing mix
1½ tablespoons seasoned flour
1 tablespoon peanut oil
4 fl oz beef consomme or stock
4 fl oz dry red wine
3 teaspoons arrowroot
1–2 tablespoons cold water
1 oz sliced Brazil nuts

Time: 1 hour 47 minutes. Serves 4–6

Cut steak into 4 inch squares. Pound lightly with meat mallet. Combine onions, celery and butter in a medium-sized bowl. Cook on high 3–4 minutes. Add ⅓ cup of stock and cook on high 1 minute. Stir in ½ cup Brazil nuts and stuffing. Allow to cool.

Spread filling over meat slices, roll up and tie with string. Coat rolls evenly with seasoned flour. Heat browning dish on high 6 minutes. Add oil and heat 1 minute. Cook roulades 6 minutes, turning during cooking. Add 4 fl oz stock and wine and cook on medium 12 minutes.

Remove string from rolls and transfer to serving plate. Blend arrowroot with water, stir into pan liquids and cook on high 3 minutes or until boiling. Strain sauce and pour over roulades. Garnish with sliced Brazil nuts to serve.

> **HINT: MEAT BALLS**
> Roll meat balls with wet hands to prevent sticking.

Ginger Meat Balls

1 lb lean ground beef
3 scallions, finely chopped
1 egg, beaten
1 teaspoon green ginger, finely chopped
⅛ teaspoon garlic salt
½ cup beef consomme
2 teaspoons arrowroot
1 tablespoon soy sauce
1 teaspoon vinegar
1 tablespoon parsley

Time: 12 minutes. Serves 4–

Combine beef, scallions, egg, ginger and salt. Form into 2 small balls. Arrange the meat balls around outer edge of 10 inch pie plate. Cook on high 7 minutes, turning onc during cooking. Remove to serving dish.

Blend consomme and arrowroot with meat juices in pi plate. Add soy sauce, vinegar and parsley. Cook on hig 2–3 minutes until sauce has thickened, stirring twice dur ing cooking. Coat meat balls with sauce and cook 2–3 min utes on high to reheat.

Calf's Liver and Bacon

12 oz calf's liver
4 large bacon slices
1 small onion, finely chopped
½ teaspoon freshly ground pepper
¼ teaspoon salt
1½ fl oz sweet vermouth
1 tablespoon tomato paste
1 teaspoon gravy powder
1½ fl oz beef consomme or stock

Mustard Cream

1 cup sour cream
3 tablespoons French mustard

Time: 16 minutes. Serves

Soak liver in cold, salted water for 10 minutes. Remov skin and cut liver into thin slices. Derind bacon slices anc cut each slice into 1 inch lengths.

Place bacon and onion in casserole and cook on high minutes, stirring after 2 minutes. Add liver and cook or high 2 minutes. Add freshly ground pepper and salt, ver mouth and tomato paste.

Blend in gravy powder and consomme. Cover and cook on medium 10 minutes, stirring and rearranging live every 3 minutes.

Serve with Mustard Cream — made by blending sou cream and French mustard.

Roasted Ribs with Sweet Sour Sauce

2–3 lb beef ribs, cut in 1 inch
   lengths
1 medium-sized onion, thinly
   sliced
1 teaspoon basil
1 cup sweet sour sauce or
   barbecue sauce
1 tablespoon lemon juice,
   strained

Sweet Sour Sauce

¼ cup brown sugar
1 tablespoon cornstarch
½ cup pineapple juice
¼ cup vinegar
2 tablespoons soy sauce

Time: 40–46 minutes. Serves 4–6

Arrange ribs in roasting dish in a single layer for even cooking. Top with onion rings and basil and cook on high 5 minutes. Reduce power to medium and cook for 15 minutes.

Rearrange and turn ribs over. Cook on medium 15–20 minutes. Drain off liquid.

To make the sauce combine sugar and cornstarch in a jug. Blend in remaining sauce ingredients and cook on high 3 minutes or until thickened, stirring every minute.

Pour sauce over ribs and cook for a further 6 minutes.

Roasted Ribs with Sweet Sour Sauce

Stuffed Peppers

1 quantity basic beef mixture,
   thawed (see recipe Basic
   Beef Mix)
1¼ cups cooked rice
8 oz tomato paste
½ teaspoon chopped basil
   leaves
1 teaspoon sugar
¼ teaspoon salt
¼ teaspoon pepper
4–6 large peppers
½ cup grated tasty cheese

Time: 12 minutes. Serves 4–6

In a 3½ pint casserole combine beef mixture, rice, tomato paste, basil, sugar, salt and pepper.

Cut tops from peppers, remove seeds and fill each pepper with mixture. Place into casserole, cover and cook on high 12 minutes. Top each with cheese during the last minutes of cooking.

T-bone Steak

2 T-bone steaks, ¾ inch thick

Time: 15 minutes. Serve

Preheat grilling plate on high 9 minutes. Butter grill
plate and cook steaks on high 3 minutes on first side
minutes on second side for rare. Serve with herb butt

Tongue

3–3½ lb beef tongue
1½ cups water
½ teaspoon salt
¼ teaspoon pepper
2 bay leaves
1 onion, quartered

Time: 73–83 minutes. Serves 4–6

Wash tongue and trim off fat. Place in a 3½ pint casserole with water, salt, pepper, bay leaves and onion.

Cover and cook on high 3 minutes. Reduce power to medium and cook 70–80 minutes, or until tender, turning tongue half way through cooking. Let stand 5 minutes before removing skin.

91

Cooking Times For Lamb

8–11 minutes per 1 lb : rare
9–13 minutes per 1 lb : medium
10–14 minutes per 1 lb : well done

Cook 5 minutes on high to begin. Finish on medium.

Shoulder Cooking Time

9–13 minutes per 1 lb : rare : first 4 minutes on high —
finish cooking on medium.
10½–14½ minutes per 1 lb : medium : first 4 minutes on
high — finish cooking on medium.
12–15½ minutes per 1 lb : well done : first 4 minutes on
high — finish cooking on medium.

Colonial Goose

1 × 4 lb leg lamb, boned

Stuffing

1 oz butter
1 tablespoon honey
4 oz dried apricots, chopped
1 onion, finely chopped
4 oz white breadcrumbs
¼ teaspoon lemon pepper
¼ teaspoon salt
¼ teaspoon dried thyme
1 egg, beaten

Marinade

1 onion, sliced
1 carrot, sliced
1 bay leaf
3 crushed parsley stalks
1 cup red wine
1 cup consomme
2 teaspoons arrowroot
1 tablespoon water

Time: 56 minutes. Serves 6–8

Combine butter and honey in a bowl and cook on high 1
minute. Blend in remaining stuffing ingredients and force
prepared stuffing into boned cavity of lamb leg. Tie firmly
with string and place meat in roasting dish. Combine marinade ingredients, pour over meat and leave in cool place
to marinate for 6 hours, turning leg occasionally. Remove
from marinade. Reserve marinade. Weigh leg to calculate
cooking time.

Place lamb on roasting rack in baking dish, fat side
down. Divide cooking time in half. Cook on high 5 minutes
then reduce power to medium for remaining first half of
cooking time. Turn roast over and cook on medium for
remaining time. Let stand 10 minutes, lightly covered with
aluminum before carving. Arrange lamb on serving plate.

Remove fat from roasting dish and deglaze dish with 3
tablespoons of strained marinade and 1 extra cup of consomme. Thicken lightly with extra blended arrowroot and
cook on high 3–4 minutes. Strain and serve with lamb.

Shoulder of Lamb Duxelle

4 lb boneless rolled shoulder of
*   lamb*
1 clove garlic, quartered
1 tablespoon melted butter
1 teaspoon ground ginger
2 oz tasty cheese
2 oz Parmesan cheese

Stuffing

10 oz mushrooms, chopped
1 tablespoon butter
¼ cup finely chopped scallions
½ teaspoon dried thyme
1 tablespoon chopped parsley
½ cup soft white breadcrumbs

Time: 36–73 minutes. Serves 8–1

To make stuffing, melt butter in bowl on high 1 minute
Add mushrooms and herbs and cook on high for 1 minute
Add scallions and breadcrumbs.

Weigh lamb. Make 4 small cuts on each side of the rolle
shoulder and insert a piece of garlic in each one. Heat bu
ter on high 1 minute and brush over lamb. Sprinkle with
ginger.

Place lamb, fat side down, on roasting rack in bakin
dish and cook on high for 3 minutes. Reduce to mediur
and continue cooking for remaining first half of cookin
time.

Turn shoulder over and continue cooking on medium fo
remaining cooking time. Remove string from shoulder. Cu
three-quarters of the way through the shoulder into slice
insert stuffing between each slice and reshape. Combin
tasty and Parmesan cheese. Sprinkle over top of shoulde
and cook on medium for 6 minutes until cheese melts an
lamb reheats. Serve with gravy.

Lamb Burgers

1 lb ground lamb
4 slices bacon
½ cup finely chopped scallions
1½ teaspoons Worcestershire
*   sauce*
½ teaspoon lamb seasoning
*   salt*
4 slices cheese

Time: 12 minutes. Serves

Arrange bacon between two layers of white paper towe
and cook on high 3 minutes.

Preheat grilling plate on high 5 minutes. Combine lamb
scallions, sauce and seasoning and shape into 4 burgers
Place on preheated grilling plate and cook on high 2 min
utes.

Cut bacon slices in half and place 2 pieces on each patty
Top each with cheese and cook on high 2 minutes for wel
done. Serve on hot toasted buns.

Lamb Casserole

1 lb lean lamb shoulder, cut
  into ¾ inch cubes
2 tablespoons all-purpose flour
½ teaspoon salt
¼ teaspoon lemon pepper
1 × 16 oz can tomato pieces
¾ cup consomme or stock
8 oz sliced mushrooms
1 medium-sized onion,
  quartered
½ teaspoon oregano
1 sprig fresh rosemary
1 × 10 oz packet frozen
  chunk-style beans, thawed

Time: 65 minutes. Serves 6

In 3½ pint casserole place lamb, flour, salt and pepper and
stir to coat lamb. Add tomatoes, consomme, mushrooms,
onion, oregano and rosemary.

Cover and cook on high 5 minutes. Reduce to medium
and cook 20 minutes. Stir, re-cover and cook on medium
30 minutes. Add beans and cook on medium 10 minutes
until beans are cooked.

Lemon Lamb Satay

1 lb lean lamb, cut into 1 inch
  cubes
½ green pepper, diced
1 medium-sized onion, cut into
  eighths
1 lemon, cut into 8 wedges
4 bamboo satay sticks

Lemon Marinade

½ cup lemon juice
½ cup olive oil
2 cloves garlic, crushed
2 bay leaves
1 teaspoon oregano
½ teaspoon salt
¼ teaspoon freshly ground
  black pepper

Time: 14 minutes. Serves 4

Combine all marinade ingredients in 3½ pint bowl. Add
lamb cubes and marinate four hours. Discard marinade.

Thread marinated lamb cubes and vegetables onto satay
sticks. Place on roasting rack and cook on medium 6 minutes. Turn over and rearrange. Cook 8–9 minutes. Serve
with lemon wedges.

Lamb Kebabs

1 lb lean boneless lamb, cut
  into 24 cubes
1 small can pineapple pieces in
  juice
2 teaspoons lemon juice
2 teaspoons soy sauce
¼ teaspoon ground ginger
¼ teaspoon dried oregano
8 cherry tomatoes
½ green pepper, cut into
  eighths
4 wooden satay sticks

Time: 10 minutes. Serves

In a bowl combine ⅓ cup pineapple juice, lemon juice, so
sauce, ginger and oregano. Stir in lamb and cover. Mar
nate overnight in refrigerator. Remove meat and discar
marinade.

Thread lamb, tomatoes, peppers and pineapple pieces o
satay sticks and arrange on roasting rack. Cook on mediu
10 minutes.

Veal Mozzarella

1 lb veal escalopes
¾ cup grated mozzarella
  cheese
1 tablespoon finely chopped
  parsley

Sauce

8 oz tomato paste
¼ teaspoon oregano
½ teaspoon basil
¼ teaspoon garlic salt
½ teaspoon sugar
⅛ teaspoon white pepper

Time: 22 minutes. Serves

Combine all sauce ingredients in a medium-sized bowl an
cook on high 2 minutes. Reduce power to medium an
cook 6 minutes. Set aside.

Place veal escalopes in a single layer in baking dish an
cook on medium 8–9 minutes. Drain.

Spoon sauce over veal. Sprinkle with cheese and parsle
and cook on medium 6–7 minutes until cheese melts.

**HINT: TESTING THE
VEAL IS COOKED**
Veal is cooked when the
internal temperature
reaches 325°–350°F. Let
stand covered until
temperature rises to
360°F.

Standing time
tenderizes veal.

Veal and Ham Terrine

½ lb veal, ground
bacon slices, rinds removed
clove garlic, finely chopped
eggs, beaten
teaspoon dried tarragon
tablespoon chopped parsley
tablespoons brandy or sherry
teaspoon salt
teaspoon pepper
cup soft white breadcrumbs
oz ham, finely chopped
cup toasted almond slivers
cup drained crushed
  pineapple

Time: 20–25 minutes. Serves 8–10

ne a loaf dish with bacon. In a bowl combine veal, garlic, gs, tarragon, parsley, brandy, salt, pepper and eadcrumbs. Place ham, almonds and pineapple into a all bowl.

Place one-third of veal mixture onto bacon and cover ith half ham mixture. Repeat with veal and ham mixtures d cover with remaining veal. Fold exposed ends of bacon er veal and cover with lid or plastic food wrap.

Stand terrine on plate to collect spillover and cook on edium-high 20–25 minutes. Let stand 10 minutes, then ol.

Remove lid. Place weight on top and refrigerate over-ght to prevent crumbling when cut. Serve sliced with lad and toast.

Veal Nicoise

lb veal steaks
medium-sized onion, sliced
  thinly in rings
tablespoons tomato paste
tablespoon flour
  teaspoon dried basil
teaspoon sugar
teaspoons chopped parsley
small clove garlic, chopped
  teaspoon salt
  teaspoon freshly ground
  black pepper
large tomatoes, peeled and
  chopped
medium-sized green pepper,
  thinly sliced
medium-sized red pepper,
  thinly sliced
cup sliced stuffed olives
whole black olives
teaspoons finely chopped
  parsley

Time: 16–18 minutes. Serves 4

Pound veal with meat mallet to tenderise and flatten to ½ inch thickness. Place slices into baking dish and top with onion rings.

In a medium-sized bowl blend tomato paste, flour, basil, sugar, parsley, garlic, salt and pepper. Stir in tomato and peppers. Spread veal with vegetable mixture and sprinkle with sliced and whole olives.

Cook on high 16–18 minutes until veal is fork tender. Sprinkle lightly with finely chopped parsley to serve.

Osso Bucco

4 × 10 oz osso bucco (shin of
  veal slices)
seasoned flour
3 tablespoons olive oil
1 small onion, chopped
1 small carrot, cut in ½ inch
  pieces
1 stalk celery, cut into ½ inch
  pieces
1 bay leaf
⅔ cup dry vermouth or white
  wine
1 can peeled tomato pieces
1 tablespoon tomato paste
½ teaspoon salt
1 teaspoon freshly ground
  black pepper
1 clove garlic, finely chopped
zest ½ lemon
2 tablespoons finely chopped
  Italian parsley

Time: 75–85 minutes. Serves 4

Heat browning casserole dish on high 8 minutes. Add oil and cook on high 1 minute. Roll each piece of shin of veal in seasoned flour and place in oil. Cook on high 8 minutes, turning every 2 minutes. Transfer meat to a plate.

Add onion, carrot, celery and bay leaf to casserole dish. Cover and cook on high 5 minutes. Add wine, stir in and cook on high for 4 minutes. Stir in tomatoes and their juice, tomato paste salt and pepper. Cover and cook on high 6 minutes.

Place meat in sauce mixture and baste. Cover and cook on high for 5 minutes. Reduce to medium and cook 44 minutes, turning and basting every 10 minutes.

Arrange meat on serving platter, puree vegetables and sauce in food processor. Correct seasoning and pour over meat.

Combine garlic, lemon zest and parsley. Sprinkle over meat just before serving. Serve with Lemon Rice (see recipe Lemon Rice).

Veal and Ham Terrine

Pork Fillets with Prune and Almond Stuffing

4 × 13 oz pork fillets
16 prunes
4 anchovy fillets
16 toasted almonds
1 tablespoon butter
1 tablespoon all-purpose flour
1 cup beef consomme
1/8 teaspoon salt
1/8 teaspoon pepper
6 tablespoons red wine
8 pickling onions, peeled

Time: 38 minutes. Serves 4

Cut each fillet lengthwise two-thirds through and open out. Remove seed from each prune. Cut each anchovy into quarters. Stuff one almond and a piece of anchovy into each prune and reshape.

Place 4 stuffed prunes into each cut fillet and tie each fillet with white string to enclose prunes. Preheat browning casserole on high for 8 minutes. Add butter and fillets and cook on high 4 minutes, turning every minute. Remove from casserole.

Blend flour into pan drippings and cook on high 1 minute. Blend in consomme, salt, pepper and red wine. Cook on high 4 minutes. Add fillets and pickling onions and mask with sauce. Cover and cook on high 3 minutes, then reduce to medium. Cook 18 minutes, turning 4 times during cooking.

Pickled Pork with Caper Sauce

5 lb lean pickled pork
1 tablespoon brown sugar
1 cinnamon stick
1 teaspoon peppercorns
6 whole cloves
3 bay leaves
1 onion, chopped
1 stalk celery, cut in 3/4 inch
    lengths
1 cup water
1/2 cup pineapple or orange
    juice

Time: 2–2½ hours. Serves 8–10

Place pork in a 3½–5 pint casserole dish. Add remaining ingredients, cover and cook on high 10 minutes. Reduce power to medium and cook for 45 minutes.

Turn pork over and cover. Cook on medium 60–90 minutes or until pork is tender. Let stand 10–20 minutes, covered; before carving. Serve with Caper Sauce.

Caper Sauce

1 tablespoon capers
2 teaspoons chopped parsley
1 tablespoon butter
1 tablespoon all-purpose flour
1/8 teaspoon salt
1/8 teaspoon pepper
8 fl oz milk

Time: 3 minutes 45 seconds. Makes 2-3 cup

Place butter into medium-sized bowl. Cook on high seconds until melted. Stir in flour, salt, pepper and ad milk. Cook on high 3 minutes or until boiling, stirring aft each minute. Fold in capers and parsley.

Sweet and Sour Pork Casserole

1½ lb pork, cut into 3/4 inch
    pieces
2 tablespoons seasoned
    cornstarch
3 tablespoons soy sauce
1/4 cup brown sugar
1/4 cup vinegar
1/4 teaspoon ground ginger
1 × 14 oz can pineapple pieces
    in juice
1 onion, chopped
1/2 red pepper, chopped
1 stalk celery, chopped
1 clove garlic, finely chopped

Time: 35 minutes. Serves

Toss pork in seasoned cornstarch into a 3½ pint casserol dish. Add remaining ingredients except peppers. Cover ar cook on high 5 minutes, stirring twice during cooking.

Add peppers, adjust seasonings and thickening if neces ary and continue cooking on medium 10 minutes. Serv with rice or fried noodles.

> **HINT: ADDING THICKENING AGENTS TO CASSEROLES**
> Pour blended cornstarch into casserole around outer edge. Cook on high 2 minutes. Stir through the other ingredients. Continue cooking 2–3 minutes.

Seasoned Shoulder of Lamb

1 boned shoulder of lamb
  — 4 lb

Seasoning

1 cup fresh breadcrumbs
1 tablespoon butter
¼ teaspoon nutmeg
¼ teaspoon salt
¼ teaspoon pepper
1 tablespoon chopped mint
pinch mixed herbs
2 tablespoons milk
2 scallions, finely cut
½ cup sliced fresh mushrooms

Peach Sauce

1 cup cranberry sauce
½ cup diced peaches
2 tablespoons sweet vermouth
  or sherry

Time: 39 minutes. Serves 4–6

Combine all ingredients for seasoning. Place seasoning on boned lamb. Roll up. Tie firmly with string or fasten with bamboo sate sticks. Place onto roasting rack, fat side down. Cook 36 minutes on high, turning halfway through cooking time. Wrap in aluminum foil and let stand for 15 minutes before carving.

Combine ingredients for Peach Sauce and cook 3 minutes on high to heat.

Pork Chops with Mustard and Apple Sauce

6 pork chops, fat removed
salt and pepper to taste
1 tablespoon oil

Mustard and Apple Sauce

1 tablespoon wholegrain
  mustard
1 small green apple, peeled,
  cored and chopped
1 tablespoon freshly chopped
  parsley
2 teaspoons white wine

Time: 22 minutes. Serves 6

Preheat browning dish on high 6 minutes. Add oil and cook chops, 3 at a time, on high 6 minutes, turning once. Repeat with remaining chops. Arrange on serving dish.

Combine sauce ingredients in a bowl, cover and cook on high 3–4 minutes. Stir and serve over chops.

Beef Olives

1 lb very thinly sliced rump
  steak
1 slice bacon, diced
1 small onion, chopped
¼ cup breadcrumbs
1 tablespoon chopped parsley
1 teaspoon grated lemon rind
1 small carrot, grated
black pepper
¼ teaspoon salt
1 egg
seasoned flour
1 oz butter
5 fl oz brown stock
5 fl oz red wine
3 teaspoons arrowroot
1 tablespoon cold water
parsley for garnish

Time: 30 minutes. Serves 3

Cut steak into 4 inch squares. Pound with meat malle
Place bacon and onion into bowl, cook 3 minutes. A
breadcrumbs, parsley, lemon rind, carrot, pepper, salt, a
egg. Blend together. Spread filling over meat slices. Roll
and tie with string. Coat meat with seasoned flour. Prehe
browning skillet 6 minutes. Add butter to melt. Add be
rolls, cook 3 minutes on high on each side. Add stock, wi
and cook covered 12 minutes medium.

Remove string from rolls, transfer to serving plate. R
serve juices and add 3 teaspoons arrowroot blended wi
1 tablespoon cold water to skillet juices. Cook on high 2
minutes to form sauce. Mask rolls with sauce. Sprink
with cut parsley.

Pepper Steak

4 thin slices fillet steak
2 tablespoons ground black
  pepper
2 tablespoons oil
2 cloves garlic, finely chopped
2 tablespoons brandy
¼ cup white wine

Time: 17 minutes. Serves

Cover steaks with ground pepper and pound with malle
Heat browning skillet 6 minutes on high. Add oil and ga
lic. Heat for 3 minutes. Press steak into pan, cook 3 mi
utes on each side. Add brandy and wine, cook 2 minute

Beef Olive

Guard of Honor

2 racks of lamb, each with 8
  cutlets

Stuffing

2 oz butter
1 small onion, finely chopped
2 cups fresh breadcrumbs
1 tablespoon chopped parsley
pinch dry mixed herbs
1 egg, beaten
1 teaspoon grated lemon or
  orange rind
garlic slivers

Time: 23 minutes. Serves 4–6

Place butter into bowl for 15–20 seconds to melt. Add onion and cook 2–3 minutes on high. Combine with remaining ingredients.

Interlace cutlet bones to form an arch. Stud with garlic slivers and season lightly. Place seasoning in center of cutlet racks, and fasten with bamboo sate sticks to retain shape. Cook 20 minutes on high. Cover with aluminum foil and allow to stand 10–15 minutes. Top cutlet bones with frills. Serve with minted Potato Balls, Glazed Carrots and a green vegetable (see Vegetables).

Potato Pie

2 tablespoons butter
1 small onion, finely chopped
1 lb cold roast lamb, ground
2 tablespoons chopped parsley
8 oz peas, cooked
8 oz cooked carrots, sliced
8 oz fresh mushrooms, sliced
1 teaspoon curry powder
5½ oz canned mushroom soup
salt and pepper
2 cups hot mashed potato
nutmeg and paprika

Time: 12 minutes. Serves 4–6

Melt butter in casserole dish for 15 seconds. Add onion and cook 3 minutes on high. Fold in lamb, parsley, peas, carrots, mushrooms, curry powder, soup, salt and pepper. Pipe potatoes over top of mixture. Sprinkle with nutmeg and paprika. Cook 9 minutes.

Garlic Brains

1 lb calves' or lambs' brains
1 tablespoon white wine
1½ oz butter
4 cloves garlic
juice of ½ lemon
chopped parsley
seasoned salt

Time: 16 minutes. Serves 2

Trim and rinse brains. Place in flat dish and add 1 tablespoon of dry white wine. Cover with plastic food wrap and cook 4 minutes on high. Turn over after 2 minutes. Cover and cut into thick slices. Heat browning skillet for 6 minutes. Add butter and chopped garlic. Cook 2 minutes. Add sliced brains and cook 2 minutes on each side. Add lemon juice, chopped parsley, seasoned salt.

Vienna Schnitzel

1 lb fillets of veal
¼ cup lemon juice
seasoned flour
1 egg, beaten
2 tablespoons milk
1 teaspoon soy sauce
1 cup breadcrumbs
1 cup oil
lemon wedges

Time: 15 minutes. Serves 2

Pound veal fillets with meat mallet until thin. Marinate in lemon juice for 20 minutes. Dust with seasoned flour. Combine egg, milk and soy sauce. Dip veal fillets into egg mixture, and coat with breadcrumbs. Preheat browning skillet for 8 minutes on high. Add oil and heat for 3 minutes. Add schnitzels, cook 2 minutes on each side. Serve with lemon wedges.

Glazed Ham Steaks

1½ lbs ham steaks
¼ cup maple syrup
¼ cup brown sugar
pinch ground cloves

Time: 17½ minutes. Serves

Combine maple syrup, brown sugar and ground cloves in small basin. Cook on high 1½ minutes, stir to dissolve sugar.

Heat browning dish on high 8 minutes. Add ham steaks. Pour over half glaze, cover and cook on high 4 minutes, turn steaks after 2 minutes and pour over remaining glaze. Cook on medium 4 minutes uncovered.

Lamb Stew

1½ lb lean lamb
3 tablespoons flour
salt and pepper
oregano
pinch of thyme
2 oz butter
1 large onion, finely chopped
2 carrots, sliced
8 oz potato balls
½ red pepper, diced
bouquet garni
1½ cups beef stock

Time: 52 minutes. Serves 4

Cut lamb into even sized pieces. Combine flour, salt, pepper, oregano and thyme. Roll lamb in seasoned flour. Heat browning skillet for 8 minutes. Add butter to melt. Add lamb pieces, cook 2 minutes on each side. Add all vegetables and bouquet garni, cook covered 5 minutes on high, stirring once during cooking. Add stock, cook covered on medium for 35 minutes. Let stand 10–15 minutes before serving.

Roast Leg of Lamb

1 × 5 lb leg of lamb
3 cloves garlic, peeled
lemon-flavored black pepper
1 teaspoon powdered ginger
variety of vegetables
1 can drained pears
1 jar mint jelly

Time: 53 minutes. Serves 8

Trim excess fat from lamb. Cut garlic in slivers and stud lamb. Sprinkle with lemon-flavored black pepper and rub lightly with ginger. Place lamb, fat side down, on a roasting rack in an oblong casserole dish or just place into casserole dish. Cover with a sheet of paper towel and cook 25 minutes on high. Turn leg over and baste with pan drippings. Cook a further 15 minutes. Wrap in aluminum foil, allow to stand for 15 minutes before carving.

During this time vegetables can be cooked in the baking dish. Suggested vegetables: whole onions, sweet potato, pumpkin, potatoes. Place vegetables in pan and baste with drippings. Cook 5 minutes on high. Turn over to cook a further 5 minutes or until tender. Fill pears with mint jelly and heat 3 minutes.

Beef Stroganoff

2 tablespoons oil
1 lb rump steak
½ teaspoon salt
½ teaspoon pepper
2 tablespoons flour
2 onions, sliced
1 clove garlic, cut finely
8 oz fresh mushrooms, sliced
5 fl oz red wine
5 fl oz beef stock
1 tablespoon tomato paste
1 carton sour cream

Time: 25 minutes. Serves 4–

Preheat browning skillet for 8 minutes on high. Add oil an heat for 2 minutes. Combine salt, pepper and flour. Cu meat into very thin slices, across grain. Roll in seasoned flour. Add to pan and cook 3–4 minutes, stirring frequentl to brown meat. Add onions, garlic and cook 3 minute Add mushrooms, wine, stock, tomato paste and cook minutes on medium. Blend in sour cream, cook to rehe 2 minutes. Serve with rice or buttered noodles.

Sauerbraten

1 × 3–3½ lb piece boneless
   sirloin

Marinade

1¾ cups cold water
½ cup red wine vinegar
1 medium onion, sliced
1 stalk celery, sliced
2 teaspoons salt
6 whole cloves
6 whole peppercorns
2 large bay leaves

Sauce (reserved marinade)

¼ cup seaoned flour
1 tablespoon brown sugar
10 gingersnap cookies, crushed

Time: 64 minutes. Serves 8–1

Mix marinade ingredients together in large casserole. Ad sirloin, cover and marinate in refrigerator 24 hours, turr ing several times. Strain marinade.

Place beef and 1 cup of the marinade into a 3 pint ca serole. Cover and cook on medium 60–75 minutes or unt fork tender, turning halfway through cooking. Let stand covered, while making sauce.

Place reserved marinade, flour and sugar into a 2 pir bowl and blend well. Cook on high 2–3 minutes, stirrin every minute. Place roast on warm serving platter. St sauce into meat drippings. Add gingersnap cookies an cook 1–2 minutes on high until boiling, stirring once.

Note: For long slow cooking of beef, cook on lo 105–120 minutes.

Roast Pork Ribs

½ lb pork spareribs

Marinade

medium onion, chopped
tablespoons dark soy sauce
tablespoons honey
tablespoons lemon juice
clove garlic, crushed
teaspoon salt
nch pepper
teaspoon curry powder
teaspoon chili powder
teaspoon ground ginger
cup oil

Time: 20 minutes. Serves 4

Combine marinade ingredients. Remove rind and excess fat from ribs. Prick with skewer and place in marinade for 2 hours. Place ribs onto a roasting rack and cook 20 minutes on high, turning after 10 minutes. Spare ribs may also be cooked in an oven bag.

Note: Chicken wings can also be cooked in this manner.

Roast Pork Ribs

Lamb Curry

1½ lb boneless leg of lamb
1 oz butter
8 oz onions, chopped
1 clove garlic, chopped
2 tablespoons curry powder
1 tablespoon flour
1 tablespoon chutney
2 teaspoons coconut
1 tablespoon raisins
2 oz chopped apple
2 tablespoons tomato paste
1 cup beef stock
salt

Time: 36 minutes. Serves 4–6

Trim lamb and cut into even sized pieces. Preheat browning skillet 6 minutes on high. Add butter and heat for 2 minutes. Cook lamb pieces 3 minutes on each side with onion and garlic. Drain off any fat, add curry powder and flour. Mix well and cook 2 minutes. Add chutney, coconut, raisins, apples, tomato paste and stock. Cook covered 20 minutes on high, stirring occasionally. Serve with plain boiled rice and cucumber sambal.

Corned Beef

4 cups boiling water
3 lb corned beef
3 cloves
1 small onion, chopped
1 cinnamon stick
¼ teaspoon nutmeg
1 tablespoon brown sugar
1 bay leaf
1 tablespoon vinegar

Defrost Cooking Cycle Method

Place water, meat and remaining ingredients into a covered casserole dish and cook on defrost cycle 1¾–2 hours, or until tender when pierced with a fork. Allow to stand 10 minutes before carving.

Oven Bag Method

Time: 1–2 hours (see instructions). Serves 6–8

Soak beef in 2 changes of cold water for 2 hours. Place meat into an oven bag with remaining ingredients and 1½ cups of cold water. Tie bag. Place in large Pyrex bowl. Pierce bag once or twice. Cook 30 minutes on high, turn meat over and cook 30 minutes on medium. Allow to stand 10 minutes before carving.

Veal Marsala

1 lb veal steak
seasoned all-purpose flour
3 tablespoons butter
½ cup Marsala

Time: 14 minutes. Serves

Pound veal with mallet to flatten. Dust with season flour. Heat browning skillet 6 minutes on high. Add butt to melt. Add veal and cook 2 minutes on each side. A Marsala and cook 3–4 minutes to form a sauce with p drippings.

Veal Cordon Bleu

4 × 4 oz slices veal
2 slices Gruyere cheese
2 slices lean ham
seasoned flour
1 beaten egg
1 tablespoon milk
1 teaspoon soy sauce
1 cup seasoned breadcrumbs

Time: 19 minutes. Serves

Pound veal slices with mallet until thin. Place 1 slice ea of cheese and ham on 2 veal slices. Top with remaini veal. Seal outer edges of veal by tapping with meat malle

Combine egg, milk and soy sauce. Dust veal wi seasoned flour, dip into egg mixture and coat wi breadcrumbs. Preheat browning skillet 8 minutes on hig Add oil and heat for 3 minutes. Cook veal for 4 minutes each side.

Stuffed Butterfly Pork Chops

4 butterfly pork chops
1 cup peeled chopped apple
¼ cup raisins
2 teaspoons orange zest
⅛ teaspoon cinnamon
1 tablespoon butter
½ cup dry breadcrumbs
2 teaspoons brown sugar

Time: 24 minutes. Serves

Combine apple, raisins, orange zest, cinnamon and butte in bowl and cook on high 3 minutes. Stir in ¼ cu breadcrumbs and all brown sugar. Pack filling into eac chop and press edges together. Coat chops with remainin breadcrumbs and arrange on the outer edge of roastin rack in baking dish.

Cook chops on high 5 minutes. Reduce power medium and cook 16 minutes or until meat is no longe pink.

Roast Pork

5 lb leg or loin of pork in one
  piece
3 tablespoons oil
1 teaspoon salt
1 teaspoon five spice powder
juice of half a lemon
apple and pineapple slices for
  garnish
apricot jam for glaze

Time: 45 minutes. Serves 6

Score rind of pork. Brush with oil. Rub salt and five spice powder into the skin and allow to stand for 15 minutes. Pour lemon juice over. Place on roasting rack in casserole dish and cook 40–45 minutes on high. (It is not necessary to turn pork over during cooking.) Wrap in aluminum foil and allow to stand 20 minutes before carving. During last 4 minutes of cooking, place slices of apple and pineapple around pork. Glaze slices with apricot jam.

Braised Pork Chops

4 shoulder pork chops
seasoned all-purpose flour
2 tablespoons oil
1 onion, sliced
3 large mushrooms, sliced
2 tomatoes, peeled and sliced
½ cup chicken stock
½ cup port wine
2 cloves
salt and pepper

Time: 23 minutes. Serves 4

Coat chops with seasoned flour. Heat browning skillet 6 minutes on high. Add oil and heat for 3 minutes. Press chops into skillet and cook 3 minutes on each side to brown. Add onion, mushrooms, tomato, stock, port, cloves, salt and pepper. Cover and cook for 8 minutes. Allow to stand 5 minutes before serving. Sauce may be thickened lightly with cornstarch.

Polynesian Kebabs

1½ lb lean boneless pork cut
  into 1 inch cubes
1 cup pineapple pieces
1 cup red or green peppers,
  diced or 1 onion, diced

Time: 20 minutes. Serves 6–8

Marinade

1 clove garlic, chopped
½ cup pineapple juice
1 cup soy sauce
¼ cup dry sherry
3 teaspoons brown sugar

Combine marinade ingredients in basin and add pork cubes. Toss to coat. Cover and marinate 2 hours or overnight. Thread pork cubes onto long satay sticks alternating with pieces of peppers, or onion and pineapple.

Heat browning dish on high 8 minutes and lightly oil. Arrange kebabs and cook on high 12 minutes turning and basting frequently.

Meat Loaf

2 bread slices, ½ in thick
1 lb ground beef
2 oz onion, finely chopped
2 oz green pepper, finely
  chopped
2 oz celery, finely chopped
½ cup grated tasty cheese
1 tablespoon chopped parsley
5 fl oz tomato juice
2 eggs
¾ teaspoon salt
dash of pepper and nutmeg
2 tablespoons Worcestershire
  sauce
2 oz tomato sauce

Time: 25 minutes. Serves 4–

Soak bread slices in water until soft. Squeeze out wate thoroughly. Mix beef, bread, onion, green pepper, ce ery, cheese, parsley and tomato juice in a bowl. Stir wel Add eggs, salt, pepper and nutmeg. Stir well again. Shap meat into a loaf and place in dish. Cook 20 minutes o high. Blend Worcestershire sauce and tomato sauce Drizzle liquid over top of loaf. Cook 5 minutes.

Note: Fruit chutney and extra grated cheese can b spread on top of meat loaf during last 5 minutes of cookin;

Tongue a la King

1½ lb cooked tongue, diced
  into ¾ inch pieces
1 tablespoon butter
3 oz sweet red pepper, diced
  into ¾ inch pieces
6 oz button mushrooms, sliced
1½ tablespoons sherry
1½ tablespoons butter
1½ tablespoons all-purpose
  flour
1 cup chicken stock
1 cup milk
⅛ teaspoon salt
⅛ teaspoon white pepper
2–3 tablespoons cream

Time: 14 minute

Combine butter, peppers and mushrooms in a 3½ pint ca serole and cook on high 2 minutes, stirring after 1 minute Drain off any liquid. Add tongue and sherry.

Place butter into a 2 pint measure and cook on high minute. Stir in flour and cook on high 2 minutes. Blend i milk and stock. Cook on high 5–6 minutes or until boiling stirring twice during cooking. Add salt, pepper and cream

Fold into vegetable mixture and cook on high 2–3 mi utes or until heated through. Serve with rice (p. 261).

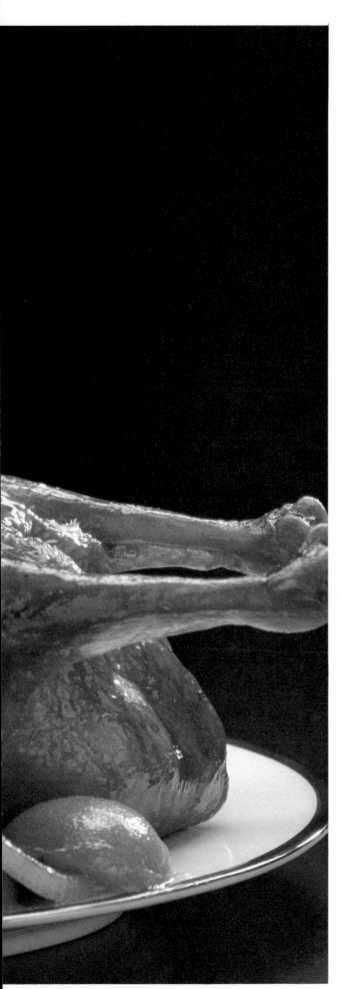

Poultry

Chicken is one of the most economical sources of protein available and when cooked in a microwave oven none of the natural tenderness and juiciness of the chicken is lost. As chicken will not brown in a microwave, baste the chicken during cooking with a mixture of barbecue or soy sauce and butter.

To roast a whole chicken place uncovered on a rack and allow 11–13 minutes cooking time for each 1 lb. Complete the first 10 minutes of cooking on high, then finish with the microwave set to medium. Baste and turn the chicken during cooking and when cooked the internal temperature should be 370°F. Try not to prick the chicken with a fork as the loss of natural juice can dry out the flesh.

For casseroles remove the skin from the breast, thighs and drumsticks.

Ducks render a great deal of fat and therefore the roasting dish should be emptied a number of times during cooking. Allow 8–9 minutes cooking time for each 1 lb and complete the first 10 minutes on high and finish on medium. After the first 10 minutes the duck can be removed from the oven and the cavity filled with a prepared stuffing. Secure the neck with a bamboo skewer. Turn halfway through cooking and before carving allow the duck to stand for 5 minutes. For both duck and turkey commence cooking breast side down.

When buying a turkey for cooking in a microwave oven make sure that there will be at least 3 inches between the turkey and the oven walls and at least 2 inches between the turkey and the oven roof.

To prevent drying out, wings, drumsticks, neck and cavity can be wrapped in thin strips of aluminum foil. Allow 10–15 minutes cooking time for each 1 lb. Cook in the same fashion as chicken and duck.

Finish cooking breast side up and remove any aluminum foil half way through cooking. When the turkey is done the internal temperature should be 360°F and the juices should run clear. Stand turkey for 20 minutes before carving.

For cooking rolled turkey breast (boned or deboned, stuffed or plain) allow 12–15 minutes for each 1 lb. Cook on high, with the breast side down, for the first 5 minutes and finish cooking on medium. Turn breast halfway through cooking time and baste. When cooked internal temperature should be 340°F. Stand for 10–15 minutes before carving.

Follow these guidelines for other turkey portions. Wings and drumsticks can be roasted, broiled or casseroled. Allow 12–16 minutes cooking time for each 1 lb, cook for the first 5 minutes on high and finish cooking on medium. Allow 16 minutes for each 1 lb when cooking hindquarters and cook on high for the first 10 minutes and finish on medium. For turkey breast steaks allow 15 minutes cooking for each 1 lb and cook on medium.

Roast Apricot Duck

Turkey Divan

1½ lb cooked turkey, diced into
　¾ inch pieces
1 cup chicken stock
1 lb broccoli heads, washed
1 tablespoon water
⅛ teaspoon salt
1 tablespoon melted butter
3 tablespoons dry sherry
2 oz grated cheese
2½ cups bechamel sauce
1 quantity hollandaise sauce (see
　recipe Eggs Benedict)
2 tablespoons dry sherry
2 oz grated tasty or Parmesan
　cheese
strip of pimiento or blanched red
　pepper strips
chopped parsley

Time: 24 minutes. Serves 6-8

Place turkey and stock in a casserole, cover and cook on high 3 minutes, stirring after 2 minutes. Set aside.

Put broccoli, water and salt in a 5 pint casserole dish. Cover and cook on high 6 minutes. Drain. Sprinkle with melted butter, 3 tablespoons sherry and cheese.

Drain turkey cubes and arrange over broccoli. Fold bechamel (see recipe following) and hollandaise sauce together, blend in remaining sherry and spoon over turkey. Sprinkle with remaining cheese.

Cook on medium 6-9 minutes until heated through and cheese melted. Garnish with pimiento strips and chopped parsley.

HINT: TURKEY IN THE MICROWAVE

The maximum size turkey suitable for cooking in a microwave oven is 12-14 lb. Larger birds should be roasted conventionally.

To test the oven for size, place turkey in oven and turn on all sides. There should be 3 inch space between turkey and oven walls and at least 2 inch between the top of the oven and the upper side of the turkey.

During cooking, baste the turkey occasionally. Check for areas that may be cooking too fast and shield these with small amounts of aluminum foil.

Cooking times remain the same whether the turkey is stuffed or unstuffed.

Turkey Chow Mein

2 boned turkey thighs, diced
　into ¾ inch pieces
1-2 tablespoons cornflour
½ cup rich chicken stock
1½ tablespoons soy sauce
1 cup thinly sliced celery
1 medium-sized onion, diced
1 × 14 oz can Chinese mixed
　vegetables, drained
8 oz fresh mushrooms, sliced
1 packet cooked chow mein
　noodles

Time: 18 minutes. Serves

Place turkey pieces in casserole. Cover and cook on hig 6-8 minutes, stirring after 3 minutes.

Blend cornflour and stock and add to casserole. Stir soy sauce and vegetables. Cover and cook on high 12 mi utes, stirring after 6 minutes. Serve surrounded by cho mein noodles.

Roast Turkey with Pineapple Stuffing

1 × 12-14 lb turkey,
　completely defrosted

Pineapple Stuffing

¼ cup chopped onion
¼ cup butter
2 cups prepared poultry stuffing
⅔ cup hot water
1 × 14 oz can crushed
　pineapple, well drained
½ teaspoon poultry seasoning

Time: 2 hours 36 minutes-3 hours 15 minute
Serves 10-

Weigh turkey and estimate total cooking time. Allow 12- minutes cooking time on medium per 1 lb.

In a 2 pint casserole cook onion and butter on high 3- minutes until onion is soft. Blend in remaining stuffing i gredients. Place stuffing into cavity of prepared turke Secure cavity and neck skin with bamboo satay sticks c to required length.

Place turkey, breast side down, in baking dish. Divi cooking time into quarters. Cook on high for first 10 mi utes. Reduce heat to medium and cook remaining part first quarter of time. Shield wings, drumsticks, cavity an neck with aluminum foil strips if necessary. Turn turke on side and cook for a further quarter of cooking tim Turn to other side. Baste with pan juices.

Turn breast side up and cook a further quarter of coo ing time. Let stand 20-30 minutes (this can be done microwave on warm setting) before carving. Turkey cooked when the leg moves freely and is soft to touc Pierce thigh with skewer; juices run clear when cooking complete. A meat thermometer placed in the thigh can al be used to check it's ready — it should register 350°F.

Bechamel Sauce

2½ cups milk
2 oz butter
2 oz all-purpose flour
salt
white pepper
pinch nutmeg
4 tablespoons cream

Time: 8½ minutes. Makes 2-3 cups

Place butter in a bowl and cook on high 1 minute. Stir in flour and cook 1 minute. Blend in milk. Cook on high 6½ minutes or until boiling, stirring twice during cooking. Season with salt, pepper and nutmeg. Fold in cream.

Step 1 Chicken Roulade. Place cheese slice on each chicken fillet

Chicken Roulade with Almond and Broccoli Stuffing

4 large chicken breast fillets,
  skin removed
2 slices sandwich cheese slices
10 oz frozen broccoli, defrosted
  and chopped
2 oz almonds or cashews,
  chopped
1 cup milk
1 tablespoon all-purpose flour
1 tablespoon white wine
2 teaspoons chopped parsley
¼ teaspoon salt
¼ teaspoon pepper
1 tablespoon grated cheese

Time: 12 minutes. Serves 4

Cut each slice of cheese in half. Pound chicken fillets to flatten. Place a piece of cheese onto each fillet and divide broccoli and almonds between the four chicken fillets. Roll up fillets around broccoli and secure with cocktail sticks. Place rolls seam side down in 8 inch square baking dish. Cover with white paper towel and cook on high 8 minutes, turning twice during cooking. Drain and set aside.

Blend milk, flour, wine, parsley, salt and pepper in a jug. Cook on high 2-3 minutes until thickened, stirring twice during cooking. Blend in grated cheese. Pour sauce over roulade and cook on high 1 minute to reheat.

HINT: STIR YOUR SAUCE
Stirring sauce during cooking ensures an even distribution of the cooked sauce and ensures a thoroughly tasty meal.

Chicken Roulade with Almond and Broccoli Stuffing

Step 2 Divide broccoli and almonds between fillets

Step 3 Roll up fillets and secure with cocktail sticks

Chicken Schnitzel with Asparagus Cream Sauce

4 large chicken breast fillets,
    skin removed
2 tablespoons butter
1 cup breadcrumbs
2 tablespoons grated Parmesan
    cheese
1 tablespoon dried parsley
    flakes
1 teaspoon paprika
2 tablespoons all-purpose flour
2 tablespoons butter
¼ teaspoon salt
⅛ teaspoon white pepper
1¼ cups milk
2 tablespoons sherry
1 cup green asparagus tips
½ cup grated cheese
pinch nutmeg

Time: 22 minutes. Serves 4

Place butter in pie plate and heat on high 1 minute. In another plate combine breadcrumbs, Parmesan cheese, parsley and paprika. Dip each fillet in butter then coat with crumb mixture. Place in a single layer in baking dish and cook on high 12–14 minutes or until tender. Rearrange fillets half way through cooking. Let stand, covered.

Place 2 tablespoons butter in jug and cook on high 45 seconds. Stir in flour, salt and pepper and cook a further minute. Blend in milk and sherry. Cook on high 4 minutes or until thickened. Blend in asparagus, cheese and nutmeg. Cook on medium 2 minutes until cheese melts. Pour over chicken to serve.

HINT: TESTING IF CHICKEN IS COOKED

Pierce thigh with cocktail stick. If liquid runs clear the chicken is cooked. Should the natural juice have a slight pink color — this may occur if chicken was frozen — the chicken requires longer cooking.

Coq au Vin

3 lb chicken thighs
4 slices bacon, diced into ¾
    inch pieces
⅓ cup all-purpose flour
½ cup red wine
½ cup chicken stock
2 tablespoons brandy
2 teaspoons chopped parsley
1 teaspoon salt
1 clove garlic, finely chopped
1 bay leaf
¼ teaspoon thyme
¼ teaspoon pepper
¼ teaspoon chicken seasoning
8 oz mushrooms, sliced
1 large onion, sliced

Time: 35 minutes. Serves

Place bacon in a 5 pint casserole dish. Cover and cook on high 4 minutes. Drain, leaving 1 tablespoon bacon fat casserole. Blend in flour. Stir in liquids and seasonings.

Add mushrooms, onion and chicken. Cover and cook on high 15 minutes. Stir and rearrange chicken. Cook 11 minutes or until chicken is tender. Let stand, covered, 5 minutes before serving.

Five Spice Chicken

1 × 3 lb fresh chicken
2 cloves garlic
4 tablespoons soy sauce
2 tablespoons peanut oil
½ teaspoon Chinese five spice
    powder
½ teaspoon salt
1 teaspoon sugar
¼ teaspoon pepper

Time: 20–30 minutes. Serves 4–

Weigh chicken and allow 8–9 minutes cooking time on high for 1 lb.

Chop garlic finely and sprinkle with salt. Mash together with side of a knife into a creamy paste. Combine with remaining ingredients in a large bowl. Place chicken into bowl and baste with marinade. Let chicken marinate hour, basting and turning every 15 minutes.

Drain chicken and place breast side down on roasting rack in baking dish. Cook on high for half the required cooking time. Turn chicken breast side up. Baste with remaining marinade. Continue cooking on high for rest of time. Carve chicken or chop up Chinese style to serve.

Coq au V

Crab Stuffed Chicken

1 × 3 lb fresh chicken
5 oz crabmeat
½ cup chopped green peppers
1 teaspoon lemon juice
¼ teaspoon pepper
2 slices bread cut in ½ inch
  cubes

Glaze

2 teaspoons soy sauce
1 tablespoon white wine
2½ tablespoons water
1 teaspoon cornstarch
⅛ teaspoon garlic salt

Time: 20–30 minutes. Serves 4–6

Weigh chicken and allow 8–9 minutes cooking time on high per 1 lb. Combine stuffing ingredients in bowl. Place inside cavity of chicken and truss with white kitchen string.

To make glaze: Blend all glaze ingredients together in a bowl and cook on high 2 minutes, stirring after 1 minute.

Place chicken on roasting rack, breast side down. Brush with prepared glaze. Cook on high for half required time. Turn chicken breast side up and baste with remaining glaze. Cook on high for remainder of time.

Chicken with Avocado

6 chicken breast fillets, skin
  removed
3 tablespoons butter
2 teaspoons soy sauce
½ cup pineapple juice
1 teaspoon chopped ginger root
1 small clove garlic, chopped
⅛ teaspoon paprika
1 large avocado, thickly sliced
1 teaspoon arrowroot

Time: 19 minutes. Serves 6

Place butter into baking dish and cook on high 1 minute. Arrange chicken breasts in butter. Blend soy sauce, ginger and garlic with ¼ cup pineapple juice, coating each breast evenly with liquid. Sprinkle with paprika and cook on high 12 minutes.

Place thick slices of avocado on fillets and cook a further 4 minutes. Mix arrowroot with remaining pineapple juice. Cook liquid on high 1½–2 minutes until thickened. Strain sauce over chicken and avocado to serve.

Step 1 Crab Stuffed Chicken. Combine stuffing ingredients

Step 2 Place stuffing in chicken

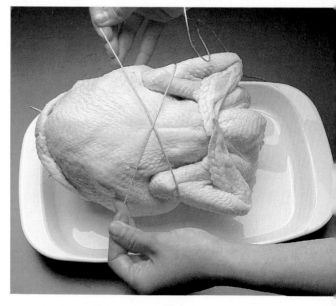

Step 3 Truss chicken with kitchen string

Crab Stuffed Chicke

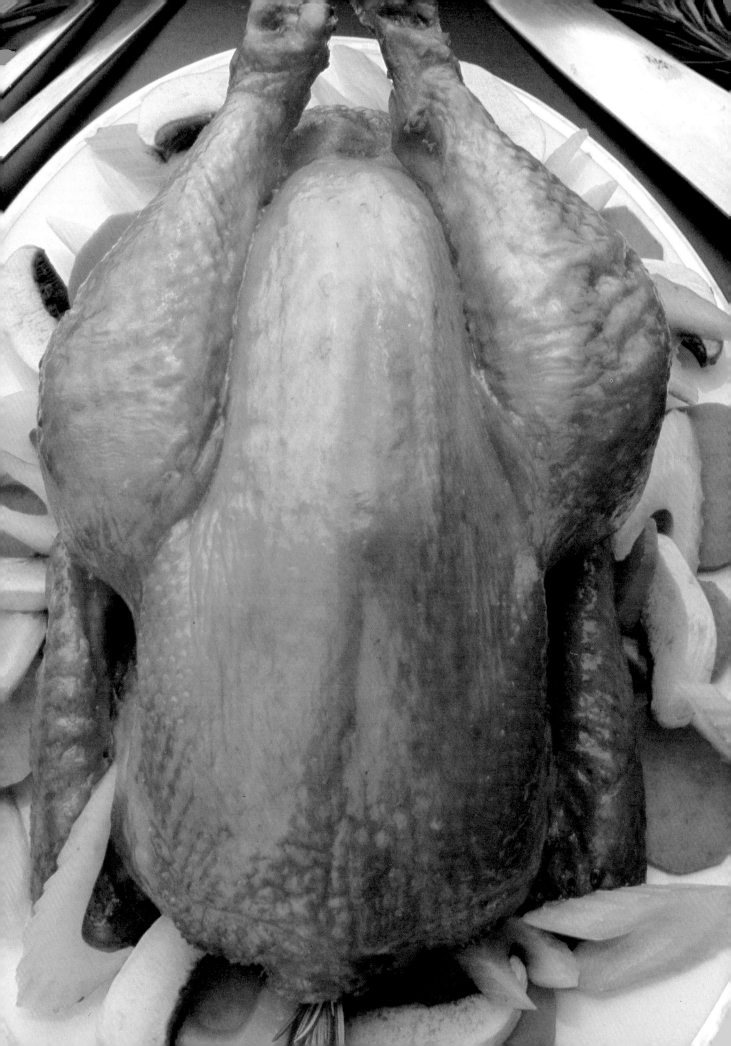

Chicken Catalan

8 large chicken breast fillets,
  skin removed
10 oz stuffed olives
8 oz fresh mushrooms, sliced
2 slices bacon, diced in ½ inch
  pieces
1 tablespoon all-purpose flour
¾ cup red wine
½ teaspoon salt

Time: 20 minutes. Serves 8

In a baking dish layer olives, mushrooms and chicken fillets. Set aside.

Place bacon in pie plate and cook on high 3 minutes. Remove bacon with slotted spoon. Blend flour into bacon drippings and stir in wine and salt. Cook on high 2–3 minutes to form sauce, stirring during cooking. Add bacon and pour over chicken.

Cover and cook on high 10–11 minutes. Rearrange chicken after 5 minutes. Let stand 5 minutes before serving.

Barbecued Drumsticks

10 chicken drumsticks, skin
  removed
¼ cup finely chopped onion
2 tablespoons finely chopped
  celery
½ teaspoon sugar
½ teaspoon dry mustard
1 teaspoon Worcestershire
  sauce
1 tablespoon vinegar
1 tablespoon barbecue sauce
¾ cup ketchup
⅛ teaspoon freshly ground
  black pepper
water

Time: 33 minutes. Serves 5

Combine all ingredients except drumsticks in jug. Cook on high 3 minutes or until hot, stirring once. Reduce to medium and cook 12 minutes, stirring every 3 minutes.

Arrange drumsticks in roasting dish. Brush with one-third of sauce and cover. Cook on high 7 minutes. Turn over and rearrange drumsticks and brush with one-third of sauce. Cover and cook on high 7 minutes. Brush with remaining sauce. Cover and cook on high 4 minutes.

> ## HINT: REMOVING SKIN FROM FILLETS
> Removing skin from chicken fillets enables the flavor of seasoning and other ingredients to penetrate the meat.

Orange Pecan Drumsticks

3–4 lb chicken drumsticks, skin
  removed
6 fl oz concentrated orange
  juice
½ cup water
1 teaspoon poultry seasoning
½ teaspoon salt
¼ cup water
2 tablespoons cornstarch or
  arrowroot
½ cup finely chopped scallions
½ cup pecan nuts

Time: 23 minutes. Serves 4–

Combine orange juice, water, poultry seasoning and salt i jug. Arrange drumsticks in roasting dish with the mea ends arranged around the edge. Pour sauce over chicker cover and cook on high 20 minutes until tender.

Combine ¼ cup water with cornstarch or arrowroot i medium-sized bowl. Remove drumsticks to serving platte Blend arrowroot into sauce. Add scallions and pecan nut Cook on high 2–3 minutes, stirring after 1 minute. Pou sauce over drumsticks. Serve with rice.

Roast Apricot Duck

1 × 5 lb duck
1 × 16 oz can apricot or
  mango halves with juice
2 teaspoons arrowroot or
  cornstarch
2 tablespoons orange juice
1 tablespoon brown sugar
½ teaspoon French mustard
¼ teaspoon salt
⅛ teaspoon curry paste
1 onion, quartered
1 stalk celery, cut in 1 inch
  lengths

Time: 45 minutes. Serves

To make glaze: combine ½ cup apricot juice from can wit arrowroot or cornstarch in 2 pint jug. Mix in remaining in gredients except apricot halves, onion and celery. Cook or high 3–4 minutes until thick, stirring until smooth Coarsely chop apricots and stir into glaze.

Weigh duck and allow 8–9 minutes cooking time on high per 1 lb. Place prepared duck breast side down on roastin rack and cook on high 10 minutes. Drain well. Fasten neck skin to back with bamboo satay stick. Place onion and cel ery into cavity and return duckling to rack breast side down. Reduce heat to medium. Cook for remaining firs half of cooking time.

Drain fat from dish, turn duck breast side up and spoor over half the apricot glaze. Cook on medium for remainin cooking time. Drain off fat and add remaining glaze. Le stand covered for 5 minutes.

Braised Lemon Chicken

2 tablespoons dark soy sauce
1 tablespoon dry sherry
1 cup lemon juice
2 teaspoons sugar
2 lb chicken breasts, cut into
    serving pieces
3 tablespoons oil
2 thin slices of green ginger
1 clove garlic, peeled and
    crushed
¾ cup water
1 tablespoon cornstarch
salt
2–3 tablespoons water

Time: 52 minutes. Serves 4–6

Mix soy sauce, sherry, lemon juice, sugar in a bowl. Add chicken pieces and marinate for 20 minutes. Preheat browning skillet for 6 minutes. Add oil and heat for 2 minutes. Add ginger, garlic, chicken pieces and cook on high 3 minutes on each side.

Place chicken, garlic and ginger in casserole dish. Add remaining marinade and water. Cook covered 15–18 minutes, stirring twice during cooking. Add blended cornstarch, cook 2 minutes. Season. Serve with plain boiled rice.

Spanish Chicken

2 lb chicken breasts, cut into
    pieces
seasoned flour, salt and pepper
4 tablespoons oil
2 onions, chopped
1 clove garlic, crushed
2 tablespoons parsley, chopped
2 tablespoons scallions,
    chopped
4 tomatoes, sliced
1 green pepper, chopped
4 oz button mushrooms
1¼ cups red wine
1 teaspoon red chili, finely
    chopped
salt
pepper
1 cup frozen lima beans,
    cooked

Time: 36 minutes. Serves 4–6

Toss chicken pieces in seasoned flour. Preheat browning skillet for 6 minutes on high. Add 2 tablespoons oil and heat a further 2 minutes. Place chicken pieces in skillet and cook 3 minutes on each side. Place chicken pieces into a 3½ pint casserole dish.

Reheat browning skillet for 2 minutes, add onions, garlic, remaining oil and cook for 2 minutes. Remove and add to chicken. Add parsley, scallions, tomatoes, peppers, mushrooms, wine, chili, salt and pepper. Cover casserole and cook 15 minutes. Add cooked beans and cook a further 3 minutes. Serve with boiled rice.

Mexican Chicken

1 large chicken, jointed, or
    chicken pieces
seasoned flour
4 tablespoons oil
3 large onions, sliced
2 cloves garlic, crushed
1 red pepper, diced
1 tablespoon sesame seeds
½ teaspoon oregano
¾ cup dry red wine
1 cup blanched almonds
1 cup stuffed olives, sliced
½–1 teaspoon chili powder (to
    taste)
1 cup chicken stock
1 cup whole kernel corn

Time: 35 minutes. Serves 4

Dust chicken pieces lightly with seasoned flour. Preheat browning skillet for 6 minutes on high. Add oil, heat for ? minutes. Add chicken pieces and cook for 3 minutes ? each side. Remove chicken and place into a 3½ pint ca? serole dish.

Place onions, garlic, peppers, into browning skillet an? cook 3 minutes, stirring after 2 minutes. Add sesame seed? oregano, wine and pour over chicken pieces. Add almond? olives, chili powder, stock, and cook covered 15 minute? Fold in corn kernels and cook 3 minutes longer.

Honeyed Chicken Live? Kebabs

1 lb chicken livers
2 tablespoons honey
1 teaspoon black pepper
2 teaspoons soy sauce
2 medium onions, cut into
    sixths
bamboo satay sticks

Time: 19 minutes. Serves ?

Marinate chicken livers with honey, pepper and soy sau? for 20 minutes. Drain. Arrange chicken livers and onio? wedges on bamboo satay sticks to cover 2½–3 inches of th? point end of each stick.

The kebabs may be cooked on a browner grill preheate? on high for 8 minutes or arranged in a roasting dish. Coo? on high 2 minutes. Reduce power to medium and cook 7–? minutes or until livers are tender.

Baste with marinade and turn kebabs twice durin? cooking.

Apricot Chicken Casserole

3 tablespoons oil
2 lb chicken breasts, cut into
    serving pieces
2 tablespoons butter
1 large onion, diced
1 green pepper, diced
2 tablespoons all-purpose flour
1½ cups apricot nectar
salt and pepper
pinch oregano
2 teaspoons chopped parsley,
3 large tomatoes, peeled and
    sliced

Time: 37 minutes. Serves 4–6

Preheat browning skillet for 6 minutes. Add oil and heat for 2 minutes. Add chicken pieces and cook for 3 minutes on high on each side. Melt butter in a 3½ pint casserole for 15 seconds. Add onion, peppers and cook for 3 minutes. Stir in flour and cook for 2 minutes. Stir in apricot nectar to form a sauce. Add browned chicken pieces and remaining seasonings. Cover with tomato slices. Cook covered 18 minutes. Serve with buttered, boiled macaroni, which has been sprinkled with toasted sesame seeds.

Chicken in Red Wine

1 chicken, cut in serving pieces
2 oz seasoned flour
3 tablespoons oil
4 oz bacon, diced
1 clove garlic, chopped
6 small onions
2 cups red wine
4 oz button mushrooms
salt and pepper

Time: 39 minutes. Serves 4–6

Coat chicken pieces lightly with seasoned flour. Preheat browning skillet for 6 minutes. Add oil and heat for 2 minutes. Place in chicken pieces pressing down on all sides to seal and color. Cook 3 minutes on high on each side.

Remove chicken from pan and place in 3½ pint casserole dish. Reheat browning skillet for 4 minutes, add bacon, garlic and onions, cover with paper towels and cook for 3 minutes. Add this mixture to chicken. Gradually blend in wine with remaining flour to form a smooth paste. Add mushrooms and cook covered 15–18 minutes on high, stirring twice during cooking.

Gourmet Chicken

2 whole chicken breasts
seasoned flour
3 tablespoons oil
¼ cup blanched slivered
    almonds
1 small onion, diced
1 clove garlic, minced
1 cup celery, diced
2 tablespoons parsley, chopped
¾ cup dry sherry
1 cup button mushrooms
1 tablespoon cornstarch
    (optional)
parsley sprigs and almonds for
    garnish

Time: 38 minutes. Serves

Cut chicken breasts into serving pieces and dust lightl with seasoned flour. Preheat browning skillet for 6 minute on high. Add oil and heat for 2 minutes. Add almond brown slightly, set aside for garnish. Reheat skillet for minutes, add chicken pieces and cook 3 minutes on eac side on high. Remove chicken and place into a 3½ pin casserole dish.

Place onion, garlic, celery, parsley into browning skille and cook 2 minutes. Add sherry, mushrooms and stir wel Pour mixture over chicken pieces and cook covered 15–1 minutes. Thicken slightly with cornstarch if necessary an cook 2 minutes longer. Serve garnished with almonds an parsley sprigs.

Golden Chicken

3 lb chicken breasts, cut into
    serving pieces
2 tablespoons curry powder
½ teaspoon salt
½ cup honey
2 tablespoons French mustard
2 cloves garlic, finely chopped
½ teaspoon ground cardamom

Time: 46 minutes. Serves 8–1

Preheat browning dish for 6 minutes. Remove skin fror chicken portions and place bone side down in casserol dish. Sprinkle with curry powder and salt. Combine honey mustard, garlic and cardamom. Cook on high 2 minute then brush or spoon over chicken portions.

Cover chicken and cook on high 10 minutes. Tur portions over and baste with honey mixture. Cook o medium 20 minutes. Rearrange pieces from outer edge t centre halfway through cooking.

Test for doneness. If underdone, cook on medium further 8 minutes or until juices run clear. Let stand 8–1 minutes before serving. Standing time can take place in conventional oven heated to 200°F to keep chicken warn Standing time: 8–10 minutes.

Crumbed Chicken Drumsticks

Time: 8 minutes. Serves 4

drumsticks
cups cooking oil
clove garlic, peeled and
  crushed
tablespoons flour
salt and pepper to taste
inch oregano
level teaspoon five spice
  powder
egg
cup milk
½ cups dry breadcrumbs
cup sesame seeds

Combine flour, salt, pepper, oregano and five spice powder. Beat egg and milk together. Combine breadcrumbs and sesame seeds.

Heat oil in pan on top of range. Add garlic, brown and remove. Roll drumsticks in seasoned flour. Coat with egg mixture, then with breadcrumb mixture. Fry drumsticks until a rich golden color. Remove and drain.

Arrange on a glass platter with the thickest part of the drumsticks to the outside edge. Cover with paper towels. Cook for 8 minutes on high, turn over after 5 minutes of cooking. Serve with fried rice (*see recipe*).

Note: This method combines the crispness of pan frying with the moist cooking of the microwave oven.

Crumbed Chicken Drumsticks

125

Red Roast Chicken

1 whole chicken
1 slice ginger
1 clove garlic, crushed

Marinade

¾ cup Chinese barbecue sauce
several drops red food coloring
½ cup dry sherry
½ cup dry sherry

Time: 25 minutes. Serves 4–6

Place ginger and crushed garlic into cavity of chicken. Combine marinade ingredients. Coat chicken with marinade and allow to stand for 2 hours. Place chicken into an oven bag. Tie loosely with string. Prick bag once or twice. Place in casserole dish and cook on high 15 minutes. Turn over and cook a further 10 minutes. Allow to stand 10 minutes before carving. Serve hot or cold with salads.

Sweet and Sour Chicken

1½ lb fresh chicken breasts
3 tablespoons oil
1 clove garlic, finely chopped
1 thin slice ginger, finely
*   chopped*

Sauce

½ cup sugar
½ cup vinegar
¾ cup pineapple juice or water
1–2 tablespoons dark soy sauce
2 tablespoons oil
1 clove garlic, finely chopped
½ red pepper, diced
½ green pepper, diced
¼ cup Chinese pickles, diced
¼ cup mushrooms, sliced
¼ cup bamboo shoots, sliced
3 scallions, cut into ¾ inch
*   lengths*
2 tablespoons cornstarch
*   blended with ½ cup water*

Time: 34 minutes. Serves 4–6

Remove flesh from bone and cut into ¾ inch dice. Preheat browning skillet for 8 minutes. Add oil and heat for 3 minutes. Add garlic, ginger and cook 1 minute. Add chicken pieces and stir to coat with oil. Cook on high 5 minutes, stir and cook a further 5 minutes.

Combine sugar, vinegar, pineapple juice, and soy sauce. Heat oil in casserole dish for 2 minutes. Add garlic, vegetables and cook for 3 minutes uncovered on high. Add vinegar mixture. Cook for 3 minutes. Blend cornstarch and water to a paste. Add to other ingredients and cook for 2 minutes. Add chicken pieces. Reheat for 2 minutes. Serve with plain or fried rice (*see recipe*).

126

Chili Chicken

2 whole chicken breasts, cut
*   into serving pieces*
4 red chilies, seeds removed
*   and finely chopped*
2 slices green ginger, finely
*   chopped*
2 cloves garlic, finely chopped
1 medium onion, finely chopped
2 teaspoons lemon or lime juice
1 teaspoon turmeric
1 teaspoon sugar
salt

Time: 20 minutes. Serves

Salt chicken pieces lightly. Combine all other ingredien in a bowl. Add chicken pieces and allow to stand 15–2 minutes. Place chicken and marinade in an oven bag. T bag loosely with string or elastic band. Cook 10 minutes high, then turn bag over and continue cooking a further minutes.

Note: The chicken in the oven bag must be in one laye not bunched up.

Chicken Curry

3 lb chicken pieces
2 tablespoons butter
1 clove garlic, chopped
8 oz onions, chopped
2 tablespoons curry powder
1 tablespoon flour
1 tablespoon tomato paste
1 tablespoon raisins
1 cup coconut milk (see recipe
*   following)*
1 tablespoon chutney
2 oz chopped mango or
*   pineapple*

Time: 43 minutes. Serves

Preheat browning casserole dish on high 6 minutes. Ad butter and cook 2 minutes. Place chicken pieces skin si down in casserole. Add onion and garlic. Cook on high minutes, turning chicken over after 4 minutes. Add cur powder and flour and stir. Cook on high 2 minutes.

Mix in tomato paste, coconut milk, chutney, raisi and mango. Reduce heat to medium and cook 25–30 mi utes or until chicken is tender. Stir and rearrange piec twice during cooking.

Coconut Milk

1 cup shredded coconut
1 cup milk or half milk, half water

Place coconut and milk in Pyrex bowl. Cook on high minutes. Allow to cool. Strain mixture through whi cheesecloth. Squeeze to extract milk. This process can repeated with a second quantity of milk. This will yield thinner milk which can be used for cooking vegetables

Roast Chicken

1 × 3 lb chicken, washed and
  dried

Stuffing

1 small onion, finely chopped
1 cup white breadcrumbs
pinch of mixed herbs
1 tablespoon butter
¼ teaspoon salt
pinch pepper
1 tablespoon chopped parsley

Basting Sauce

1–2 tablespoons melted butter
1 teaspoon soy sauce

Time: 33 minutes. Serves 4–6

Saute onion in butter, 3 minutes on high. Add remaining ingredients. Place stuffing into cavity. Truss chicken to a neat shape. Baste with 2 tablespoons melted butter mixed with 1 teaspoon soy sauce. Place in an oven bag. Tie loosely with string and prick bag once or twice. Cook 15 minutes on high, breast side down. Turn over and cook a further 15 minutes. Let stand in bag for 10 minutes before carving.

Note: Baked rabbit can also be cooked in this way.

Chicken Satay

1 lb chicken breasts
1 cup pineapple pieces
1 cup button mushrooms
1 cup red pepper diced same
  size as pineapple

Marinade

3 tablespoons soy sauce
1 tablespoon dry sherry
1 tablespoon brown sugar
½ teaspoon powdered ginger
2 teaspoons grated onion

Sauce

1 cup pineapple juice
1 tablespoon cornstarch

Time: 16 minutes. Serves 4–6

Debone chicken. Cut into ¾ inch cubes. Combine marinade ingredients, add chicken pieces and marinate for 1 hour. Arrange chicken pieces, pineapple and vegetables on bamboo skewers. Preheat browning skillet for 8 minutes. Add 2 tablespoons oil and heat for 2 minutes. Arrange skewers in oil and cook 3 minutes on high, turn and cook a further 3 minutes. Place on serving platter. Heat pineapple juice and cornstarch to form a sauce. Spoon over chicken satay and serve.

Roast Orange Duck

1 × 4 lb duck
1 clove garlic
2 tablespoons butter, melted
  and mixed with 2 teaspoons
  soy sauce
1 onion, peeled and cut into
  quarters
1 orange, unpeeled, cut into
  quarters
¼ cup dry sherry
½ cup orange juice
½ teaspoon ground ginger
1 teaspoon salt
parsley
1 tablespoon cornstarch
2 tablespoons water

Time: 33 minutes. Serves

Wipe duck inside and out with a damp cloth. Cut garlic half and rub skin with it. Brush with butter and soy mixture. Place onion and orange into cavity and fasten with bamboo skewer. Place duck in shallow glass baking dish. Cover loosely with plastic food wrap and cook 15 minutes on high. Pour sherry, orange juice, ginger and salt over duck. Re-cover and cook a further 15 minutes. Allow stand 10 minutes. Remove orange and onion.

Blend 1 tablespoon cornstarch with a little water and add to pan drippings. Cook a further 3 minutes. Carve duck and garnish with orange segments and parsley. Mask with thickened orange sauce.

Note: The duck can also be cooked in an oven bag.

Roast Turkey with Apple Dressing

turkey, approximately 10 lb

Time: 80 minutes. Serves 8–10

Clean and prepare turkey for cooking. Place turkey, breast side down in a glass baking dish. Put Apple Dressing (see recipe) inside cavity of turkey. Cover bottom half of wings and legs with small pieces of aluminum foil. Secure legs and wings close to body with string. Cover turkey lightly with plastic food wrap — this keeps the inside tender and juicy.

Cook turkey for 40 minutes on high then remove aluminum, turn turkey over, cover and cook a further 40 minutes. When cooking time is up, rest turkey 15–20 minutes before carving.

Note: If turkey cavity is filled with Apple Dressing, add 1 minute per pound to cooking time.

Apple Dressing

cup butter
2 cups celery, finely chopped
cup onion, finely chopped
teaspoon salt
teaspoon sage
–¾ cup water
cups dry breadcrumbs, more
if needed
cups peeled and chopped
apple

Time: 3 minutes.

Melt butter in a large casserole, saute celery and onion 2–3 minutes on high, stirring after every minute. Mix salt, sage, and water together. Pour over breadcrumbs and toss lightly. Add breadcrumbs to vegetables, and stir in apples. Stuff turkey just before roasting.

Alternative Stuffings for Turkey

Stuffing for Cavity

4 oz butter
2 oz onion, finely chopped
4 oz fresh white breadcrumbs
fresh or dry mixed herbs
1 tablespoon chopped parsley
turkey liver, chopped
salt and pepper

Time: 4 minutes

Place butter and onion into casserole dish or bowl. Cook 4 minutes on high, add remaining ingredients, mix well and place into cavity. Truss turkey firmly. A small amount of aluminum may be placed on the wings and drumsticks for half of the cooking time to prevent drying out. Cover the whole turkey with plastic wrap to retain natural juices.

Stuffing for Neck Cavity

1 lb ground sausage meat
4 oz water chestnuts, diced
salt and pepper

Combine ingredients and place into neck cavity. Fasten with bamboo skewer.

HINT: EASY ROASTING
Average sized birds require basting and turning to ensure even cooking. Larger birds like turkey take longer to cook and often baste themselves in the process. Special oven bags can be bought to speed up cooking time and prevent loss of juices. Poultry pieces should be prepared with the larger parts angled out to allow even cooking

Roast Turkey

Seafood

afood cooked in a microwave oven takes on new
mensions of flavor, appearance and texture. The entire range
shellfish, whole fish and fillets can be cooked with
inimum fuss and handling.
Fresh shellfish can be opened easily with the aid of a
icrowave oven, then cooked in their own shells and juices.
ways prick oysters, mussels, scallops and fish eyes (when

whole fish are being cooked) as this allows steam to escape
and prevents bursting.
Frozen fish can be thawed on a defrost setting, but if time
permits it is preferable to use a warm setting. Defrost and cook
fillets with the thickest portion of the fish at the outer edge of
the dish. Cook covered and in a single layer.

Coconut Jumbo Shrimp Cutlets

uncooked jumbo shrimp
easoned all-purpose flour
egg, beaten
tablespoon milk
cup shredded coconut
slice green ginger
cup peanut oil

Time: 20 minutes. Serves 2

eel shrimp, leaving tail intact. Split shrimp down the back
nd remove intestinal tract. Continue to cut ⅔ through the
rimp and press shrimp to form a cutlet shape. Beat egg and
ilk together. Dip each shrimp in flour, egg and milk. Coat
ith shredded coconut.
Heat browning casserole dish on high 8 minutes. Add oil
nd ginger and heat on high 3 minutes. Add cutlets and cook
-5 minutes until tail turns pink. Drain on paper towel.
Serve with curry sauce (see recipe following) and lemon
ices.

Curry Sauce

tablespoon butter
finely diced onion
teaspoon curry powder
finely chopped small, red chili
tablespoon all-purpose flour
cup chicken stock
½ teaspoons fruit chutney
tablespoon heavy cream

Time: 5 minutes. Makes 1 cup

elt butter in a jug. Cook on high 40 seconds. Stir in onion
nd cook on high 30 seconds. Blend in curry powder and heat
r 30 seconds on high. Add chili and stir in flour. Heat on high
) seconds.
Add chutney, blend in stock and cook on high 4 minutes,
irring twice. Stir in cream.
Serve hot or cold.

Garlic Scallops

1 lb prepared scallops
2 scallions, finely chopped
4 cloves garlic, finely chopped
1 fresh hot chili, finely chopped
½ teaspoon chili powder
4 tablespoons peanut oil

Time: 15 minutes. Serves 4–6

Combine scallions, garlic, chili and oil in casserole dish. Add
scallops and toss to coat. Leave to marinate 10 minutes. Cover
and cook on high 5 minutes. Rearrange scallops halfway
through cooking to ensure they are evenly done. Serve with
lemon rice (see recipe Lemon Rice).

HINT: PREPARING SCALLOPS AND OPENING MOLLUSC SHELLS
To prepare scallops remove the beard, which is brownish colored and usually found near the coral. The intestinal tract should also be removed. Split large scallops in half before cooking.
Fresh scallops, clams and oysters in the shell may be opened in the microwave oven. First clean the shells and soak in cold water for 10 minutes. Place 6 shells at a time around edge of pie plate, cover with lid or plastic wrap and cook on high for 45 seconds or until shells have just opened. Continue to heat any unopened shells, checking every 15 seconds. Insert knife between shells to open.

oconut Jumbo Shrimp Cutlets

Curried Smoked Cod Supreme

1 lb smoked cod
1 tablespoon butter
8 oz onions, sliced
2 teaspoons curry powder
2 tablespoons butter
2 tablespoons all-purpose flour
2 cups milk
½ teaspoon salt
¼ teaspoon pepper
¼ cup white wine
2 tablespoons mayonnaise
½ cup grated cheese
½ teaspoon paprika

Time: 25 minutes. Serves 6

Place cod fillets into plastic bag or baking dish. Cook on high 5 minutes. Remove any bones and skin, flake fish with a fork and set aside.

Melt butter in a bowl on high for 1 minute. Add onions and cook 4–5 minutes, covered, on high. Stir twice during cooking. Add curry powder, cook 1 minute on high and set aside.

Melt 2 tablespoons butter in jug on high 1 minute. Stir in flour and cook 2 minutes on high. Stir in milk and cook on high 5–6 minutes until boiling, stirring twice during cooking. Add salt, pepper, wine and mayonnaise.

Place a layer of sauce in an 8 × 8 inch casserole dish. Cover with onions and the flaked cod. Cover evenly with remaining sauce. Sprinkle with grated cheese and paprika and cook on medium 6 minutes. Let stand 3 minutes before serving.

Swiss Style Mussels

12 mussels on shell
2 tablespoons butter
3 tablespoons Gruyere cheese
1 tablespoon finely diced red
    pimiento
pinch cayenne pepper
3 tablespoons Parmesan cheese

Time: 3 minutes. Serves 2

Place butter in a medium-sized bowl. Heat the microwave on high 1 minute. Fold in cheese, pimiento and cayenne.

Arrange mussels around outer edge of plate and prick each with a toothpick. Spoon over Gruyere butter, sprinkle with Parmesan and cook on medium 2–3 minutes.

HINT: USING PLASTIC BAGS
Plastic bags may be secured with an elastic band. Prick once or twice to allow hot air to escape during cooking.

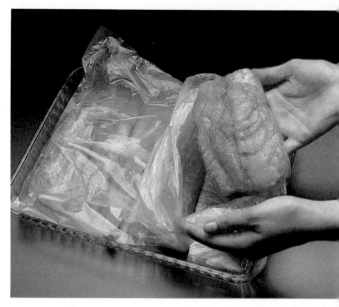
Step 1 Curried Smoked Cod Supreme. Cook cod fillets in plastic bag

Step 2 Add curry powder to cooked onions

Step 3 Cover onions and flaked cod with sauce

Shrimp Creole

b uncooked shrimps, shelled
and deveined
× 16 oz can tomato pieces
medium-sized onion, diced in
½ inch pieces
green pepper, diced in ½ inch
pieces
teaspoon salt
teaspoon white pepper
teaspoon chili powder
bay leaf

Time: 13 minutes. Serves 4–6

ombine all ingredients except shrimp in a 3 pint casserole
sh. Cover and cook on high 9 minutes, stirring once. Stir
shrimp, cover and cook on high 4–5 minutes, stirring
ice during cooking.
Avoid overcooking as this toughens shrimp. Remove bay
af before serving.

Lobster Newburg

cooked lobster tail
tablespoons butter
tablespoons all-purpose flour
cup cream
tablespoons dry vermouth or
riesling
cup sliced fresh mushrooms
teaspoon salt
teaspoon onion salt
teaspoon cayenne pepper
teaspoon nutmeg
egg yolks
teaspoon paprika
teaspoon chopped parsley
mon wedges

Time: 8 minutes. Serves 2–4

emove meat from lobster tail, split in half lengthwise and
emove intestinal tract. Cut meat into ¾ inch cubes. Place
utter in a 3½ pint casserole dish. Cook on high 1 minute.
ir in flour and cook an extra minute on high.
Add cream, vermouth (or Riesling), mushrooms and
asoning. Cook on high 5 minutes, stirring twice during
oking.
Beat egg yolks in a small bowl. Add 1 tablespoon of the
uce and whisk. Stir yolks into remaining sauce.
Fold in lobster and cook on high 1–2 minutes until hot.
poon into lobster shell or ramekins. Sprinkle lightly with
aprika and garnish with parsley and lemon wedges to
erve.

Shrimp Creole

Salmon Burgers with Parsley Sauce

1 × 16 oz can salmon, drained
2 cups white breadcrumbs
2 tablespoons butter, melted
1 onion, finely chopped
1 egg, beaten
¼ cup cream
2 tablespoons lemon juice,
    strained
3 teaspoons chopped parsley
1 teaspoon chopped dill
salt
lemon pepper
1½ cups dry breadcrumbs
½ cup toasted sesame seeds

Time: 15 minutes. Makes 12

Place butter and onion in a medium-sized basin. Cook on
high 3 minutes. Cool. Blend in salmon, breadcrumbs, egg,
cream, juice, herbs, salt and pepper.
Use an ice cream scoop to form the mixture into even
portions. Combine dry breadcrumbs and seeds and roll
each portion in crumbs to coat evenly. Shape into patties.
Preheat broiling plate for 7 minutes, then cook burgers
2½ minutes on each side.
Serve on toasted buns with parsley sauce (*see recipe following*) or with a vegetable platter.

Parsley Sauce

8 fl oz warm milk
1 bay leaf
3 peppercorns
⅛ peeled onion
1 tablespoon butter
1 tablespoon all-purpose flour
¼ teaspoon onion salt
⅛ teaspoon white pepper
1 tablespoon finely chopped
    parsley

Time: 9½ minutes. Makes about 3 cups

Place milk, bay leaf, peppercorns and onion into a jug.
Cook on medium-low 5 minutes to infuse flavors. Melt butter in a medium-sized bowl on high 1 minute. Stir in flour
and cook on high 1 minute. Blend in strained milk, salt and
pepper. Cook on high 2½ minutes or until boiling, stirring
every minute. Fold in parsley.

**HINT: TOASTING
SESAME SEEDS**
1 tablespoon butter
3 tablespoons sesame
    seeds
Place butter in pie plate
and cook on high 30
seconds. Stir in sesame
seeds and cook on high
3–4 minutes, stirring
every minute until
golden. Drain on white
paper towel.

Crab Stuffed Flounder Fillets

8 thin, evenly sized, flounder
    fillets
10 oz flaked crabmeat
1 tablespoon butter
½ cup chopped onion
½ cup chopped peppers
4 tablespoons breadcrumbs
1 teaspoon parsley
½ teaspoon salt
½ teaspoon lemon pepper
¾ cup tomato juice
½ teaspoon chopped basil
    leaves
1 teaspoon lemon juice
4 lemon slices

Time: 22 minutes. Serves 4

Step 1 Crab Stuffed Flounder Fillets. Combine butter, onion and peppers

Combine butter, onion and peppers in a bowl and cook on high 4 minutes, stirring once during cooking. Stir in crabmeat, breadcrumbs, parsley, salt and lemon pepper.

Arrange 4 flounder fillets in a roasting dish, cover each evenly with stuffing mixture then place a second fillet on top.

Combine tomato juice, basil and lemon juice in a bowl and cook on high 2 minutes. Spoon sauce over fillets and top with lemon slices. Cook on medium 16 minutes or until fish flakes easily.

Step 2 Stir in crabmeat and breadcrumbs

Garlic Oysters

12 oysters in shell
2 tablespoons butter
1 clove garlic, finely chopped
1 teaspoon finely chopped red
    chili
⅛ teaspoon lemon pepper
1 tablespoon finely chopped
    parsley
2 tablespoons toasted
    breadcrumbs

Time: 4 minutes. Serves 2

Heat butter on high 1 minute. Add garlic, chili and lemon pepper. Heat on medium 1 minute.

Prick oysters with a cocktail stick. Spoon a little garlic butter onto each oyster. Sprinkle with parsley and breadcrumbs.

Arrange oysters around the outer edge of a plate and cook on medium 2–3 minutes.

Step 3 Cover each fillet with stuffing and place another fillet on top.

rab Stuffed Flounder Fillets

Fillets of Bream Caprice

bream fillets
bananas, peeled and halved
  lengthwise
easoned all-purpose flour
 oz butter, melted
ry breadcrumbs
½ cups peanut oil
slice green ginger

Time: 15 minutes. Serves 4

oat bream fillets with seasoned flour, dip in melted butter
nen coat with breadcrumbs. Lightly coat banana halves
vith seasoned flour.

Preheat browning casserole dish on high 6 minutes. Add
il and green ginger. Cook on high 6 minutes until ginger
; brown. Remove ginger.

Place fillets into oil and cook 3 minutes. Turn over and
dd banana pieces. Cook on high 2 minutes. Remove and
rain on white paper towel.

Place half a banana on each portion of fish and serve
vith orange cream (see recipe following).

Orange Cream

1 cup sour cream
4 tablespoons mayonnaise
2 teaspoons Dijon mustard
½ teaspoon finely grated
  orange zest
2 teaspoons orange juice or
  Grand Marnier
2 tablespoons chopped
  scallions or chives

Beat sour cream until smooth. Stir in mayonnaise and mustard. Add orange zest, orange juice or Grand Marnier. Garnish with scallions or chives and serve with fish.

> **HINT: PREPARING OYSTERS AND MUSSELS**
> Before microwaving oysters and mussels, always prick each one about 4 times to allow steam to escape and prevent splitting.

Oysters Kilpatrick

? oysters on the half shell
slices bacon, diced without
  rind
-3 tablespoons
  Worcestershire sauce
lt and pepper to taste

Time: 5 minutes. Serves 1-2

ash oysters and shell to remove any grit. Dry with a
ean cloth. Place diced bacon on white kitchen paper.
over with a second piece of paper. Cook 3 minutes on
gh. Pierce oysters with toothpick. Top with bacon.
rinkle with sauce. Season to taste. Cook 1-2 minutes.

Oysters Mornay

? oysters on the half shelf,
  pierced with toothpick

auce

tablespoons butter
tablespoons flour
/3 cups milk
 cup Parmesan cheese, grated
 cup Swiss cheese, grated

Time: 6 minutes. Serves 1-2

it butter into small ovenproof dish and cook 15 seconds
 melt. Stir in flour, then milk. Cook 3 minutes on high or
itil mixture boils. Stir sauce after 1 minute. Stir in cheese.
over and cook until cheese melts. Spoon sauce over each
ster on the shell. Dust lightly with paprika, or a little
xtra grated cheese. Cook 1-2 minutes and serve with
mon wedges.

Garlic Shrimp

-6 tablespoons peanut oil
cloves garlic, finely chopped
scallions, finely chopped
fresh hot red chili, sliced
  without seeds, or ½ teaspoon
  chili powder
lb shelled uncooked shrimp

Time: 4 minutes. Serves 4

ombine oil, garlic, scallions and chili in microwave oven
ish. Add shrimp and toss to coat with oil. Allow to stand
0 minutes. Cook 2 minutes on high. Stir and cook until
ey turn pink, another 2 minutes.

Fillets of Flounder with Pernod Sauce

¾ oz butter
6 fillets of flounder
fish seasoning
juice of half a lemon
2 tablespoons Pernod
⅓ cup cream
sprinkling of dry basil
chopped chives for garnish

Time: 9 minutes. Serves 4-6

Melt butter in an oblong dish for 15 seconds. Sprinkle
fillets lightly with seasoning and place in butter. Pour over
lemon juice and Pernod. Cook covered 6-7 minutes on
high. Remove to plate, reheat liquids, add cream, basil and
cook 1½ minutes. Spoon over fillets. Sprinkle with
chopped chives and serve.

Salmon Ring

1 × 16 oz can red salmon
½ cup chopped onion
¼ cup salad oil
⅓ cup dry breadcrumbs
2 eggs, beaten
1 teaspoon dry mustard
½ teaspoon salt

Time: 9 minutes. Serves 6

Drain salmon, reserving ⅓ cup liquid. Cook onion in oil for
2½ minutes. Combine onion, dry breadcrumbs, salmon
liquid, eggs, mustard, salt and flaked salmon in a basin and
mix well. Place into a microwave ring pan and cook for 6
minutes on high. Give pan a quarter of a turn after 3 minutes. Let stand for 5 minutes before serving.
  Note: Tuna may be used instead of salmon.

ysters Kilpatrick

Smoked Salmon Quiche

6 oz smoked salmon, thinly
   sliced

Pie Dough

2 cups flour
1¼ cups butter
½ teaspoon salt
¼ cup cold water

Custard

1 cup cream
4 egg yolks
2 scallions, finely chopped
salt, cayenne pepper, and
   nutmeg to taste

Time: 31 minutes. Serves 6

Sift dry ingredients in bowl. Rub in butter and mix to a firm dough with water. Knead lightly and roll out to fit an 8 inch pie plate. Chill for 15 minutes. Cook for 6 minutes on high.

Blend together custard ingredients, pour into cool pie dough shell and carefully float salmon slices on the surface. With a teaspoon, carefully lift some of the custard over the top of the salmon. Bake on the defrost cycle for 25 minutes until center is set. Stand 3 minutes before serving.

Salmon Stuffed Mushrooms

12 medium to large mushrooms
6 tablespoons flaked red
   salmon
6 tablespoons soft breadcrumbs
2 teaspoons scallions, finely
   chopped
2 teaspoons parsley, finely
   chopped
2 teaspoons lemon juice
2 tablespoons butter, melted
grated Parmesan cheese

Time: 5 minutes. Serves 6

Remove stems from mushrooms. Chop stems finely. Combine salmon, breadcrumbs, stems, scallions, parsley, lemon juice and butter. Fill caps with mixture. Sprinkle with cheese. Arrange mushrooms in a circle on the outer edge of a glass platter. Cook 5 minutes on high.

Whole Fish with Black Bean Sauce

1 whole fish, approximately
   1½ lb, or fish fillets
fish seasoning (optional)

Sauce

1 tablespoon oil
1 slice green ginger, finely chopped
1 clove garlic, finely chopped
1 tablespoon black beans
½ teaspoon dry sherry
½ teaspoon sugar
2 teaspoons soy sauce
1 cup fish stock or water
1 tablespoon cornstarch
water
3 scallions, finely chopped
red pepper for garnish

Time: 11 minutes. Serves 4

Trim off fins and tail with a pair of scissors. Remove t[he] eyes. Check that all scales have been removed. Wash w[ell] and dry with kitchen paper. A small amount of fish seaso[n]ing may be sprinkled into cavity. Place fish onto a plate a[nd] cover with plastic food wrap. Cook approximately 6 minutes on high or until flesh flakes easily.

Heat oil in a bowl for 2 minutes. Add ginger, garl[ic] beans, and stir. Cook for 1 minute on high. Add sher[ry] sugar, soy sauce and stock. Cook 1 minute. Blend cornflo[ur] and water, stir into mixture. Cook another 2 minutes. S[tir] in shallots. Spoon over fish. Serve garnished with shredd[ed] red pepper.

Melba Toast with Curried Salmon

4 oz canned red salmon,
   drained
3 tablespoons mayonnaise
3 tablespoons finely chopped
   peanuts
3 tablespoons canned crushed
   pineapple, drained
½ teaspoon curry paste
Melba toast (see recipe)

Time: 1 minute. Serves

Combine all ingredients in a bowl and spoon onto roun[ds] of Melba toast.

Arrange on a plate lined with paper towel and cook [on] high 1 minute.

Baked Orange Fish

1 large orange
1 small clove garlic
1 tablespoon butter
1 small onion, finely cut
1 tablespoon finely chopped
    parsley
salt and pepper
1 cup fresh bean sprouts, roots
    removed
¾ cup orange juice
1 whole fish (1½–2 lb)

Time: 9½ minutes. Serves 4

Peel orange and cut into segments. Cut garlic into small pieces and half the orange segments into dice. Place butter, onion, garlic, orange segments, parsley, salt and pepper into a microwave oven dish and cook covered on high for 2 minutes. Add bean sprouts.

After trimming fins and tail, place fish on a baking dish, removing eyes and checking for any scales which may have been missed. If the fish is large it may be scored 2 or 3 times on each side to ensure even cooking. Season cavity with salt and pepper. Stuff cavity with onion and orange mixture. Cover fish with plastic wrap and cook 5 minutes on high. Pour juice over fish and arrange remaining segments over fish neatly. Continue cooking 2½ minutes until flesh flakes easily.

Note: Allow 5 minutes per 1 lb cooking time.

Whole Fish with Chinese Pickle Sauce

1 whole fish, approximately
    1½ lb

Chinese Pickle Sauce

2 teaspoons ketchup
½ teaspoon salt
2 teaspoons soy sauce
2 cups pineapple juice
½ cup diced Chinese mixed
    pickle
1 slice pineapple, diced
2 tablespoons vinegar
3 tablespoons brown sugar
small piece pepper, diced
1–2 tablespoons cornstarch

Time: 15 minutes. Serves 4–6

Prepare and cook the fish in the same way as Whole Fish with Black Bean Sauce (see recipe).

Combine all ingredients in a bowl except cornstarch. Cook 4–5 minutes on high until boiling. Stir after 3 minutes. Thicken with blended cornstarch. Cook 2 minutes, serve over fish.

Note: Allow 5 minutes per 1 lb cooking time.

Scallops in Oyster Sauce

1½ tablespoons oil
1 slice green ginger, finely chopped
1 clove garlic, finely chopped
1 lb scallops
1 tablespoon dry sherry
2 teaspoons soy sauce
½ cup fish stock
2 tablespoons oyster sauce
1 teaspoon sugar
3 teaspoons cornstarch
2 scallions, cut into ¾ inch
    lengths
½ teaspoon salt

Time: 7 minutes. Serves

Heat oil in an ovenproof dish for 1 minute. Add ginge garlic and scallops. Cook for 3 minutes on high. Ad sherry, soy sauce and cook 1 minute. Blend the stock, oy ter sauce, sugar and cornstarch. Add to dish, stir to blen and cook 2 minutes until boiling. Fold in scallions, salt an serve with plain boiled rice.

Scallops with Barbecue Sauce

1 lb prepared scallops
1 egg white, lightly beaten
2 teaspoons seasoned cornstarch
2 tablespoons peanut oil
1 slice green ginger, finely
    chopped
1 clove garlic, finely chopped
½ onion, cut in ¾ inch pieces
½ red pepper, cut in ¾ inch
    pieces
½ green pepper, cut in ¾ inch
    pieces
2 tablespoons Chinese
    barbecue sauce
1 tablespoon dry sherry
2 scallions, cut in ¾ inch pieces

Time: 12 minutes. Serves

Combine scallops, egg white and cornstarch in a mediun sized bowl. Preheat browning casserole dish on high 5 min utes. Add oil, ginger, garlic, onion and peppers and coc on high 3 minutes, covered.

Add scallops, barbecue sauce and sherry. Cook on hig 4–5 minutes, stirring twice during cooking. Add scallion

Serve in a parsley rice (see recipe Parsley Rice Ring) ri (p. 50).

Coquilles St. Jacques

4 tablespoons butter
1 small onion, finely chopped
8 oz scallops
2 teaspoons lemon juice
½ teaspoon salt
marjoram
dash paprika
6 tablespoons white wine
2 tablespoons flour
½ cup cream
2 oz mushrooms, sliced thinly
fresh white breadcrumbs
1 teaspoon chopped parsley

Time: 9½ minutes. Serves 4

Combine 1 tablespoon butter and onion in a medium sized casserole dish. Cook uncovered 1 minute. Stir in scallops, lemon juice, seasoning and wine. Cook, covered 3 minutes on high. Drain liquid and reserve. Melt 3 tablespoons butter for 30 seconds. Blend in flour then stir in reserved liquid and cream. Heat, uncovered, 2 minutes or until sauce thickens. Add scallop mixture, mushrooms and spoon into 4 individual ramekins, or scallop shells. Sprinkle with breadcrumbs and parsley and heat uncovered 3 minutes.

Fresh Trout with Asparagus Sauce

2 whole trouts, approximately 8
    oz each
2 small branches of fresh dill
fish seasoning
1 scallion, cut finely
1 tablespoon dry vermouth
4 tablespoons fish stock or
    white wine
1 lemon, peeled and sliced
butter

Time: 7 minutes. Serves 2

Wash and dry trout, remove eyes. Place fresh dill into cavities and season. Place in a glass dish, sprinkle with scallions, vermouth, fish stock and cover with slices of lemon. Dot lightly with butter. Cover with plastic food wrap and cook 6-7 minutes on high.

Asparagus Sauce

1 (10 oz) can green asparagus spears
8 tablespoons chicken stock
salt and pepper to taste
1 tablespoon fresh cream

Time: 2 minutes. Serves 2

Combine asparagus with stock, salt, pepper and cream. Puree in a blender until smooth. Correct seasonings. Pour into glass jug. Cook 2 minutes on high. Mask trout with sauce.

Curried Shrimp

2 tablespoons butter
¼ cup crushed onion
1 tablespoon fresh ginger,
    grated
¼ cup plain flour
1 tablespoon curry powder
1 cup milk
1 cup coconut milk
2 teaspoons lemon juice
1 lb uncooked shrimp

Time: 13 minutes. Serves 4

Place butter, ginger and onion in 3½ pint casserole a cook 2 minutes on high. Stir in flour and curry powder. S to a smooth paste. Add both milks and cook 5 minute stirring every minute. Blend in remaining ingredients. M well and cook 6 minutes, stirring after 2 minutes. Ser with plain boiled rice, toasted coconut and mango chutne

Simple Fish and Vegetable Pie

1 lb white fish: barramundi,
    jewfish, etc.
4 oz fresh peas
4 oz diced carrots
1 onion, finely chopped
freshly ground black pepper
salt to taste
2 tablespoons chopped parsley
2 tablespoons butter
2 tablespoons cornstarch
2 cups milk
½ teaspoon mixed herbs
paprika
¼ cup grated Cheddar cheese

Time: 35-40 minutes. Serves 8-

Place fish in shallow dish. Cover and cook on medium minutes. Stand covered 5 minutes.

Combine peas, carrots and onion in small bowl. Cov and cook on high 8 minutes. Stand covered 5 minutes.

Combine pepper, salt, parsley and butter. Cook on hi 45 seconds. Blend in cornstarch, milk and mixed herl Cook on high 3-5 minutes. Stir and cook on high anoth 1-2 minutes. Stir again.

Flake fish and add to vegetables and sauce. Pour mixtu into shallow dish, top with paprika and grated chees Cook on high 2-3 minutes to melt cheese. Serve hot. Stan ing time: 10 minutes.

Fresh Trout with Asparagus Sauc

Desserts

Without doubt the crowning glory of any meal is dessert and with the microwave on your side the variety of desserts you can prepare is endless. Even better for the host or hostess is the advantage of being able to prepare desserts well in advance of the guests arriving.

Keep these hints in mind when preparing your sweet dinner finale: fruit pies can be started in the microwave and finished on the convection setting; flan cases can be pre-baked, frozen and then quickly thawed on the defrost setting; and a whole range of imaginative dessert sauces can be prepared and frozen in containers till you need them.

Fruit Pizza

2 cups self-rising flour
1–2 tablespoons sugar
½ teaspoon salt
1½ tablespoons butter
¾ cup milk

Topping

4 oz cream cheese, softened
¼ cup sugar
1 teaspoon grated lemon zest
6 cups sliced fresh fruit (kiwi
    fruit, strawberries, mango,
    peeled grapes, etc.)
⅔ cup apple or orange juice
2 teaspoons arrowroot or ⅔ cup
    fruit gel

Time: 12–15 minutes. Serves 12

Sift flour into a bowl and add sugar and salt. Cut butter into small cubes and rub into flour. Add milk, blending mixture with a table knife.

Turn dough onto floured board and knead lightly. Roll dough into a 12 inch circle and place onto a lightly greased round pyrex plate.

Set convection oven to 425°F and bake pizza base 12–15 minutes until well browned. Allow to cool.

Place softened cream cheese into bowl and beat in sugar until dissolved. Add lemon zest and spread mixture evenly over pizza crust. Arrange sliced fruits on top.

Combine juice and arrowroot in small bowl. Cook on high 2–2½ minutes until thickened and clear, stirring after each minute. Cool until warm. Spoon over fruit and chill until set.

Fruit Pizza

Strawberry Cheese Cake

1½ tablespoons butter
4 oz cookie crumbs
1 lb cream cheese, softened
½ cup superfine sugar
2 egg yolks
1 teaspoon grated lemon zest
1 tablespoon lemon juice,
  strained
2 stiffly beaten egg whites

Topping

1 cup sour cream
1 tablespoon sugar
1 teaspoon vanilla extract
1 punnet strawberries
1 jar fruit gel

Time: 23 minutes. Serves 8–12

Place butter in bowl and soften on high 1 minute. Stir in cookie crumbs and cook on high 2 minutes. Press crumb mixture into base of flan dish.

In a large bowl beat cream cheese, sugar, egg yolks, zest and juice until creamy. Avoid overbeating. Fold in stiffly beaten egg whites, using a metal spoon. Pour into prepared dish and cook on defrost 20 minutes. Allow to cool.

In a small bowl beat sour cream, sugar and vanilla until sugar dissolves. Spread over cheese cake. Wash and dry strawberries, place upright on cheese cake and coat evenly with fruit gel. Chill several hours before serving.

Custard Sauce

12 fl oz milk
3 tablespoons sugar
2 tablespoons custard powder
2 egg yolks
1 teasoon vanilla extract
cinnamon sugar

Time: 6–7 minutes. Makes about 4 cups

Combine milk, sugar and custard powder in jug and cook on high 4 minutes until sauce thickens, stirring after 2 minutes.

Beat egg yolks in basin with whisk. Blend in 2 tablespoons of custard mixture and whisk egg mixture into remaining custard. Cook on defrost cycle for 1–2 minutes. Blend in vanilla.

Sprinkle surface of custard with a little cinnamon sugar to prevent skin forming.

Step 1 Strawberry Cheese Cake. Press biscuit mixture into base of flan dish

Step 2 Use a metal spoon to fold in egg whites

Step 3 Pour mixture into cookie base

Rhubarb Pie

1½ lb rhubarb, cut into 1 inch
    lengths
½–¾ cup sugar
2 tablespoons custard powder
pinch salt
1 teaspoon mixed spice
2 oz raisins

Dough

1½ cups all-purpose flour
1 teaspoon baking powder
½ teaspoon salt
½ cup butter, cut in small
    cubes
2 teaspoons sugar
3–4 tablespoons cold water
1 tablespoon sugar

Time: 17–20 minutes. Serves 6–8

Combine rhubarb, sugar, custard powder, salt, mixed spice and raisins in a bowl.

Sift flour, baking powder and salt and place in food processor. Add butter and 2 teaspoons sugar and blend to a crumb texture, adding water gradually until dough forms a ball. Chill dough 15–20 minutes.

Roll out two-thirds of dough, line 9 inch pie plate and place rhubarb mixture onto dough, piling center high. Roll out remaining dough and brush edge of dough in pie plate with cold water. Place remaining dough over rhubarb and seal edges. Cut air vents in top, brush with water and sprinkle with 1 tablespoon sugar.

Cook on high 8 minutes, then convection at 400°F for 7–10 minutes until dough is well browned. Serve with cream or custard sauce (*see recipe Custard Sauce*).

Orange Sponge Pudding

2 tablespoons butter
2 tablespoons sugar
1 egg
¾ cup self-rising flour
¼ cup milk
1 tablespoon orange juice or
    Grand Marnier
1 tablespoon grated orange zest
orange sauce (see recipe
    following)

Time: 4–5 minutes. Serves 4–6

Cream butter and sugar; beat in egg. Fold in flour, milk, orange juice and zest. Lightly grease china pudding basin and place a small circle of greaseproof paper in the bottom. Top with sponge mixture and cook on high 4–5 minutes. Turn out onto serving plate. Mask with sauce

Orange Sauce

2 tablespoons sugar
1 tablespoon cornflour
⅔ cup strained orange juice
⅓ cup water
1 tablespoon Grand Marnier
2 tablespoons butter
1 tablespoon grated orange zest
2 teaspoons strained lemon
    juice

Time: 2½ minut[es]

Blend sugar, cornflour and orange juice in jug and cook [on] high 2–2½ minutes, stirring twice during cooking. Mix [in] remaining ingredients and serve warm over pudding.

Pears with Chocolate Sauce

6 firm pears
1 tablespoon lemon juice,
    strained
¼ cup sugar
2 tablespoons dry sherry
2 tablespoons Grand Marnier
6 oz cooking chocolate pieces
1½ oz butter

Time: 14 minutes. Serves

Peel pears, leaving stems intact. De-core from the base [by] cutting a circle with paring knife. Brush with lemon jui[ce] to prevent discoloring.

In a 2 pt casserole combine sugar, sherry and Gra[nd] Marnier. Place pears on sides with the thicker en[d] towards the outside. Add remaining lemon juice and cove[r]. Cook on high for 6 minutes. Turn pears over and bas[te]. Cover and cook a further 6 minutes or until tender. R[e]move pears. Reserve poaching liquid.

Measure ½ cup poaching liquid and return to casserol[e]. Add cooking chocolate pieces and cook on high 2 minute[s]. Add butter and whisk till smooth.

Fill each pear with custard sauce (*see recipe Egg Custar[d]*[)]. Place upright on serving dish. Pour remaining custa[rd] around pears and spoon chocolate sauce over top.

> **HINT: MELTING CHOCOLATE**
> When melting chocolate test it with a skewer to confirm that it has in fact melted, and not just softened. When reheating melted or softened chocolate be careful to avoid burning.

Egg Custard

3 tablespoons sugar
1 tablespoon all-purpose flour
½ cup milk
½ cup light cream
6 egg yolks
1 teaspoon Grand Marnier
1–2 teaspoons superfine sugar

Time: 3 minutes. Makes about 2 cups

Combine sugar and flour in a bowl and beat in milk and cream. Cook on high 2 minutes, stirring every 30 seconds. Beat egg yolks, add to milk and cream sauce.

Cook on high 30–45 seconds, stirring after each 15 seconds. Beat in Grand Marnier. Sprinkle lightly with a little superfine sugar to prevent a skin forming on the sauce.

Pavlova Roll

2 teaspoons melted butter
2 teaspoons cornflour
6 egg whites
1½ cups superfine sugar
¾ teaspoon vanilla extract
1 teaspoon white vinegar
½ cup toasted almond slivers
1 tablespoon cinnamon sugar
2 cups fresh strawberries
10 fl oz whipped cream

Time: 3 minutes. Serves 6–8

Place butter in small bowl and cook on high 15 seconds to melt. Lightly grease tray and line base with wax paper. Regrease and dust lightly with cornflour and shake off excess.

Beat egg whites until firm peaks form. Add sugar, one tablespoon at a time, beating until dissolved. Blend in vanilla and vinegar.

Spread meringue evenly into prepared 12 × 12 inch tray and sprinkle with toasted almonds. Cook on high 3 minutes and allow to cool.

Sprinkle a large sheet of wax paper with cinnamon sugar and turn pavlova onto it. Slice 1½ cups of strawberries and fold into whipped cream. Spread cream over two-thirds of the pavlova.

Roll up as for a Swiss roll. Pipe rosettes of cream on top and garnish with remaining strawberries, cut into fans. Chill before serving.

HINT: MAKING STRAWBERRY FANS
Wash and hull strawberries and using a sharp thin-bladed knife make 5–6 cuts in each extending only ⅔ into the strawberry from the top. Carefully separate slices until strawberry takes on a fan-shape.

Step 1 Pavlova Roll. Spread meringue evenly into tray

Step 2 Sprinkle with roasted almonds

Step 3 Roll up pavlova with wax paper

Grasshopper Torte

⅓ cup butter
1 packet chocolate flavored
    plain cookies, crumbed
4 cups white marshmallows,
    diced
¾ cup milk
¼ cup green creme de menthe
2 tablespoons white creme de
    cacao
2 teaspoons gelatin
2 tablespoons cold water
1 cup stiffly beaten cream

Time: 3 minutes. Serves 8

Place butter in glass bowl and cook for 45 seconds on high. Stir in cookie crumbs. Put half the mixture into a 9 inch round glass dish. Chill. Place marshmallows and milk into a large bowl. Cook 1½–2 minutes to melt marshmallows. Stir in creme de menthe and creme de cacao.

Blend gelatin and water in small bowl. Heat 15 seconds on high. Blend into mixture. Cool. Fold in whipped cream. Pour into crumb-lined dish. Top with remaining crumbs. Chill until firm. Cut into wedges and pipe with whipped cream.

Pineapple Meringue Pie

Pastry

4 oz butter
⅓ cup sugar
2 cups all-purpose flour, sifted
3 drops vanilla extract
2 teaspoons water
1 egg yolk

Filling

1 (16 oz) can crushed pineapple
1 egg yolk
2 tablespoons custard powder
1 tablespoon arrowroot
¼ cup orange juice

Meringue

3 egg whites
½ cup superfine sugar

Time: 13 minutes. Serves 8

Rub butter into sugar and flour. Add vanilla, water and egg yolk. Knead lightly and let rest 15 minutes. Roll out pastry and line a 9 inch pie plate. Prick well and cook for 4 minutes on high. Allow to cool.

Place pineapple into a casserole dish and cook 4 minutes until boiling. Beat egg yolk, add custard powder, arrowroot and orange juice. Mix into hot pineapple and cook for 2 minutes on high. Cool and spoon into pastry case.

Beat egg whites, adding sugar, 1 tablespoon at a time, until soft peaks form. Pipe or spread over pineapple filling and cook to set for 2–3 minutes. Place under grilling plate for a few minutes if a light golden color is required.

Savarin

2 oz butter
3½ oz superfine sugar
3 eggs
4 oz self-rising flour
2 tablespoons milk or cream

Syrup

7 fl oz water
8 oz sugar
5 tablespoons Grand Marnie

Time: 6 minutes. Serves

Beat softened butter and sugar to a cream. Add eggs, or at a time. Add flour, all at once. Fold in milk or crean Grease and line base of micro-ring dish. Grease again. Pou in mixture and cook 5–6 minutes on high. Turn out on cooking rack.

Boil water and sugar to form a syrup. Add Gran Marnier. Spoon warm syrup over cake until all is absorbed Place on serving platter. Fill center with fresh fruit sala Decorate with whipped cream and extra fruit.

Apricot Upside Down Cake

Base

2 oz butter
⅓ cup brown sugar
14 apricot halves
7 glace cherries, halved

Cake

2½ oz butter
½ cup sugar
1 egg
½ cup corn syrup
⅓ cup milk
1½ cups all-purpose flour
1 teaspoon bicarbonate of soda
1 teaspoon ground ginger
1 teaspoon ground cinnamon
pinch salt

Serving Suggestion

rum-flavored whipped cream
chopped pecans

Time: 12 minutes. Serves

Cream butter and brown sugar. Lightly grease a 10 inc ring mold with melted butter and line base with waxpro paper.

Spread butter mixture over base. Place one cherry ha into hollow of each apricot center and lie them, cut sic down, on batter mixture.

For cake, cream butter and sugar, add egg, corn syru and milk. Sift dry ingredients together and blend into mi ture. Spread carefully over apricot layer. Cook uncovere on high 10–12 minutes.

Serve with rum flavored whipped cream sprinkled wit chopped pecans.

Baba au Rhum

Fruit

1 tablespoon raisins
1 tablespoon currants
1 tablespoon golden raisins
1 tablespoon rum

Baba Batter

2 oz butter
3½ oz superfine sugar
3 eggs
4 oz self-rising flour
2 tablespoons milk

Syrup

½ cup sugar
1 cinnamon stick
1 cup syrup from tinned
   apricots
2 tablespoons lemon juice
4 tablespoons rum

Time: 11 minutes. Serves 8

Combine fruit and rum and set aside. Cream butter and sugar. Add eggs, one at a time. Add flour all at once and fold in milk and fruit. Place batter in greased and lined glass Baba mold. Cook 5–6 minutes on high. Turn out on a serving platter.

Combine sugar, cinnamon stick and syrup together and cook 5 minutes on high. Add lemon juice and rum. Cool.

Spoon syrup over Baba. Serve decorated with whipped cream, apricots and glace cherries.

Apple Crumble

6 cooking apples, peeled and
   sliced
½ cup water
½ cup sugar
½ teaspoon cinnamon
2 oz soft butter
¼ cup flour
½ cup coconut
½ cup brown sugar

Time: 9 minutes. Serves 6–8

Place apples, water, sugar and cinnamon into a 2 pint casserole dish, cover and cook 5 minutes on high. Rub butter into flour, coconut and brown sugar then sprinkle over apples. Top with extra cinnamon and cook 3–4 minutes. Serve with Custard Sauce (*see recipe*).

Pineapple Coconut Cake

2 oz butter
¾ cup sugar
vanilla extract
1 egg
½ cup milk
1 cup well-drained crushed
   pineapple
½ cup coconut
1½ cups flour
1 teaspoon baking powder
½ teaspoon salt

Time: 6–9 minute

Cream butter, sugar and vanilla until light and fluffy. Be in egg and fold in milk, crushed pineapple, coconut an sifted dry ingredients. Grease and line micro-baking dis Pour mixture into dish and cook 6 minutes on high or minutes on medium.

Pineapple Ginger Cake

2 oz butter
⅓ cup brown sugar
6 small slices of canned
   pineapple
6 maraschino cherries

Cake

2½ oz butter
½ cup superfine sugar
1 egg
½ cup corn syrup
⅓ cup milk
1½ cups flour
1 teaspoon baking soda
1 teaspoon ground ginger
1 teaspoon ground cinnamon
pinch salt

Time: 10 minutes. Serves

Cream 2 oz butter and brown sugar together and sprea into the bottom of a baking dish. Place pineapple rings in mixture with a cherry in the center of each ring.

Cream together 2½ oz butter and white sugar, add eg corn syrup and milk. Sift dry ingredients together. Blen all into a creamy mixture. Spread over pineapple slice Cook uncovered 10 minutes on high.

Note: Other fruits may be used: sliced mangoes, peach or apricots.

Pineapple Coconut Cake (see recip
this sectio

Baked Bread and Butter Custard

1 oz butter
2 cups milk
5 eggs
¼ cup raw sugar
1 teaspoon vanilla extract
4 slices white bread, crusts
    removed, then buttered
nutmeg
2 tablespoons golden raisins

Time: 62 minutes. Serves 6

Place butter into milk and heat for 2 minutes. Beat eggs, sugar and vanilla, add milk and butter mixture. Sprinkle buttered bread lightly with nutmeg, cut into cubes, and place into a greased baking ring with raisins. Pour custard over bread and cook uncovered 60 minutes on defrost.

Rice Custard

Time: 22 minutes

Note: 1 cup of precooked rice can be used in place of the buttered bread.

Queen Pudding

4 slices of buttered, stale plain
    cake
5 eggs
2 tablespoons sugar
2 cups warm milk
vanilla extract
strawberry jam

Time: 63 minutes. Serves 6

Cut cake into cubes. Place into well-buttered baking ring. Beat eggs, sugar and vanilla, add warm milk. Pour over cake cubes and cook 60 minutes on defrost.

Spread top of custard with strawberry jam. Top with piped meringue (see recipe Pineapple Meringue Pie) and cook 2–3 minutes on high. Sprinkle with sugar lightly colored with a few drops of pink food coloring.

Caramel Tart

1 precooked pastry case (see
    recipe Pineapple Meringue
    Pie)
2 tablespoons butter
1 cup brown sugar
4 egg yolks
3 drops vanilla extract
pinch salt
2 tablespoons flour
2 cups milk
meringue (see recipe Pineapple
    Meringue Pie)

Time: 8 minutes. Serves

Beat butter and sugar until fluffy. Beat in egg yolks. A vanilla, salt, fold in sifted flour, stir in milk. Cook 4–5 mi utes on high, stirring every minute until mixture thicker Spoon into pastry case. Top with meringue and cook 2 minutes on high.

Chocolate Souffle

6 teaspoons gelatin
¾ cup sugar
3 eggs, separated
1 cup milk
2 oz melted cooking chocolate
    (chop or grate chocolate, and
    cook ¾-1 minute to melt)
1 cup whipped cream

Time: 7½ minutes. Serves

In a large bowl, combine gelatin with ½ cup sugar. Stir egg yolks and beat in the milk. Heat on defrost for 6½–7 minutes or until gelatin dissolves, stirring occasionally. S in chocolate and chill, stirring occasionally until mixtu mounds slightly.

Beat egg whites until soft peaks form, gradually add maining sugar and beat until stiff. Fold in the chocola mixture with whipped cream. Pour into souffle dish wi a collar. Chill. To serve, garnish with extra whipped crea and almond slivers.

Chocolate Souff

Strawberry Marshmallow

4 egg whites
1 cup superfine sugar
½ teaspoon vanilla extract
¾ teaspoon white vinegar
3 teaspoons butter, melted
cornstarch

Filling

½ cup strawberry jam
2 teaspoons brandy
1 pint strawberries, hulled,
    washed and dried
whipped cream

Time: 4 minutes. Serves 8

Beat egg whites until soft peaks form. Add ⅓ cup sugar, beat until dissolved. Gradually add remaining sugar. When dissolved, add vanilla and vinegar, beating 1 minute.

Grease a 9 in pie plate with melted butter, dust well with cornstarch and shake off any excess.Spoon meringue into pie plate leaving outside edge higher than the center. Cook 3 minutes on high. Place under preheated grilling plate until pale golden if desired.

Heat jam to melting point, 1 minute on high, then sieve. Blend in brandy. Cut strawberries in halves, coat lightly with jam. Spread top of pavlova with cream, pile strawberries on top of cream. Pipe rosettes of cream around outside edge.

Strawberry Cream Dessert

2 pints ripe red strawberries
4 eggs, separated
1 tablespoon gelatin
8 tablespoons sugar
1 carton whipped cream

Time: 7 minutes. Serves 6-8

Wash and hull strawberries. Place 1½ pints into a blender and puree. Blend puree, egg yolks, gelatin and sugar. Place into a glass bowl and cook on defrost 7 minutes until gelatin dissolves, stirring constantly. Chill until slightly set. slightly set.

Beat cream to form stiff peaks. Fold into strawberry puree and beaten egg whites. Pour into individual glass dessert dishes to set. Decorate with whipped cream and remaining strawberries.

Peaches Flambe

1 oz butter
1 can drained peach halves
2 tablespoons Grand Marnier
1 oz sugar
3 extra tablespoons Grand
    Marnier for flaming

Time: 5½ minutes. Serves

Heat butter in glass serving dish for 1-2 minutes. Ad peach halves and Grand Marnier. Sprinkle with sugar ar cook 3 minutes on high. Heat extra Grand Marnier in gla jug for 25 seconds, flame and pour over peaches. Ser with vanilla ice cream.

Lemon Meringue Pie

1 precooked pastry case (see
    recipe Pineapple Meringue
    Pie)
meringue (see recipe Pineapple
    Meringue Pie)

Filling

½ cup cornstarch
½ cup sugar
¾ cup water
⅓ cup lemon juice
⅓ cup butter
3 egg yolks
grated rind of 1 lemon

Time: 7 minutes. Serves

Combine cornstarch, sugar, water, juice of lemon and bu ter in a casserole dish and cook 2 minutes on high, stir ar cook another 2 minutes. Cool. Beat in yolks and lemo rind. Place in pastry case. Top with meringue, cook 2 minutes. Cool.

Strawberry Pavlov

Baked Honey Pears

4 firm pears
4 tablespoons chopped dates
2 tablespoons chopped walnuts
3 tablespoons honey
¼ teaspoon cinnamon

Time: 8 minutes. Serves 4

Peel pears. Cut off caps ¾ inch from top. Core each pear without cutting right through. Remove seeds. Combine dates, walnuts, honey and cinnamon. Fill pear centers with date mixture, replace caps. Arrange in a circle on a glass plate and cook 6–8 minutes on high. Pears can be served whole: remove cap and top with whipped cream, or cut in half, served with a rosette of whipped cream.

Apple Tea Cake

2 oz butter
¾ cup sugar
vanilla extract
1 egg
¾ cup milk
1½ cups flour
2 teaspoons baking powder
½ teaspoon salt
1 green apple, peeled, cored
   and thinly sliced
2 teaspoons brown sugar
2 teaspoons cinnamon

Time: 6–9 minutes

Cream butter, sugar and vanilla until light and fluffy. Beat in egg and fold in milk and sifted dry ingredients except the apple, brown sugar and cinnamon. Prepare the micro-baking dish, grease it first, then line it with greaseproof paper and grease it again. Arrange thinly sliced apples and lightly dust with mixture of brown sugar and cinnamon. Pour batter on top of apples. Cook 6 minutes on high or 9 minutes on medium.

HINT: FRUITFUL VITAMINS

To retain the natural goodness of fruit, it must be cooked with care. Most fruits can be simply prepared to taste delicious and provide a healthy vitamin supplement.

Apple and Raisin Strudel

2 tablespoons butter
4 sheets filo pastry
4 tablespoons ground almonds
   or cake crumbs
4 large cooking apples
¼ cup raisins
¼ cup sugar
1 teaspoon cinnamon
2 teaspoons grated lemon zest
1 beaten egg

Time: 6 minutes. Serves 6

Place butter into bowl. Cook on high 1 minute or until melted. Brush 1 sheet of filo pastry lightly with butter and sprinkle with 1 teaspoon ground almonds. Place another sheet of filo pastry on top and repeat, brushing with butter and sprinkling with ground almonds until all pastry is used. Reserve some almonds for filling.

Peel, core and thinly slice apples and place in a bowl. Add raisins, sugar, cinnamon, zest and remaining ground almonds and blend together.

Cover two-thirds of pastry with apple mixture. Brush uncovered pastry with beaten egg and roll up. Brush with remaining butter and sprinkle with extra cinnamon.

Cook in roasting dish on high 6–8 minutes or on preheated broiling plate 6 minutes on high. Cook strudel 3–4 minutes on each side. Transfer to serving plate and dust with icing sugar mixture.

Ginger Puff Sponge

2 eggs
2 oz sugar
1 teaspoon corn syrup
1 oz cornstarch
1 oz flour
2 level teaspoons ground ginger
1 level teaspoon cinnamon
1 level teaspoon cocoa
¼ level teaspoon baking soda
   of soda
½ level teaspoon cream of
   tartar

Time: 2½ minutes

Beat eggs until thick and creamy, gradually adding sugar, beating until dissolved. Add corn syrup and beat until well mixed. Fold in sifted dry ingredients. Place into a well greased micro-baking ring and cook for 2½ minutes on high, turning every minute. When cold, split and fill with cream.

Meringue-topped Chocolate Cheese Cake

Base

1 cup cookie crumbs
½ cup melted margarine (to
  melt margarine put in oven
  ¾–1 minute)

Filling

12 oz cream cheese (to soften
  cheese, cut up and place in
  oven on defrost 1 minute)
2 eggs
½ cup superfine sugar
1 teaspoon vanilla extract
2 oz melted chocolate (to melt
  chocolate, cut up and place
  in oven and cook 1 minute)

Topping

2 egg whites
5 tablespoons superfine sugar
⅓ cup coconut
2 teaspoons cornstarch

Time: 9 minutes

Combine base ingredients and press evenly into an 8 inch Pyrex pie plate. Chill until firm.

To make filling, beat cream cheese using an electric mixer until smooth. Add eggs one at a time. Add sugar, vanilla, and beat until creamy smooth. Pour into crumb crust. Swirl in melted chocolate to give a marble effect. Cook 3 minutes.

Whip egg whites until stiff, using an electric beater, gradually adding sugar, beating to dissolve. Fold in coconut (can be lightly toasted if desired) and cornstarch. Pipe onto cheese cake and cook 3 minutes. Serve cold.

> ### HINT: CAKE CONTAINERS
> Cake mixtures should not fill the container more than half way or they will spill over. Cooking in a microwave makes rising agents more active.

Banana Cake

2 oz butter, melted
¼ cup milk
1 egg, beaten
½ cup mashed banana
½ cup brown sugar
1 cup self-rising flour
½ cup chopped nuts

Topping

¼ cup brown sugar
¼ cup chopped nuts
1 tablespoon all-purpose flour
2 tablespoons coconut
pinch cinnamon
½ oz softened butter

Time: 10½ minute

Combine butter, milk, egg, banana, and brown sugar in basin. Mix well. Fold in flour and nuts. Pour into a grease and lined 8 inch Pyrex souffle dish. Combine topping i gredients and sprinkle in souffle dish. Cook on mediu 10½–11½ minutes. Let stand 5 minutes before turning ou

Marble Cake

2 oz butter
¾ cup sugar
vanilla extract
1 egg
¾ cup milk
1½ cups all-purpose flour
2 teaspoons baking powder
½ teaspoon salt
red food coloring
cocoa
baking soda

Time: 6–9 minute

Cream butter, sugar and vanilla until light and fluffy. Bea in egg, fold in milk and sifted dry ingredients alternatel Divide the mixture into 3 separate bowls:

Leave one plain.

Add a few drops of red food coloring to the second on

Add 2 tablespoons cocoa, a pinch of baking soda and tablespoon milk to the third.

Drop into greased, lined micro-baking ring in alternat colors. Lightly mix with a metal skewer to blend color Cook 6 minutes on high or 9 minutes on medium.

Marble Cak

Carrot Cake

½ cup butter or margarine
½ cup firmly packed brown
 sugar
1 egg
1 cup firmly packed fresh
 grated carrot
1 dessertspoon crystallized
 ginger
½ cup seeded raisins
½ cup golden raisins
1½ cups double sifted flour
1 teaspoon baking powder
½ teaspoon soda
½ teaspoon cinnamon
½ teaspoon nutmeg
¾ cup milk

Frosting

8 oz confectioners' sugar
3 oz cream cheese
3 tablespoons butter
1 teaspoon vanilla extract
1 teaspoon sherry

Time: 9 minutes

Cream butter or margarine and brown sugar. Beat in egg until well blended. Stir in carrots, ginger, raisins and golden raisins. Sift together flour, baking powder, soda, cinnamon and nutmeg. Stir into the mixture with milk. Blend well. Turn into a well greased micro-ring dish and cook in oven 6 minutes on high then 3 minutes on medium. Serve cold with lemon frosting or hot with lemon sauce.

Beat all frosting ingredients until fluffy — spread over cake. Decorate with mandarin quarters or small marzipan carrots.

Orange Tea Ring

2 oz butter
¾ cup sugar
vanilla extract
1 egg
3 tablespoons orange juice
3 tablespoons milk
2 teaspoons orange rind, grated
1½ cups flour
2 teaspoons baking powder
½ teaspoon salt

Time: 6–9 minutes

Cream butter, sugar and vanilla until light and fluffy. Beat in egg and fold in orange juice, milk, orange rind and dry ingredients alternately. Drop into a lined and greased micro-baking ring. Cook for 6 minutes on high or 9 minutes on medium. Cool and top with orange frosting.

Date Loaf

2 tablespoons butter or
 margarine
½ cup raw sugar
1 egg
⅔ cup milk
½ cup dates
½ cup walnuts, chopped
1½ cups self-rising flour
pinch salt
½ teaspoon cinnamon
½ teaspoon ginger
1 teaspoon mixed spice

Time: 6–9 minut

Beat butter and sugar to a cream. Add well-beaten egg. A milk gradually. Add chopped dates and nuts. Stir in light the sifted flour, salt, and spices. Spoon mixture into pr pared micro-baking dish. Cook 6 minutes on high or minutes on medium.

Date and Cherry Slice

8 oz chopped dates
2 oz chopped glace cherries
4 oz butter
1 oz crystallized ginger,
 chopped
1½ oz brown sugar
2 oz pecans, roughly chopped
3 cups Rice Crispies
6½ oz cooking chocolate
1 tablespoon butter

Time: 6–6½ minutes. Makes 2

Place dates, butter, cherries, ginger, sugar and pecan nut in a medium-sized bowl. Cook on medium for 5 minute Stir in Rice Crispies, press mixture into a lightly greased × 8 inch dish and chill until firm.

Chop chocolate into cubes and place in a basin with bu ter. Cook on high 1–1½ minutes until soft. Stir unt smooth. Spread chocolate over slice and chill until set. C into small serving pieces.

Black Forest Cherry Cake

1 packet chocolate cake mix

Filling

1 can black cherries, stoned
⅓ cup Kirsch
2 tablespoons arrowroot
3 tablespoons cherry syrup
10 fl oz cream
dark chocolate, grated
red cherries

Time: 12 minutes

Make cake as directed on packet. Grease and line a microwave baking ring. Pour cake mix into prepared dish. Cook in oven 5½–6 minutes on high. Turn onto a cake cooler and cover before cake is cold.

Place cherries, 2 tablespoons of Kirsch and syrup from cherries into a bowl to cover. Cook 4 minutes on high or until boiling. Blend arrowroot with 3 tablespoons syrup. Stir into cherry mixture, cook 2 minutes and allow to cool.

Split cake into 3 layers. Spread cherry mixture over base layer, top with second layer and set aside. Whip cream with remaining Kirsch. Spread half over second layer, top with third layer of cake. Spread top and outside edges lightly with cream. Mark top into serving sections, then dust top and sides with grated chocolate. Pipe a rosette of cream on edge of each marked section and top with a whole red cherry.

Black Forest Cherry Cake

Lemon Sponge Roll

egg yolks
cup sugar
cup water
ice and rind 1 lemon
cup all-purpose flour
egg whites
teaspoon cream of tartar
inch salt
fted confectioners' sugar
cup lemon spread jam

Time: 6–7 minutes. Serves 6–8

eat egg yolks with ½ cup sugar, water and lemon juice nd rind. Fold in sifted flour. Set aside.

Whisk egg whites till stiff. Beat in remaining ½ cup ugar, cream of tartar and salt. Fold egg white mixture with gg yolk mix. Pour mixture into greased and lined oblong ish. Cook on medium 5 minutes, then a further 1–2 minutes on high.

Turn cake immediately onto sheet of plastic wrap. prinkle with confectioners' sugar. Remove paper lining. oll up cake with plastic wrap. Cook on cake rack for ½ our.

Carefully unroll, spread cake with lemon, reroll without lastic wrap. Dust surface with confectioners' sugar and erve.

HINT: TOASTING NUTS

Almonds take 3–4 minutes on high, stirring once or twice to allow even toasting. Smaller nuts will take half the time.

Chocolate Bars

1 cup Cornflakes
1 cup sifted self-rising flour
1 cup coconut
¾ cup sugar
2 heaped teaspoons cocoa
pinch salt
6 oz butter, melted

Chocolate Icing

2 tablespoons butter
2 tablespoons cocoa
6 tablespoons icing sugar
⅛ teaspoon vanilla extract

Time: 8 minutes. Makes 25

Blend all ingredients together in bowl. Press into greased 8 × 8 inch square casserole and cook on medium-high 8 minutes.

Combine chocolate icing ingredients in basin and beat with electric hand mixer until smooth. Spread evenly over bars while still warm. When set, cut into squares.

Apricot and Almond Balls

1 cup chopped dried apricots
1 cup chopped, toasted
  almonds
½ cup butter
1 cup sugar
⅓ cup flour
½ teaspoon salt
2 eggs
3 cups wheat flakes, finely crushed
1 teaspoon vanilla extract
½ cup confectioners' sugar

Time: 6 minutes. Makes 50

Place butter into a mixing bowl and soften on high for 1 minute or until melted. Blend in sugar, flour, salt and eggs. Stir in apricots and cook on high 5 minutes or until very thick, stirring every 2 minutes. Cook for 5 minutes.

In a large bowl, combine wheat flakes and almonds. Stir in apricot mixture and vanilla until well blended. Shape into 1 inch balls. Roll balls in icing sugar to coat and chill until firm.

Sauces and Jams

Sauces are very quick and easy to make in the microwave. And they are delicious served with meats, vegetables and desserts. Be sure to stir frequently. You can even leave the wooden spoon in the bowl in the oven to make this a very simple operation. Use a large glass-type container when making sauces to prevent boiling over. When thickening a sauce, remember that arrowroot will make a more transparent sauce than cornstarch.

There's just nothing like homemade jams and fruit butters. With a microwave oven, jam-making is so quick and easy. But remember to stir for even cooking.

Basic White Sauce I

1 small onion, peeled
6 whole cloves
20 fl oz milk
1 bay leaf
2 oz butter
2 oz flour
salt and pepper

Time: 10½ minutes. Makes about 2 cups

Stud onion with cloves. Pour milk into a glass jug, add onion and bay leaf. Cook on high for 4½ minutes to heat and infuse flavors.

Place butter into a glass jug or casserole and cook 1 minute to melt. Add flour and stir with wooden spoon. Cook 1 minute.

Stir in milk to blend. Cook for 4 minutes, stirring after 2 minutes. Remove onion and bay leaf. Season with salt and pepper.

Parsley Sauce

2 tablespoons parsley, chopped
1 quantity Basic White Sauce I

Time: Fold 2 tablespoons of parsley into Basic White Sauce I.
Serve with seafood, vegetables, or corned meats.

Onion Sauce

Basic White Sauce I ingredients
2 oz onion, diced

Melt butter in Basic White Sauce I. Add onion and cook 3–4 minutes before adding the flour.
Add milk and cook as above.
Serve with roast mutton, corned beef, or corned ox tongue.

Egg Sauce

2 hard-boiled eggs
1 quantity Basic White Sauce I

Dice eggs finely. Fold into Basic White Sauce I. A little fine cut parsley may also be added.

Cheese Sauce I

1 quantity Basic White Sauce I
2 oz grated tasty cheese
1 egg yolk, beaten

Add 2 tablespoons of Basic White Sauce I to egg yolk and beat quickly. Return to remainder of sauce, along with cheese. Reheat for 2 minutes if necessary. Do not allow to boil.
Serve with seafood or vegetables.

Basic White Sauce II

2 tablespoons butter
2 tablespoons flour
½ teaspoon salt
little white pepper
8 fl oz milk

Time: 4 minutes. Makes about 1 cup

Place butter in a glass bowl. Cook for 45 seconds or until melted. Stir in flour, salt and pepper. Add milk and cook on high approximately 3 minutes until boiling, stirring from time to time.
Note: Use a wooden spoon when stirring.

Mushroom Sauce (see recipe this section

172

Cheese Sauce II

Time 4 minutes. Makes about 1 cup

Ingredients are the same as Basic White Sauce I except that you add ¼ teaspoon dry mustard with the flour. After sauce has cooked, stir in ½ to 1 cup shredded cheese until melted.

Hollandaise Sauce

⅓ cup butter
2 tablespoons lemon juice
2 egg yolks
¼ teaspoon salt

Time: 1 minute 45 seconds

Place butter into a small bowl, heat for 45 seconds on high. Stir in lemon juice and egg yolks, beat with whisk until well mixed. Cook 60 seconds, whisking every 15 seconds. Stir in salt halfway through.

Basic Brown Sauce

1 oz butter
2 oz carrot, diced
2 oz onion, diced
1 oz celery, diced
1½ oz pre-browned flour
1 tablespoon tomato paste
1 bayleaf
20 fl oz brown stock

Time: 12 minutes

Place butter into a casserole, cook 1 minute to melt. Add carrots, onion and celery, cook 4 minutes on high. Blend in flour and cook 1 minute. Add tomato paste, bay leaf, blend in stock and cook 3 minutes, stir well and cook another 3 minutes. If slower cooking is required, cook sauce on defrost 15–20 minutes, stirring from time to time. Strain.

Serve with roast meats or as a base for other sauces.

Demi Glace Sauce

10 fl oz brown sauce (see recipe)
8 fl oz brown stock
1½ fl oz Madeira

Time: 6 minutes

Combine ingredients in a jug. Cook 4–6 minutes on high, stirring twice during cooking time.

Chasseur Sauce

1 oz butter
1 scallion, cut finely
2 oz mushrooms, sliced
1½ fl oz dry white wine
4 oz tomatoes, chopped, deseeded
10 fl oz Demi Glace Sauce (see recipe)
parsley, chopped
salt and pepper to taste

Time: 13 minut

Cook butter in a casserole for 1 minute. Add scallions a cook 2 minutes on high. Add mushrooms and cook cover 2 minutes. Drain off butter. Add wine and cook 2–3 mi utes until boiling and reduced to half. Add tomatoes, De Glace Sauce and cook 5 minutes. Add parsley, salt a pepper.

Serve with steaks, chicken, barbecued food or lamb.

Port Wine Sauce

10 fl oz Demi Glace Sauce (see recipe)
3 tablespoons port wine
1 oz butter

Time: 6 minut

Cook Demi Glace Sauce in jug for 3–4 minutes on hig Add port wine and cook 2 minutes. Blend in the butte

Serve with roast or barbecued meats.

Curry Sauce

1 oz butter
1 clove garlic, chopped
2 oz chopped onion
1 tablespoon curry powder
1 oz flour
2 teaspoons tomato paste
14½ fl oz chicken stock or fish stock for seafood
2 oz apple, chopped
1 tablespoon fruit chutney
1 tablespoon golden raisins
1 tablespoon chopped almonds
salt and pepper

Time: 11 minut

Cook butter in casserole 1 minute to melt. Add garl onion and curry powder. Cook 3 minutes on high, blend flour and cook 1 minute. Add tomato paste and stoc blend with wooden spoon. Add remaining ingredients a cook 4–6 minutes, stirring after 2 minutes.

Serve with seafood, poultry, hard-boiled eggs or veg tables.

Mint Sauce

oz sugar
oz arrowroot
sh salt
fl oz warm water
-3 drops green food coloring
teaspoon finely chopped mint
drops peppermint extract

Time: 9 minutes

ombine sugar, arrowroot and salt in a 4 cup glass
easure. Stir well, add water. Cook for 6 minutes on high,
rring after first 2 minutes and then after every minute.
ing to boil. Add food coloring, chopped mint and extract.
eat for 30 seconds.

Apple Sauce

lb cooking apples
tablespoons water
oz butter
oz sugar
teaspoon cinnamon or
nutmeg

Time: 12 minutes

el, core and slice apples. Place into a casserole with
gar, butter and water. Cook covered for 12 minutes on
gh or until a puree is formed. Stir twice during cooking.
rain, stir in nutmeg or cinnamon.
Serve with roast pork or poultry.

Fresh Tomato Sauce

medium onion chopped
large clove garlic
lb fresh tomatoes, peeled and
chopped
bay leaves
teaspoons sugar
teaspoon dry basil
tablespoons tomato paste
tablespoon butter
cup stock
lt
pper

Time: 14 minutes

elt butter in Pyrex dish 30 seconds. Add onion, garlic.
ook 4 minutes on high. Add remaining ingredients. Cook
high 10 minutes, remove bay leaves. Puree mixture.

HINT: SAUCE TALK
Sauces are simple in a
microwave. You can
usually make them in the
jug you want to serve
them in and they do not
need the constant
attention required when
using your conventional
oven. Occasional stirring
of milk-based sauces is
essential to avoid spillage.

Veloute Sauce

This is a basic sauce, a little darker in color. Chicken, fish or veal stock is used in place of milk.

2 oz butter
2 oz flour
20 fl oz of stock (suitable for
*   sauce required)*
salt and pepper

Time: 11 minutes

Place stock into a glass jug and cook on high for 4 minutes. Place butter into a jug or casserole dish, cook 1 minute to melt. Stir in flour with wooden spoon. (A wooden spoon may be left in sauce during cooking for ease of stirring.) Cook 2 minutes. Blend in stock. Continue cooking for 4 minutes, stirring well after 2 minutes. Add seasonings.

Mushroom Sauce

Veloute Sauce ingredients (see
*   recipe)*
4 oz sliced button mushrooms
*   (canned mushrooms can be*
*   sliced and used if a mild*
*   flavor is required)*
1 egg yolk, beaten
4 tablespoons fresh cream

Melt butter in a jug or casserole. Add mushrooms and cook for 1 minute on high. Blend in flour and cook another 1 minute. Blend in warm stock (veal or chicken) and cook 4 minutes to thicken.

Stir after 2 minutes. Combine egg yolk and cream. Add 2 tablespoons of sauce, blend well and fold into remaining sauce. Season with salt and pepper.

Use with steak, veal or chicken.

Supreme Sauce

Veloute Sauce ingredients with
*   chicken stock (see recipe)*
1 oz mushroom trimmings
1 egg yolk
2½ fl oz fresh cream
squeeze lemon juice

Time: 8 minutes

Using basic Veloute Sauce ingredients, cook butter to melt and add mushrooms and cook 2 minutes on high. Blend in flour, cook another 1 minute. Blend in stock and cook 4 minutes. Stir after 2 minutes. Add seasonings, stir well and strain. Blend cream and egg yolk. Add 2 tablespoons sauce, mix well and return to remaining sauce, add lemon juice.

Serve with hot, boiled chicken or as a basic sauce for pastry or bread cases.

176

Aurora Sauce

1 quantity Supreme Sauce (see
*   recipe)*
1 tablespoon tomato puree

Time: 8 minut

Add puree to Supreme Sauce to enrich flavor and color Serve with chicken, poached eggs or pasta dishes.

Basic Custard Sauce

12 fl oz milk
3 tablespoons sugar
2 tablespoons custard powder
2 egg yolks
1 teaspoon vanilla extract

Time: 6 minut

Combine custard powder and sugar with milk. Heat 4 mi utes on high until sauce thickens, stirring twice. With wire whisk quickly beat in the egg yolks, heat for 1–2 mi utes on defrost, then flavor with vanilla.

Chocolate Sauce

10 fl oz milk
½ oz cocoa
½ oz cornstarch
2½ oz sugar
1 teaspoon butter

Time: 5 minut

Blend cornflour, cocoa with 3 tablespoons of milk. Pla remaining milk into a jug and cook 3 minutes on high boil. Blend in cornstarch mixture and cook 2 minute Blend in sugar and butter.

Jams

There is such a huge range of commercial sauces, jams and condiments now available that home production has largely fallen out of favor. In country areas where people still maintain vegetable gardens and fruit trees, the arts of jam- and pickle-making have survived. But even in the cities fruit in season suitable for jam or fruit chutney can often be bought in bulk very cheaply. Jam-making has a reputation for being tricky but this is not justified. If a few basic rules are observed it is really quite a simple procedure.

Fruit butters are traditional country fare, made with a fruit pulp (no butter) and cooked to a firm smooth texture. Tart fruit such as apples, quinces or cranberries may be used. Serve as jam, or with cold meats.

Bottling and Storing

Use jam jars or any clean, undamaged heatproof containers. Make sure that they are not chipped or cracked, and always wash and sterilize first. Warm the jars in a gentle oven before filling — this will prevent cracking. Store in a cool, airy cupboard or pantry.

Making Jam

Pectin content: The setting qualities of fruit vary according to their acidity and the amount of pectin they contain. Here is a guide to help you:

High pectin: blackcurrants; red and white currants; oranges; gooseberries; crab apples; lemons; grapefruit; plums and quinces.

Medium pectin: apricots; greengages; loganberries; raspberries and blackberries.

Low pectin: rhubarb; strawberries, cherries; figs; marrow; grapes; peaches; pears and melons.

If you are using fruit with a low or medium pectin content, you will have to add additional pectin. This is available commercially in liquid or powdered form. Or you can add some citric acid or lemon juice. The amount of pectin you add will vary according to the type of fruit but as a general guide, you will need 1½–3 fl oz liquid pectin to 1 lb fruit, or 1 fl oz lemon juice to 2 lb fruit.

Setting Tests

You will have to test the jam for setting after cooking it for the specified time. Be careful not to cook the jam beyond the setting point, or you are liable to spoil the flavor, color and texture. Fruits vary slightly but, generally speaking, when the jam is boiled to a temperature of 105°C (221°F) the sugar concentration is about 65 per cent, and the jam will set and keep well. You can measure the temperature with a sugar thermometer, but it is always a good idea to test it as well. There are two methods:

Flake test: stir the jam with a wooden spoon, then remove and hold at right angles to the pan. Allow the jam clinging to the spoon to drip back into the pan. Setting point is reached when the drops collect at the spoon's edge and form large flakes.

Saucer test: drop a little jam onto a cold saucer and place in a refrigerator for about 1 minute. It should set and form a wrinkled skin on the surface when you draw a finger across.

Plum Jam

lb plums
crystal sugar
juice 3 medium lemons

Time: 32½ minutes

Cut plums into small pieces removing stones. Place into a dish and cook approximately 20 minutes on high until a pulp is formed. Allow 1 cup sugar for every cup pulp. Warm sugar in oven for 30 seconds. Add sugar and lemon juice to fruit pulp. Cook approximately 12 minutes until a gel is formed, stirring occasionally. Pour into sterilized jars. Cool slightly, label, date and seal.

Apple and Pear Jam

lb apples, peeled and sliced
lb pears, peeled and sliced
sugar
juice 3 lemons

Time: 32 minutes

Place peeled and sliced apples and pears into a dish and cook approximately 20 minutes on high until a pulp is formed. Allow 1 cup sugar for every 1 cup of pulp. Warm sugar in oven for 30 seconds. Add sugar and lemon juice to fruit pulp. Cook approximately 12 minutes, stirring occasionally until a gel is formed. Pour into sterilized jars. Cool, label, date and seal.

Strawberry Jam

1 lb strawberries
1½ cups crystal sugar
juice small lemon

Time: 20 minutes

Chop strawberries roughly, place into oven with sugar and lemon juice. Cook approximately 20 minutes on high, stirring occasionally. Remove and pour into sterilized jars, label, date and seal.

Orange Marmalade

1½ lb oranges
1 lemon
3 cups sugar, heated

Time: 50 minutes

Wash and dry fruit. Cut in half, squeeze out the juice. Cut peel into very thin strips. Place peel into a large Pyrex bowl. Make up the juice to 3 cups with water. Pour over fruit. Cover and cook on high 20 minutes. Add sugar to cooked peel. Cook on high for 30 minutes or until jam is at setting consistency. Bottle while hot.

Lemon Butter

Rind and juice of 1 large lemon
2 oz butter
⅓ cup sugar
2 × 2 oz eggs
pinch salt

Time: 8 minutes

Combine all ingredients in a medium sized bowl. Cook covered on defrost for 6–8 minutes, stirring occasionally until thickened. Store in hot, sterile jars, in a cool, dry place.

Breads, Muffins and Biscuits

ost yeast breads can be proven and baked in a microwave [ov]en but as microwaves cook using moist heat, a baked loaf [wi]ll not form a crisp, golden crust. But the clever cook can [cr]eate a mock crust by sprinkling greased loaf dishes with [oa]tmeal, crumbed crisp savory cookies, poppy seeds, toasted [ses]ame seeds, rye or whole wheat flour, cracked wheat, [cr]ushed dried onions, wheat germ or seasoned breadcrumbs. [Dried or fresh yeast when mixed with warm water and [su]gar can be proven on a warm setting only (a defrost setting will kill the yeast) and usually takes 10–15 minutes for the mixture to double in bulk.

Breads made with baking powder should be cooked in lined and greased ring molds, bar or loaf dishes.

Here's a couple of hints to make muffin and biscuit cooking easier and more successful: cook muffins in double thickness patty cake papers; and quick Sunday afternoon biscuits should be baked (only 1 minute per side) on a preheated browning dish.

Zucchini Loaf

[2] cups unpeeled, grated
  zucchinis
[¾] cup self-rising flour
[1 t]easpoon baking soda
[pin]ch salt
[1½] teaspoons cinnamon
[1] cup vegetable oil
[2 e]ggs
[1 t]easpoon vanilla extract
[2 t]ablespoons molasses
[1] cup sugar
[2 t]ablespoons wheat germ
  (optional)

Time: 6–9 minutes.

[Bl]end all ingredients in mixing bowl on low speed for 2 min[ut]es. Beat on medium speed 1 minute. Spread mixture into [lin]ed loaf tin and sprinkle top with wheat germ.

[ ]Shield ends of loaf with 2 inch strips of aluminum foil cover[in]g 1 inch of batter. Cook on medium 6 minutes. Increase [po]wer to high and cook 2–3 minutes.

Mango Gingerbread

[2] cups peeled, sliced fresh mango
[1 p]acket commercial gingerbread
  mix
[¼] cup butter
[¾] cup brown sugar
[1 t]ablespoon milk

Time: 13–16 minutes

Cook butter on high 1–1½ minutes in an 8 × 8 inch square dish. Blend in sugar and milk and cook on high 2 minutes, stirring twice. Arrange mango slices in rows on top. Prepare gingerbread as directed on package. Spoon batter evenly over fruit and cook on medium 6 minutes.

Increase power to high and cook 4–6 minutes until gingerbread springs back when touched. Cool 5 minutes. Loosen edges and turn out on platter. Cut into serving squares. If desired, top with whipped cream or ice cream to serve.

Pumpkin Pecan Bread

1 cup all-purpose flour
¾ cup brown sugar
1 teaspoon baking powder
1 teaspoon baking soda
1 teaspoon salt
1 teaspoon mixed spice
1 teaspoon cinnamon
½ cup vegetable oil
2 eggs
½ cup chopped pecans
1 cup mashed, drained pumpkin

Time: 18 minutes

Blend all ingredients in mixing bowl on low speed 20 seconds; beat on medium for 1 minute.

Spread mixture into lined loaf dish. Shield ends of dish with 2 inch strip of aluminum foil covering 1 inch of mixture. Cook on medium 9 minutes. Remove foil. Cook on high 2–3 minutes. Let stand 5 minutes before turning out.

[Ma]ngo Gingerbread and Zucchini Loaf

Soda Bread

2 tablespoons white
  breadcrumbs
2 cups all-purpose flour
1 cup raisins
1 tablespoon sugar
2 teaspoons baking soda
½ teaspoon salt
2 tablespoons butter
⅔ cup buttermilk
1 beaten egg

Topping

1 tablespoon butter
2 tablespoons white
  breadcrumbs
1 tablespoon rolled oats
¼ teaspoon cinnamon

Time: 9½–10½ minutes

Lightly butter a 1¾ pint souffle dish and coat inside with breadcrumbs. Blend flour, raisins, sugar, baking soda and salt in mixing bowl.

Place butter in small bowl and cook on high 45 seconds until melted. Stir butter, buttermilk and egg into flour mixture. Spread in souffle dish.

Place butter in bowl and cook on high 45 seconds. Stir in breadcrumbs, rolled oats and cinnamon. Spread over top of bread. With a sharp knife cut a 1 inch 'X' on top of bread. Cook on medium-high 8–9 minutes until top springs back when touched. Let stand 5 minutes before serving.

Carrot and Bran Muffins

1 cup bran flakes
¾ cup milk
2 cups finely grated carrot
1 cup whole wheat flour
2 tablespoons brown sugar
2 tablespoons vegetable oil
1 tablespoon lemon juice
1 teaspoon baking powder
¼ teaspoon cinnamon
¼ teaspoon salt
1 egg, beaten

Time: 6–9 minutes. Makes 12–14

Combine bran, milk and carrot and let stand 5 minutes. Blend in remaining ingredients. Line muffin rings or cups with double paper liners. Half fill each with muffin mixture and cook on high. Takes 3–4½ minutes for each 6 muffins. Repeat with remaining mixture.

> ## HINT: KEEPING FLOUR PRODUCTS FRESH
> When bread, loaves and muffins are cooked and cool, wrap immediately in plastic wrap to retain moisture and prevent drying.

Step 1 Soda Bread. Coat buttered souffle dish with breadcrumbs.

Step 2 Stir buttermilk, egg and butter into flour mixture

Step 3 Cut a 1 inch cross on top of bread

da Bread

Savory Biscuit Roll

cups self-rising flour
teaspoon cayenne pepper
easpoon salt
oz softened butter
oz grated cheese
egg
cup milk
ablespoon milk
ablespoons poppy seeds

lling

oz ham, shredded
ickles, grated
easpoons butter
ablespoons finely chopped
parsley
mall onion, finely chopped
oz grated cheese
ablespoon ketchup
t and pepper to taste

Time: 6–7 minutes

Sift flour, cayenne pepper and salt into a bowl. Add butter, cheese, egg and ¾ cup milk and blend together with a table knife to form a dough. Roll out on a lightly floured board to a rectangle 8 × 12 inch.

Combine filling ingredients in a bowl and spread over prepared biscuit leaving a ½ inch strip on one long edge. Brush edge with 1 tablespoon milk. Roll up and allow to rest on glazed edge to seal. Place rolled dough onto lightly floured round plate.

Join the two ends together to form a circle. Cut two-thirds of the way through roll at 1 inch intervals. Brush with milk and sprinkle with poppy seeds. Cook on high 6–7 minutes. Let stand 4 minutes before serving. Fill center with vegetable sticks and parsley.

> ### HINT: DEFROSTING BREAD
> To defrost a 1½ lb loaf of bread. Remove metal tie from bread bag. Place wrapped bread into oven. Microwave on high 45 seconds. Turn loaf over. Microwave for a further 30 seconds. Let stand in bag for 6 minutes.

Microwave Cooking for One
Easy and Delicious Recipes for the
Solo Cook

ou get home, you are tired, in a hurry and starving. No time
or messy pans. This section is designed for the person living
lone who has a few of the basic culinary skills and a
icrowave. With a microwave you can even cook and eat off
e same plate! It's as though this marvel of modern invention
as specifically designed for the Solo Cook.

The recipes in this section have been devised by nutritionist
vonne Webb as a culinary survival guide for the Solo Cook

who wishes to spend the minimum time shopping, preparing
and cooking a delicious and nutritious meal. The easy-to-
prepare recipes will delight both the eye and the taste buds —
so much so that the Solo Cook might even consider recipes for
two.

**All recipes in the 'Microwave Cooking for One'
cooked on 'High' unless stated otherwise.**

Mediterranean Lamb

Solo Snacks

Many of these recipes are substantial enough to serve as light meals.

When a cheese topping is called for do not cook for too long or the cheese will become rubbery and tough.

Curried Eggs

1 clove garlic, crushed
½ teaspoon curry powder
1 teaspoon ghee
2 tablespoons tomato puree
1 slice lemon
1 teaspoon apricot jam
2 eggs
¼ cup milk

Time: 8½ minutes

Combine garlic, curry powder and ghee in a cup and cook on high 30 seconds. Add tomato puree, lemon and jam. Mix well and cook 1 minute.

Beat together eggs and milk in a glass bowl. Stir in all other ingredients.

Cook on low for 5 minutes until egg is beginning to set. Stir with a fork to break up egg mass then cook for 2 minutes on high.

Stuffed Mushrooms

4 large fresh mushrooms, washed
1 medium-sized dill pickle
2 scallions
3 tablespoons ricotta cheese

Time: 2 minutes

Wash mushrooms and remove stalks. Chop pickle, mushroom stalks and scallions and mix with ricotta cheese.

Stuff mixture into inverted mushroom caps and cook on high 2 minutes. Serve with sliced fresh fruit.

Variation: Finely diced ham and red pepper may be added to the mushroom stuffing.

Winter Hearty

½ can peeled tomatoes
2 canned frankfurters, drained
*   and chopped*
½ can pea and ham soup

Time: 3 minute

Stir tomatoes and frankfurters into soup. Cook in mediu sized glass bowl 3 minutes on high.

French Collation

½ red or green pepper, seeded
*   and cut into strips*
1 hard-boiled egg
½ can anchovy fillets
mayonnaise
bread roll

Time: 1½ minute

Chop egg and mix with anchovies, pepper, and mayonnais Cook on high 1½ minutes. Cut roll in half. Scoop bread o of crust and fill with mixture.

Stuffed Mushrooms

Step 1 Wash mushrooms and remove stalks. Chop stalks, pickle and scallions

Step 2 Mix chopped ingredients with ricotta cheese

Step 3 Stuff mixture into inverted mushroom caps

Stuffed Mushroom

Empty Cupboard Surprise

1 can sweet corn
1 cup any cooked vegetable (a
    mixture is best)
½ cup any chopped, leftover
    meat (optional)
1 egg

Time: 3 minutes

Drain sweet corn and mix with vegetables and meat. Place in small glass bowl and break egg on top, piercing yolk with toothpick.

Cook 3 minutes on high or until egg is set. Cover and let stand for 2 minutes before eating.

Prince's Pocket

1 small wholewheat pita
    (pocket or Lebanese) bread
1 small can mushrooms in
    butter sauce
small handful walnuts,
    chopped
1 tomato, thinly sliced
chicken leftovers

Time: 2-4 minutes

Mix mushrooms, chicken, tomato and walnuts and cook on high 2 minutes. Fill pita bread with mixture. Reheat on low for 2 minutes (optional).

Asparagus Snack

1 egg
½ cup milk
1 teaspoon grated lemon rind
½ can asparagus spears,
    drained
2 slices bread

Time: 2½ minutes

Beat egg and milk together. Add lemon rind. Arrange bread on a dinner plate and place half the asparagus on each slice. Pour custard mixture over asparagus so it soaks into the bread. Cook on high 2½ minutes.

Penjas

3 thick slices liverwurst
    sausage
1 onion, chopped
1 can diced pepper
½ cup cooked, diced vegetables
1 tomato
½ cup grated Parmesan cheese

Time: 2-3 minute

Line base of ramekin or small soup plate with liverwur; sausage. Cover with chopped onion and diced peppe then vegetables, then thickly sliced tomato.

Sprinkle with Parmesan cheese and cook 2-3 minutes o high, or until cheese has begun to melt.

Pate

6 oz liverwurst sausage
1 tablespoon unsalted butter
¼ teaspoon dried oregano
1 tablespoon cognac

Time: 2½ minute

Mash sausage, butter and oregano together. Place in sma glass bowl and cook 2½ minutes on high. Remove an pour cognac over pate and let stand until cool.

Danish Delight

ham steak or 1 thick sliced,
    canned ham
1 onion, chopped
1 tablespoon vinegar
½ cup apricot nectar
1 teaspoon cooking oil

Time: 4½ minute

Heat oil in a glass jar for 30 seconds. Add chopped onio vinegar and apricot nectar. Cook on low 2 minutes. L stand.

Arrange ham on serving plate. Cover with sauce an cook another 2 minutes on high.

Polenta

½ cup yellow cornmeal or
    polenta
2 cups water
½ cup grated Parmesan cheese
pinch cayenne pepper

Time: 6½ minut

Measure cornmeal into a large glass mixing bowl. Ad water and stir well. Cook 4 minutes on high. Add chee; and pepper and cook 1½ minutes on high.

Let stand, covered, for 5 minutes. Wrap in greasepro paper, refrigerate and cut into slices when required. reheat, place slice on paper towel and heat for 50 second

Jamaican Toast

2 slices wholewheat or kibble
    bread
sweet chutney
2 slices ham
1 banana
½ onion, chopped
1 dill pickle or gherkin, sliced
several slices mozzarella cheese
    or more if required
sour cream, paprika and dill
    for garnish

Time: 2–3 minutes

Spread each slice of bread with chutney and cover with ham. Arrange slices of banana on each, then onion and dill pickle. Cover with mozzarella cheese.

Cook 2–3 minutes on high until cheese has melted and is bubbling. Garnish with a dollop of sour cream sprinkled with paprika and a spray of dill.

White Elephant

2 slices rye bread
2 slices wholewheat or kibble
    bread
2 tablespoons Pate (see recipe
    above)
3 oz ricotta cheese
1 can sweet corn, drained
1 medium-sized dill pickle,
    sliced
1 pickled or cocktail onion

Time: 6 minutes

Spread the 4 slices of bread with pate. Cover slices 1 and 3 with corn and dill pickle. Cover slice 2 with ricotta cheese and pickled onion cut in half.

Heat each slice for 2 minutes on high. Stack bread slices so that outer 2 layers of filling are corn and center one is cheese.

Leftovers with Tomato

½ cup chopped, cooked leftover
    meat
½ cup chopped, cooked leftover
    vegetables
1 cup diced tomato
1 egg
½ cup grated Parmesan cheese

Time: 5 minu

Combine meat, vegetables and tomato in glass bowl. B egg and pour over mixture. Cook on high 3 minutes.

Top with grated cheese and cook 2 minutes or u cheese has melted. Serve with rice for a hearty a nourishing meal.

Baked Beans

1 small can baked beans
1 small can diced peppers
¼ teaspoon curry powder
1 tablespoon tomato flakes

Time: 1½ minut

Empty baked beans into mixing bowl. Drain peppers, r taining liquid. Mix tomato flakes with 2 tablespoons of th liquid until dissolved. Add curry powder.

Combine all ingredients, cover with greaseproof pap and heat 1½ minutes on high.

Jamaican Toast

Step 1 Spread chutney on bread and cover with ham

Step 2 Add banana, onion and dill pickle

Step 3 Cover with mozzarella cheese and cook until bubbling

The Virtue of Vegetables

The microwave oven performs best with vegetables. If cooked properly they retain flavor, color and nutrients. Use the minimum of water in cooking. Instead of using salt try various herbs for extra flavor. Oregano and dill enhance tomatoes.

Sprinkle coriander on zucchini.

Try a meatless meal sometime. Simply dress up the vegetables for the main meal and add cheese or eggs for protein.

Herbed Tomato

1 large ripe tomato
pinch oregano
1 teaspoon dried dill

Time: 1½ minutes

Wash tomato and cut in half. Sprinkle halves with oregano and dill. Arrange on paper towel and cook on high 1½ minutes.

Winter Tomato Savory

1 tomato
1 teaspoon Stilton or blue vein
  cheese
1 teaspoon chopped chives or
  parsley

Time: 1 minute

Cut tomato in half and place on flat serving plate. Cook on high 1 minute. Crumble cheese on top of tomato halves and cook on low for 1 minute. Sprinkle with chopped chives before serving.

Willy Nilly

¼ cup diced broccoli stalks
¼ cup diced cauliflower stalks
1 onion, chopped
1 potato, peeled and diced
¼ cup (at least) diced, leftover
  meat
1 packet French onion soup
dash angostura bitters
1 cup water

Time: 5 minutes

Add water to French onion soup powder. Mix well to eliminate lumps. Add angostura bitters and mix. Add other ingredients.

Place in small glass bowl and cover with lid or greaseproof paper. Cook 5 minutes on high.

Artichoke Hearts

1 can artichoke hearts
2 tablespoons unsalted butter
1 tablespoon vinegar
1 teaspoon horseradish

Time: 2½ minut

Heat butter with vinegar for 30 seconds in a glass jar. A horseradish and mix well. Arrange artichoke hearts serving plate. Pour sauce onto each heart and cook for minutes.

Zucchini with Cheese

2 small zucchinis (unpeeled)
1 tablespoon grated cheese
pinch coriander
Parmesan cheese
cracked black pepper

Time: 2 minu

Cut zucchini lengthwise. Sprinkle with coriander, gra cheese and Parmesan cheese and pepper. Place on serv dish, cover and cook 2 minutes on high.

Corn on the Cob

1 fresh corn cob
1 tablespoon unsalted butter
pinch nutmeg

Time: 4 minut

Remove silk from cob and place on serving dish. Dot co with butter and cover with husks. Place on paper tow double thickness. Cook 4 minutes on high. Allow to co slightly before eating.

Zucchini with Chee

192

Silver Beet Parcels

3 silver beet or spinach leaves
1 cup cooled mashed pumpkin
¼ cup chopped chives or
  parsley
1 egg

Time: 3 minutes

Wash and drain leaves and remove white stalks. (Keep stalks for soup or a leftover dish.) Arrange each leaf flat on a dinner plate and heat for 30 seconds until tender.

Combine pumpkin, chives and egg. Mix well. Spoon pumpkin mixture onto center of each leaf. Fold edges of spinach over filling and roll up securely.

Arrange parcels on dinner plate and cook 2½ minutes on high or until heated through.

Easy Asparagus with Butter Sauce

1 can diced pepper, drained
½ cup unsalted butter
1 clove garlic, crushed
juice 1 small lemon
pinch cinnamon

Time: 2½ minut

Choose a good brand of asparagus with thin green spea Remove from can, drain and place on serving dish.

Melt butter in a cup for 30 seconds. Pour melted but over asparagus. Pour over lemon juice and sprinkle w cinnamon. Cook 2 minutes on high.

Herbed Carrots

1 cup diced or sliced frozen
  carrot
½ cup canned cream of celery
  soup
½ cup canned cream of
  mushroom soup
pinch dried thyme
pinch dried marjoram or
  oregano
few button mushrooms
  (optional)
½ cup breadcrumbs
1 teaspoon unsalted butter
1 tablespoon chopped fresh
  parsley or basil
Parmesan cheese (optional)

Time: 6½ minutes

Mix first 5 ingredients with button mushrooms if used and place in a glass bowl or casserole dish. Melt butter in a cup for 30 seconds. Toss breadcrumbs into butter, stir and sprinkle over mixture.

Cook 6 minutes on high. Serve garnished with fresh parsley or basil and Parmesan cheese.

Vegetable Soup

½ can celery soup
½ can water
1 stalk celery, chopped
½ cup frozen lima beans
½ cup frozen broccoli, broken
  into florets
1 zucchini, chopped
½ cup chopped white meat

Time: 2½ minut

Combine all ingredients in a large bowl. Cover with grea proof paper and cook 2½ minutes on high.

Herbed Carrots

Step 1 Combine carrot, soups and herbs in a glass bowl

Step 2 Toss breadcrumbs in melted butter, sprinkle over mixture and cook 6 minutes

Step 3 Garnish with herbs and Parmesan cheese

Herbed Carr

Rice and Pasta

Rice cooks in the microwave in about ⅔ of the normal cooking time.

If you decide to cook extra and freeze the leftovers, simply defrost in the microwave for 2 minutes. Cold rice is delicious as a salad served with a vinaigrette dressing or with mayonnaise.

Easy Paella

½ cup cooked rice
½ onion, chopped
½ small can shrimp or a few
  fresh uncooked shrimp, shelled
½ cup any cooked, diced fish
1 tomato
½ cup white wine
pinch oregano

Time: 3 minutes

Combine first 4 ingredients and place in a large glass mixing bowl. Pour over wine. Slice tomato and arrange on top of rice mixture. Sprinkle with oregano. Cook on low 3 minutes.

Variation: To give this dish the full Spanish treatment, color the rice with saffron and add some fresh peas.

Rice with Leftovers

1 cup cooked rice
½ can asparagus cuts, drained
1 cup cooked white meat pieces
1 small can whole mushrooms in
  butter sauce
1 can diced peppers, drained
2 tablespoons fresh chopped basil
  (optional)

Time: 2½ minutes

Combine all ingredients in a mixing bowl and heat 1½ minutes on high. Mix and cook for 1 minute more. Serve with vegetables for a hearty meal.

Mediterranean Medley

⅓ cup long grain rice
1 can tomatoes, drained
few olives (optional)
handful of raisins
1 clove garlic, crushed
½ cup grated Parmesan cheese
chopped fresh basil for garnish

Time: 5 minutes

Add equal quantity of boiling water to rice in a bowl large enough to allow rice to swell. Put aside for 40 minutes. When rice is soft, mix all ingredients together. Cook on low 5 minutes or until rice is tender. Garnish with basil.

Spinach Fettucine with Sardines

7 oz spinach fettucine
1 small can sardines or
  anchovies
1 tablespoon grated Parmesan
  cheese
¼ red pepper

Time: 10½ minute

Place fettucine in glass mixing bowl and cover with ho water. Cook on high 10 minutes. Drain off water.

Empty can of sardines, including oil, into bowl. Mix we and heat for 30 seconds. Garnish with pepper sliced into thi strips, and Parmesan cheese.

Step 1 Cover fettucine with hot water, cook 10 minutes and drain

Step 2 Mix anchovies through fettucine and heat on high 30 seconds

Simple Fried Rice

 cup long grain rice, pre-soaked
 onion, chopped
 small can mushrooms in butter
 sauce
 small can shrimp
 cup chopped almonds or
 toasted slivered almonds
 egg
 ced scallions (optional)

Time: 5½ minutes

ombine onion, mushrooms, shrimp and almonds in a large
ass bowl. Cover and cook 2½ minutes on high. Mix beaten
g into rice and stir in shrimp mixture. Cook, covered, 3
inutes. Let stand before serving. Garnish with scallions.

Fried Rice

Step 1 Combine onions, mushrooms, shrimp and almonds in a large glass bowl, cover and cook 2½ minutes

Step 2 Mix beaten egg into rice, stir in shrimp mixture and cook, covered, 3 minutes

197

Main Meals in Moments

Meat, fish and chicken are still the most popular dishes for main meals — especially if the Solo Cook has only had a light luncheon. These recipes cooked in the microwave will provide a substantial and nourishing meal in half the time of conventional cooking.

As meat does not brown in the microwave to the same extent as in conventional ovens, fruits, sauces and vegetables come into their own both to mask and beautifully compleme the flavor of the meat. Take care not to overcook meat, fish and chicken. Cooking times given are only approximate. Remember, it's best to undercook, check, then cook a little more if necessary.

Lemon Fish

1 frozen fish fillet
1 small onion, chopped
2 slices lemon

Time: 2–3 minutes

Place fish on serving plate. Sprinkle over onion and top with lemon slices. Cook on paper 2 minutes on high. Check. Depending on size, a minute more cooking time may be required.

Mackerel with Mushroom Sauce

1 can cream of mushroom soup
1 cup milk
½ teaspoon cumin
1 can mackerel
½ cup wheat cereal

Time: 3 minutes

Mix soup with milk and cumin until smooth. Place mackerel in medium-sized glass bowl or casserole dish. Pour soup mixture over fish. Sprinkle crumbs on top to cover. Cook 3 minutes on high.

Shrimp with Vegetables

7 oz shelled, cooked shrimp,
    fresh or frozen
½ cup chopped onion
2 cauliflower florets
2 broccoli florets
1 medium-sized carrot, thinly
    sliced
¼ cup coarsely chopped
    pepper
½ can peeled tomatoes
½ can onion soup
1 tablespoon sherry

Time: 6 minut

Combine shrimp, onion, cauliflower, broccoli, carrot and ca sicum. Place in a large glass bowl, cover with greasepro paper and cook on high 3 minutes.

Meanwhile, mix tomato, soup and sherry together and s mixture into vegetables. Cook 3 minutes more. Let stand f 2 minutes before serving.

This amount is enough for 2 meals. Refrigerate half. Befo next serving, add 1 tablespoon water and reheat for 2 minute

Shrimp with Vegetables

Step 1 Place shrimp, onion, cauliflower, broccoli, carrot and peppers in bowl, cover and cook 3 minutes

Step 2 Mix together tomatoes, soup and sherry

Step 3 Stir into vegetable mixture and cook 3 minutes

Shrimp with vegetable

Fillet Steak with Piquant Sauce

piece eye fillet of beef
-4 anchovy or sardine fillets
egg
teaspoon brandy
teaspoons Dijon mustard
onion, chopped
tablespoon chopped dill
  pickles
slice fresh or canned
  pineapple

Time: 3½ minutes

ook steak on serving dish on high 2 minutes. Meanwhile,
ake sauce by mashing sardines or anchovies in a bowl with
g, brandy and mustard. Mix well. Add onion and pickles.
When meat is ready, remove from oven and cover com-
etely with sauce. Return meat to oven and cook on low
½ minutes. Let stand 1 minute before serving.
Serve with pineapple rings. Snow peas, mushrooms and
erry tomatoes make ideal accompaniments.

Beef in Red Wine

cup cooked beef, cut into thin
  strips
cup red wine
whole peppercorns
tablespoons vinegar
  cup golden raisins
  cup walnuts
opped scallions for garnish

Time: 4 minutes

a medium-sized glass bowl mix wine and vinegar and
ld peppercorns and golden raisins. Marinate beef in the
ixture for 15 minutes. Stir in walnuts. Cook 2 minutes on
gh, stir and cook for another 2 minutes. Garnish with
allions and serve with any short pasta.

Beef and Vegetable Kebabs

1 tablespoon teriyaki sauce
1 tablespoon honey
½ clove garlic, crushed
1 tablespoon dry sherry
pinch ground ginger
1 beef steak, thick cut
6 cherry tomatoes
4 scallions
½ pepper
6 button mushrooms

Time: 1–2 minutes

Combine first 5 ingredients in a bowl. Cut steak into cubes
and add to the mixture. Marinate for 1 hour.
   Wash and dry tomatoes. Trim scallions and cut pepper
into squares. Wash and trim mushrooms.
   Thread beef and vegetables alternately on skewers. Cook
on medium 1½ minutes. Brush kebabs with marinade and
heat a further 20 seconds on high. Serve with a crisp salad
or fried rice.

Pork and Bitters

1 pork chop or piece pork fillet
Dijon mustard
1 potato, peeled and sliced
2 medium-sized onions, sliced
¼ cup diced celery
½ can tomato puree
1 teaspoon angostura bitters
1 jar stewed apple baby food
cherry tomatoes for garnish

Time: 13½ minutes

Rub pork with mustard. Let stand. Arrange vegetables in
layers in a glass bowl or casserole. Add tomato puree, and
angostura bitters. Cook on low 10 minutes. Remove vegetables from oven, cover and let stand. Cook meat on serving dish 2½ minutes on high. Pork must be well cooked.
   Arrange vegetables around pork and pour over apple.
Heat for 1 minute. Garnish with cherry tomatoes.

Beef in Red Wine

Step 1 Mix wine and vinegar in a
medium-sized bowl and add
peppercorns and golden raisins

Step 2 Marinate beef in mixture for
15 minutes

Step 3 Add walnuts and cook
4 minutes stirring once during
cooking

llet Steak with Piquant Sauce

Lamb with Mushrooms

2 lamb chops
1 can mushrooms in butter
  sauce
1 can French onion soup
½ cup water

Time: about 3 minutes

Add water to soup and mix well. Stir in mushrooms. Place lamb chops on serving dish and cover with sauce. Cook 3 minutes on high or until well done.

Apricot Lamb

1 lamb chop
1 tablespoon apricot jam

Place lamb chop on serving dish and cover with apricot jam. Cook 2 minutes on high.

Mediterranean Lamb

1 cup diced, cooked lamb
½ cup Ratatouille (see recipe)
black olives and dill for garnish

Place lamb in small glass bowl and cook on low 3 minutes. Spoon Ratatouille over and cook on high another 3 minutes. Garnish with black olives and dill.

Mustard Chicken

1 cooked chicken piece
1 tablespoon mustard powder

Time: 1½ minut

Rub chicken over with mustard powder. Cook on servi dish on high 1½ minutes.

Chicken Tropicana

1 cup chopped cooked chicken
1 banana, peeled
1 can mango or 1 fresh mango,
  peeled and sliced
1 can tomatoes
½ cup ginger wine or white wine
1 clove garlic, crushed
1 small choko, peeled and cored

Time: 4 minut

Chop banana and choko into bite size chunks. Combir with chicken, mango, tomato and garlic and mix wel Place mixture into a large glass bowl. Cover with pap towel and cook on low for 4 minutes.
   Allow to stand for 3 minutes before eating to allo diffusion of flavor. Zucchini may be used instead of chok choko.

Chicken Curry

¼ teaspoon turmeric
¼ teaspoon powdered ginger
¼ teaspoon cayenne pepper
2 tablespoons cold pressed
  sunflower oil
1 chicken breast

Time: 3 minut

Combine spices with oil in a cup and heat for 50 second Let stand. Arrange chicken on dinner plate. Pour ov curry mixture and cook on high 2 minutes. Serve with ric

Chicken Medley

1 cup chopped cooked chicken
  or 1 whole chicken breast,
  chopped
1 can cream of chicken soup
1 tomato, chopped
¼ cup sliced, stuffed olives
1 jar stewed apple baby food
1 clove garlic, crushed
1 tablespoon sherry

Time: 3 minut

Combine all ingredients and mix well. Place in a large gla bowl. Cover with greaseproof paper and cook 3 minutes o high.

Fruity Desserts

There's no need for the Solo Cook to stop at one course. Fruit is nature's sweet convenience food, both delicious and nutritiously high in vitamin C, some B group vitamins and carotene. These tempting recipes are for those evenings whe a dessert is favored over a piece of raw fruit.

Champagne Peaches

2 canned peach halves
1 cup champagne or white grape
juice
1 clove

Time: 2½ minutes

Place all ingredients in a glass jar. Liquid should cover the peaches, if not, add extra liquid. Cook on high 2½ minutes. Cover with lid and refrigerate when cool. Will keep at least 48 hours.

Gingered Banana Ice Cream

1 serve ice cream
½ cup chopped unsalted walnuts
or macadamia nuts
3 tablespoons honey
3 tablespoons water
1 teaspoon unsalted butter
1 tablespoon chopped ginger in
syrup
1 banana, sliced

Time: 2 minutes

Place ice cream in a dessert plate and sprinkle with nuts. Put in freezer. Combine honey, water, butter, ginger and banana in glass jar and cook 2 minutes on high until mushy. Cool. Pour over ice cream and eat immediately.

Pears in Wine

2 whole pears
1 cup white wine
pinch cinnamon

Time: 7 minutes

Wash pears. Prick skin in a few places with a fork and place in small glass bowl. Add wine and cinnamon. Cook on low for 5 minutes. Turn pears over and cook for 2 minutes on high.

Creme de Menthe Pear.

2 canned pear halves
2 teaspoons lemon juice
2 tablespoons creme de menthe
1 serve ice cream
shreds of orange peel, blanched

Time: 1 minu

Drain pear halves, reserving syrup. Pour syrup into large gla jar. Add lemon juice and creme de menthe and heat on hi 1 minute. Add pears to liquid in jar. Put on lid and invert that liquid pours over fruit. Serve either hot or cold with i cream. Rum and a pinch of nutmeg can be substituted for t creme de menthe. Garnish with orange peel shreds.

Remaining pears in can can be stored for 2–3 days in r frigerator and served as an accompaniment to lamb or por

Note: Whole, peeled, fresh pears may be substituted f canned pear halves.

Baked Pawpaw

1 small firm pawpaw, yellow
but not quite ready for eating
2 tablespoons Cointreau
¼ cup chopped unsalted nuts
1 tablespoon honey

Time: 2 minut

Split pawpaw in half and scoop out seeds. Do not pee Spoon 1 tablespoon Cointreau into each cavity. Combi nuts with honey and pour into cavity.

Place on paper towel and cook 3 minutes on high. L stand 2 minutes before serving.

Hot Apple Slice

Hot Apple Slice

bought apple slice
ablespoon honey
nnamon

Time: 1 minute

ush honey over top of apple slice and sprinkle cinnamon
er sparingly. Heat 1 minute on high. Check that slice is
ated through completely.

Hot Pineapple Rings

2 canned pineapple rings
½ cup pineapple juice
small pinch powdered ginger

Time: 2 minutes

Place ring side-by-side on serving plate. Stir ginger into
juice in can. Mix well. Pour juice over rings and cook 2
minutes on high.

Spirited Nightcap

orange and cinnamon teabag
liqueur glass Grand Marnier
  or Chartreuse
slice orange

Time: 1 minute

Make 1 cup orange and cinnamon tea. Add liqueur and orange. Stir and reheat 1 minute.

Cherries in Kirsch

can pitted cherries
liqueur glass Kirsch
inch cinnamon

Place cherries in glass jar and cover with juice. Cook until mixture just begins to boil, then add cinnamon and Kirsch. Screw lid on tightly and leave for ½ hour until cherries are cool and flavors have diffused.

Mulled Wine (Gluhwein)

½ cup claret
½ cup port
1 tablespoon currants
¼ teaspoon cinnamon or 1
  cinnamon stick
strawberry and lemon garnish

Time: 2 minutes

Combine all ingredients in a measuring jug and heat on high 2 minutes. Serve in a tall glass with a strawberry and a lemon twist.

Venus Potion

1 rosehip teabag
1 liqueur glass Marsala
1 clove

Time: 2½ minutes

Make 1 cup rosehip tea and pour into measuring jug. Add Marsala and clove. Heat on low 2½ minutes. Let stand 5 minutes before removing clove. Reheat if required.

Mulled Wine (Gluhwein)

The Magic of Microwave Entertaining

The Magic of Microwave Entertaining compiled by Douglas Marsland and Jan Wunderlich shows just how simple it is to cook in stages and serve up an elegant dinner party for eight or a large buffet lunch for family and friends. Recipes and menus are included for all entertaining occasions. Try them. Then try out your own.

Dinner Parties

Entertaining friends and family with a superb dinner is something we all love to do. First come the decisions: Who? When? What to serve? Then there are the busy preparations. You can make your microwave your number one helper and throw a thoroughly modern dinner party by mastering the simple steps of sequential cooking. The recipes in this book are all perfect candidates for microwave sequential cooking and the selected menus with their preparation timetables will show you how to get the most out of your microwave.

Roasted Rosemary Leg of Lamb

The Ground Rules for Success

It's a trend, a revolution, a national craze. I'm not talking about aerobics or punk fashions — those fads are passe. I mean the expanding passion for gourmet cooking, and its concomitant — the dinner party. Unfortunately, another major trend of modern life is an ever-increasing lack of spare time. A particularly vicious circle? No.

Whipping up an elegant three course dinner in a few hours isn't just a fiction perpetrated by those prototypes of a superior form of humanity who inhabit television commercials. Ordinary mortals can accomplish such wonders, too. With a little bit of forward planning, the correct use of kitchen appliances, the microwave and organization, good fast food can prove to be synonymous with good, sophisticated, and highly enjoyable food.

Giving a dinner party is a little like show business. There's a lot of behind-the-scenes action and sleight of hand. When you orchestrate a dinner party, keep it within your scope and abilities. Don't try to do too much, have too many courses. Three courses is all you should attempt, making one or preferably two of them dishes you can do ahead or put together at the last minute. Always make a shopping list before you start, and draw up a plan of action down to the last detail.

Planning makes perfect
Begin your planning by selecting the main dish, then plan other foods around it. Do think of color. Consider a meal of lobster bisque, chicken in a creamed sauce and creme caramel. If there is anything good to say about it, well, it would be perfect for someone with a stomach ulcer.

Texture and taste are the next considerations. Something crunchy, something smooth. A crisp mignonette and watercress salad is a better partner for veal fillets with avocado and Hollandaise Sauce (*see recipe*) or veal zurichoise (a class Swiss dish of veal strips, cream and mushrooms), than a vegetable salad breaststroking in mayonnaise.

Go for choices like suavely sauced turkey, Venison (*see recipe*) or Chicken Breasts (*see recipe*) preceded by a Basil-Scented Tagliatelle Entree (*see recipe*). Hide a few surprises in some of your dishes. Fresh dill with fresh peas, grated carrot in rice, slivers of ham with broccoli, a dash or slurp of wine in a creamy fish dish. Roasts are perfectly sound choices for a dinner party, but they need an imaginative accompaniment.

A successful menu is always provocative to the palate, nev 'beige'.

It's old advice, but when preparing for a dinner party nev attempt a dish for the first time. Murphy's Law bedevils t dinner party cook. Simple first courses, such as soup, pas flan, prosciutto and melon, salads and seafood, that can made ahead of time are invaluable, because odds on the ma course and accompaniments will take up the lion's share your attention.

It's fast, it's efficient, it's microwave
The microwave oven has been a success story, and with go reason. It's fast, it's efficient, it's today. Unfortunately far many people view the microwave as a thing apart, restricti its use to heating pre-cooked foods or 'doing' the vegetabl However, cooks that learn the techniques of sequential m crowave cooking are more than seven steps ahead in throwi the thoroughly modern dinner party. Used alone or in co junction with a conventional oven and range, the microwa can be your number one helper.

Microwave sequential cooking involves partially cooki one item while you prepare another, removing the first d from the oven while you micro-cook its successor, and th returning the first dish to the oven to complete calculat cooking time. Meats, casseroles, potato and rice dishes are perfect candidates for sequential cooking, as are recipes t can be divided into several steps. In short, do everythi ahead, then simply heat when you want to serve.

A good example of a 'step' recipe is a vegetable acco panied by a sauce. The vegetable is cooked first, then t sauce is prepared, and finally the two are reheated togeth As a general rule of thumb, you can sequence foods in t following order: desserts and foods that need to be pre-cook large cuts of meat, potatoes and small cuts of meat; and th foods that need to be reheated. For an average dinner par plan a menu that includes two or three recipes cooked in t microwave.

Smooth, satiny microwave sauces

The making of sweet and savory sauces is one of the areas where the microwave really comes into its own. Beautifully smooth and satiny, many can be measured, mixed and cooked in the same bowl or casserole. With no pots, pans or potential scorching and sticking involved, microwave owners are far more likely to create delicious sauces that make entertaining that much easier.

Perhaps the most versatile microwave sauce is the Basic White Sauce (see recipe) based on a roux. A good all-purpose sauce with myriad permutations, it can be made with fish, beef or chicken stock; milk or cream; or a mixture of white wine and milk. Chopped herbs such as dill, basil, chives and parsley, grated cheese, mustard, curry powder, chopped anchovies, shrimp, and flaked crab are just a few of the additions you can make to this versatile sauce to serve with poultry, veal, fish and beef. Simply cooked meats become superlative with a good, well-flavored sauce.

Sweet cornstarch sauces, egg-based custards, chocolate and fruit sauces are also quick and easy to make in the microwave. Again, even the simplest fruit compote or pudding can be transformed into a knock-your-eye-out dessert with a well-made sweet sauce.

Fruits in season

Always take advantage of what the season has to offer. Melon, grapefruit and figs all make perfect first courses when combined with smoked chicken, baby mozzarella, ham or smoked beef. Fruits can also stand in as a quick, easy touch of glamour dessert. Envisage fresh strawberries with champagne, pineapple in kirsch or plums in marsala. Similarly vegetables of the moment can front up in simple puree soups, souffles, as crepe fillings, pureed, or tossed in butter and herbs.

Cheese makes a superbly simple last course, especially if you have planned an ambitious main course. Camembert, Brie and chevre are popular choices. Always allow cheese to mellow at room temperature for full enjoyment.

Setting the mood

Never let anyone tell you that great food tastes the same in Pyrex as on porcelain. Because the eye is partner to the plate, it usually tastes better on the latter. Pay attention to table setting. A white cloth is the ideal napery, setting off just about every pattern. You don't need to own heirloom china, just a set that suits food and matches.

Always polish cutlery first — there is nothing more off-putting than knives and forks carrying the legacies of your last dinner party. Polished glasses are another must. Offer people a choice of red or white wine and lay out two glasses right from the beginning. Flowers make superb centerpieces, but steer clear of highly scented ones. Fruit is also a top table decoration, with the added bonus that you can eat it afterwards.

Many a good meal has been spoiled by Tchaikovsky's 1812 Overture or Janis Ian's Seventeen. Choose background music carefully. Never play music with 'peaks' and 'troughs'. You don't want people's appetites blunted by crescendos and painful memories.

My final advice for a successful dinner party? Invite the people you like, not the ones you think you ought to ask.

Food and Wine Chemistry

The old rules of choosing between red and white wines are becoming less trustworthy. What use are they in the face of exotic ethnic foods? What help do they give the poor benighted soul in a restaurant trying to order a bottle of wine when one person has ordered crab, another has decided on roast beef and yet a third has plumped for chicken?

Play it safe or take a risk?

The chief aim of wine is to accentuate the flavors of the food, and likewise food should always enhance the character of the wine. Such rigid formulas as red wine with red meat and game and white wine with white meat and fish will always be 'safe' choices, but they should never become, nor were they ever intended to be, rigid concepts. Anyone truly interested in food should be willing to experiment, take a few gastronomic risks with other more interesting combinations and even attempt a few apparently 'strange' ones. That said, let's take a look at the important parameters that still have to be borne in mind.

Wine and food partnerships

Champagne, dry vermouth, dry sherry and rosé all make good opening wines for dinner, especially when the first course is smoked fish, an egg or vegetable dish or traditional type hors d'oeuvres. They are not sweet and therefore do the job of perking up the palate for what is to follow.

Depending on the richness of the ingredients, pates and terrines respond well to dry, fruity reds and whites and rose. The more strongly flavored meat varieties obviously require stronger reds. Most pasta meals marry well with light reds and tangy whites, but if a heavy meat sauce or filling is involved a fuller bodied red is more suitable. Well-flavored rice dishes such as paella and dough main courses are also best matched with red wine.

As a general rule, light, slightly acid dry whites such as chablis, white burgundy and fumé blanc are the number one choices for fish, although a good rosé is a solid selection for baked or highly seasoned fish dishes.

As chicken is to the cook what an empty canvas is to the painter, it can accommodate a great variety of wines depending on the cooking method and other ingredients involved. Light dry reds are good with highly seasoned or casseroled dishes, but in general slightly sweet white wines are the preferred choices. Turkey and duck have stronger tastes than chicken and easily merit a full-bodied white or light red.

Beef has always had an almost symbiotic relationship with full, dry reds but if a dish is highly seasoned, or you have used a budget cut, a really great wine would be wasted. The traditional wines with veal, pork and ham are rosé or slightly sweet whites, but if you like spices with these meats, young fruity reds are a much better choice.

Dessert souffles, creams and mousses go well with champagne, sweet whites, and in some cases, cream sherry and madeira. Fresh fruit and fruit-based concoctions are beautiful with sauternes. Peaches are excellent with Barsac, apricots meld best with port. But take care with apple and orange desserts. Because of their acid/sugar ratio apples need a fruity white to achieve a good balance of taste. The citric acid in oranges is so dominant that only a low acid red can cope successfully.

Chart your own course

Fiery spices are well-known palate paralysers, therefore hot Asian curries and other highly spiced foods are infinitely better suited to beer or plain water. This should never be a blanket rule, however, as mild curries respond well to a good traminer.

Chinese food has also failed to 'demand' the right wine. For example, highly spiced Szechwan food needs beer, while milder Peking-style food can deal with a slightly sweet, fruity wine. Gastronomes exploring the different cuisines of China are still advised to chart their own course.

Champagne

You often hear the cry 'champagne goes with everything', but anyone who has ever washed down a chocolate dessert with it knows that this commonly held belief simply is not true. This is not to say that you cannot serve champagne throughout a meal, because if there is one wine which can claim to suit most things it is certainly champagne, but never let this deter you from making a superior wine selection. If you do want to give an air of profligacy to the whole meal, choose a rosé champagne. Its fuller taste makes it the most suitable choice, especially for light meats such as chicken, veal and fish.

Suggestions of good wine and food partnerships should never be the death knell of spontaneity. Celestial unions such as Roquefort and sweet dessert wines, hot oyster dishes with light reds and dry sherry with seafood are just a few of the pleasures we owe to iconoclasts who went against conventional wisdom.

Menu Number 1

Elegant Dinner Party for 4 or 6

Brie and Smoked Salmon Flan
Fillet of Beef with Oyster Sauce
Parsley French Potatoes
Broccoli and Carrot Saute
Pistachio Orange Souffle

This dinner menu is beautifully balanced at all levels — color, texture, theme, and taste. The light familiar flan is given an unusual twist by the use of smoked salmon and is a perfect foil for the richer, more traditional main meal.

Brie and Smoked Salmon Flan (top); Broccoli and Carrot Saute; Fillet of Beef with Oyster Sauce (center); Pistachio Orange Souffle and Parsley French Potatoes (bottom)

212

Preparation Timetable

Week ahead: Prepare and cook pie dough for Brie and Smoked Salmon Flan. Allow to cool, then wrap securely in plastic. Freeze.

Day ahead: Take pie dough from freezer. Remove wrap and thaw. Prepare and cook souffle. Spoon mixture into prepared souffle dishes and allow to set in refrigerator. Do not decorate until just before serving.

Prepare filling for flan and pour into crust. Cook. Allow flan to cool and then cover with plastic wrap. Do not refrigerate.

Place white wine into refrigerator to chill. Check tablecloth, napkins, glassware, dinnerware and cutlery. Ensure that all are clean, polished and ready to use. Prepare any after-dinner chocolates and store in an airtight container.

3 hours before: Set table and arrange flowers. Prepare tray for pre-dinner drinks and hors d'oeuvres.

2 hours before: Prepare ingredients for Broccoli and Carrot Saute. Cook recipe for 5–6 minutes. Remove from microwave, cover and allow to stand.

1 hour before: Prepare Fillet of Beef. Cook steaks for 10–15 minutes. Remove from browning dish and place onto a microwave-safe platter. Cover and set aside. Cook Oyster Sauce omitting the oysters. Cover sauce with plastic wrap, ensuring that wrap rests on sauce to stop skin forming.

30 minutes before: Prepare and cook Parsley French Potatoes for 8 minutes. Uncover and drain. Add butter and sprinkle with parsley and celery salt. Cook on high 2 minutes. Remove from oven and set aside.

Open red wine to allow it to breathe.

15 minutes before: Cut flan into portions and place onto entree plates. Garnish with parsley and a lemon twist.

Time for dinner: Serve Brie and Smoked Salmon Flan.

Reheat covered Broccoli and Carrot Saute 2 minutes on high. Remove from oven and heat Oyster Sauce 2 minutes on high. Set aside. When reheated do not remove coverings from dishes.

Reheat uncovered Fillet of Beef on high 3 minutes. Remove from oven and cover with aluminum. Reheat Parsley French Potatoes on high 2 minutes. While potatoes are reheating, arrange Fillet of Beef and Broccoli and Carrot Saute onto dinner plates. Add oysters to sauce and pour over beef. Serve potatoes separately. Heat fresh bread rolls for 30 seconds. Enjoy your meal.

Garnish Pistachio Orange Souffle with orange slices and extra crushed pistachio nuts and serve.

The final touch: While your guests are resting after the superbly microwaved meal you may be able to tempt them with Irish coffee and chocolates.

HINT: COOKING IN BATCHES

To make entertaining easier, use your conventional oven as a warming drawer when cooking large quantities in batches in your microwave.

NOTE: RECIPE TIMES

Recipes in this book are timed for cooking in average sized ovens. If you are using a smaller wattage oven add an extra minute or two to cooking times. For one of the more powerful ovens, take off a minute or two.

Brie and Smoked Salmon Flan

Pie Dough

1½ cups flour
salt to taste
2 teaspoons ground black pepper
2 teaspoons mixed herbs
1 oz butter
½ oz shortening
cold water

Filling

4 oz smoked salmon
4 oz Brie round, sliced
10 fl oz cream
3 eggs
2 tablespoons mixed herbs
1 teaspoon pepper
6 scallions, chopped paprika

Time: 23 minutes. Serves

Combine flour, salt, black pepper and mixed herbs. Rub butter and shortening. Mix through enough water to for a soft dough. Knead dough lightly on a floured board, r out and line individual pie dishes or a 9 inch pie pla Trim edges and prick base of dough with fork. Cook dough on high 6–8 minutes. Allow to cool slightly befo filling.

Layer salmon then cheese on pie dough base. Combi remaining filling ingredients, except paprika, and pour in crust. Sprinkle top lightly with paprika and cook medium 10–15 minutes.

Fillet of Beef with Oyste Sauce

6 fillet steaks
1 tablespoon butter
1 clove garlic, crushed

Oyster Sauce

1 tablespoon oil
1 tablespoon cornstarch
1 tablespoon parsley, chopped
salt and pepper
dash Worcestershire sauce
1 cup dry white wine
dash medium-sweet sherry
24 oysters

Time: 32 minutes. Serves

Preheat browning dish on high 7 minutes. Add butter ar garlic. Cook 1 minute more then sear steaks. Cook steak 3 at a time, on high for 9 minutes, turning once.

Combine all ingredients for sauce and cook on high 3 minutes. Stir vigorously then add oysters.

Arrange steaks on a microwave-safe dish, reheat on hi; 30–60 seconds and serve with sauce.

Parsley French Potatoes

4 medium-sized potatoes, peeled
1 tablespoon butter, melted
1 tablespoon freshly chopped parsley
celery salt

Time: 11 minutes. Serves 4–6

Cut potatoes into ¼ inch thick slices and layer in shallow dish. Cover and cook on high 8 minutes. Uncover and drain. Pour over melted butter and sprinkle with parsley and celery salt. Cook on high 3 minutes and serve.

...e and Smoked Salmon Flan: **Step 1** Layer salmon and brie on pie ...ugh

Broccoli and Carrot Saute

1 lb broccoli spears
3 carrots, peeled
2 tablespoons butter
freshly ground black pepper
1 tablespoon oregano
juice and rind of 1 lemon

Time: 8 minutes. Serves 4

Trim broccoli and cut into 1 inch spears. Cut carrots into 1 inch julienne strips.

Combine all ingredients in a shallow dish. Cover and cook on high 6–8 minutes. Allow to stand covered for 5 minutes.

...ep 2 Combine remaining filling ingredients

Pistachio Orange Souffle

10 eggs, separated
2 cups sugar
½ cup orange juice
½ cup lime juice
grated rind 2 oranges
pinch salt
2 tablespoons gelatin
¼ cup water
2 cups cream
½ cup pistachio nuts, crushed

Garnish

orange slices
extra crushed pistachio nuts

Time: 5½ minutes. Serves 6

Place egg yolks in mixing bowl and beat with electric mixer until fluffy. Add sugar and continue to beat till creamy. Cook on high 4 minutes, stirring occasionally. Add orange, lime juice and rind and blend thoroughly. Set aside.

Place gelatin and water into small bowl and cook on high 1½ minutes. Stir and set aside to cool. Whisk egg whites till stiff then add pinch salt. Whip cream.

Fold together gelatin, egg yolk mixture, egg whites and cream. Divide mixture between 6 individual 20 fl oz souffle dishes and chill for 2 hours.

Decorate with orange slices and crushed pistachio nuts.

...ep 3 Spoon egg mixture into crust

215

Menu Number 2

Dinner Party to Delight 4 or 6

Classic French Onion Soup
Parsley Veal Escalopes
Lemon Artichoke with Buttered Peas
Cauliflower with Almonds
French Cherry Tart

Our second dinner party menu is a well-rounded combination of the traditional and the inventive, is visually exciting, but simplicity to prepare. The onion soup entree is a tried and true winner, a stand-by of French cooking. The main meal combines flavors and textures that will delight and surprise your guests. The crunchy-topped veal is beautifully complemented by the vegetable dishes. For a rich but clean finish the cherry tart is perfection. Let the mellow mood of the evening slowly settle with coffee, liqueurs and chocolates.

French Cherry Tart (top right);
Cauliflower with Almonds and Parsley
Veal Escalopes (center, left to right);
Classic French Onion Soup (bottom)

Preparation Timetable

Week ahead: Prepare and cook pie dough for French Cherry Tart. Allow to cool then wrap securely in plastic wrap. Freeze.

Day ahead: Take pie dough from freezer. Unwrap and thaw. Prepare cherry filling for tart and set aside.

Prepare bouillon for Classic French Onion Soup. Allow to cool and then refrigerate.

Prepare artichokes. Trim and place lemon slices between leaves. Arrange in dish, pour over melted butter, cover and refrigerate.

Core cauliflower and place head on plate, cover and refrigerate.

Arrange cherries and pour filling into pastry base for French Cherry Tart. Cook then allow to cool. Do **not** refrigerate.

Place white wine in refrigerator to chill. Check tablecloth, napkins, glassware, dinnerware and cutlery. Ensure that all are clean and polished. Prepare any after-dinner chocolates and store in an airtight container.

3 hours before: Set table. Arrange flowers or table decoration. Set up tray for pre-dinner drinks and hors d'oeuvres.

Cook onions for Classic French Onion Soup. Slice bread, grate cheese and set aside.

Prepare parsley and breadcrumb mix for Parsley Veal Escalopes. Coat veal and place ready to cook in shallow dish and cover. Cook cauliflower and set aside, keeping covered. Cook artichokes and peas. Toss together and set aside in serving bowl, covered.

1 hour before: Reheat bouillon, covered, on high 15 minutes and set aside.

30 minutes before: Uncork red wine and allow to breathe. Add onions to bouillon and cook on high 15 minutes, keep covered.

15 minutes before: Heat butter and almonds for cauliflower, pour over cauliflower. Cook Parsley Veal Escalopes for 6 minutes. Keep covered and set aside.

Place French Cherry Tart on serving dishes and whip cream.

Time for dinner: Reheat soup on high 5 minutes then top with bread and cheese, cook further 1–2 minutes on high and serve piping hot.

For the main course reheat veal uncovered on high 2 minutes then reheat artichoke and peas, covered, on high 2 minutes. Reheat cauliflower and almonds on high 2 minutes, covered. When all dishes have been reheated, arrange veal on platter and serve with uncovered artichokes and peas and cauliflower. Enjoy your dinner.

Serve French Cherry Tart for dessert with whipped cream, then tempt your guests with after-dinner chocolates, liqueurs and coffee.

Classic French Onion Soup

5 medium onions, peeled and
   thinly sliced
3 tablespoons butter
2 pt beef bouillon
½ teaspoon salt
freshly ground black pepper
6 slices French bread
¼ cup grated Gruyere cheese

Beef Bouillon

2 pt water
1 carrot, chopped
½ cup chopped turnip
2 leeks, chopped
1 bouquet garni
1 lb soup beef with bone
1 teaspoon salt
freshly ground black pepper

Time: 58 minutes. Serves 4-

To make bouillon: combine water, carrot, turnip, leek, bouquet garni, beef and bone, salt and pepper in 6 pt ca serole. Cover and cook on high 15 minutes, then a furthe 15 minutes on medium. Remove all vegetables, mea bones and bouquet garni. Set stock aside.

Place onions and butter into 3½ pt casserole dish. Cove and cook on high 5 minutes. Add bouillon, salt and peppe Cover, cook on high 10 minutes, then a further 10 minute on medium.

To serve: Uncover. Top soup with French bread an sprinkle over grated cheese. Cook on high 3 minutes an serve immediately.

Parsley Veal Escalopes

freshly ground black pepper
2 oz butter
4 tablespoons chopped parsley
2 cups soft whole wheat
   breadcrumbs
juice ½ lemon
1 egg, beaten
6 veal steaks

Time: 10 minutes. Serves 4-

Combine pepper, butter, parsley, breadcrumbs, lemo juice and egg. Blend thoroughly.

Arrange veal steaks topped with parsley mix in a shallo dish. Cook covered on medium high 6–8 minutes, then further 2 minutes on high uncovered.

Lemon Artichoke with Buttered Peas

lemon, sliced
whole artichokes, trimmed
oz butter, melted
eshly ground black pepper
lb fresh peas, shelled
onion, finely chopped
tablespoons butter
ice ½ lemon

Time: 20 minutes. Serves 4-6

ut lemon slices in half and place between artichoke aves. Arrange artichokes in shallow dish, pour over elted butter, sprinkle with black pepper and cover with astic wrap. Cook on high 6-8 minutes then allow to stand minutes.

Place peas, onion and butter into shallow dish. Cover d cook on high 10-12 minutes. Stand 5 minutes.

Remove outer leaves from artichoke, cut artichoke earts in quarters. Toss together artichoke leaves, hearts, as and lemon juice and serve hot.

Cauliflower with Almonds

whole head cauliflower
oz butter
cup almond flakes
eshly ground black pepper

Time: 16 minutes. Serves 6-8

ore cauliflower, keeping florets in shape of cauliflower. ace head on serving plate and cover in plastic wrap. Cook high 12-14 minutes. Stand 5 minutes covered.

Place butter, almonds and pepper in shallow dish. Cook high 1-2 minutes. Stir.

Uncover cauliflower, pour over butter, almonds and pper mix and serve hot.

French Cherry Tart

× 9 inch pie dough (see recipe Hazelnut Pie)
eggs
cup superfine sugar
tablespoons ground almonds
tablespoons sour cream
× 20 oz can pitted black cherries, drained
teaspoon nutmeg
hipped cream

Time: 21 minutes. Serves 6

eat together eggs, superfine sugar, 2 tablespoons ground lmonds and sour cream till fluffy.

Arrange cherries in a layer on base of pie dough. Pour ver egg mixture. Sprinkle remaining almonds and nutmeg ver pie. Cook on medium 15-20 minutes. Stand 5 min-tes. Serve with whipped cream.

French Cherry Tart: **Step 1** Beat together eggs, superfine sugar, almonds and sour cream

Step 2 Arrange cherries in pie crust

Step 3 Pour egg mixture over cherries

Hors d'oeuvres

ors d'oeuvres — tempting, bite-sized portions that stimulate
th eye and appetite. Choose a single dish, simply served or
er a range with mouth-watering contrasts in color, texture
d flavor.

Crab Mousse

ablespoon gelatin
ablespoons cold water
oz crabmeat, flaked
easpoons lemon juice
ablespoons white wine
cup mayonnaise
cup sour cream
teaspoon cayenne pepper
acket toast squares
ers

Time: 1 minute. Serves 8–10

ce gelatin and water in cup or small bowl and cook on high
ninute. Stir and allow to cool slightly.
Combine crabmeat, lemon juice, wine, mayonnaise, sour
am and peppers. Gradually add gelatin mixture and blend.
oon mixture into a prepared 4 cup mold. Chill for 2 to 3
urs. When firm, unmold. Slice thinly, place on toasts and
nish with capers.

hrimp and Curry Toasts

easpoon cornstarch
easpoons curry powder
t and pepper to taste
oz uncooked shrimp, shelled,
deveined and mashed
< ½ inch slices day-old whole
wheat bread
gg white, lightly beaten
z pecan nuts, crushed
cup whole wheat breadcrumbs
cup oil

Garnish

1 tablespoon fresh chopped
 parsley
½ lemon, finely sliced
extra shrimp

Time: 14 minutes. Serves 4

move crusts from bread. Combine cornstarch, curry pow-
r, salt and pepper. Add mashed shrimp, mix and spread
er bread slices. Brush with egg white.
Mix together pecan nuts and breadcrumbs. Sprinkle evenly
er shrimp topping, pressing firmly into surface. Cut slices
o quarters.
Preheat browning dish on high 6 minutes. Add oil and place
uares 4 at a time on skillet, shrimp side down. Cook 1 min-
e each side on high. Drain, cool and serve garnished with
non twists, chopped parsley and extra prawns.

Piri Cashews (top left); Crab Mousse
enter) and Shrimp and Curry Toasts (bottom)

Crab Mousse: **Step 1** Combine crabmeat, lemon juice and wine

Step 2 Add mayonnaise and sour cream

Step 3 Gradually blend in gelatin mixture

Piri Piri Cashews

2 teaspoons butter
6 oz unsalted cashews
½ teaspoon cayenne pepper
½ teaspoon salt
dash nutmeg

Time: 5½ minutes. Serves 4

Melt butter in mixing bowl on high for 30 seconds. Add
cashews stirring until coated with butter. Cook 5 minutes on
high. Drain.
 Combine cayenne pepper, salt and nutmeg and sprinkle
over cashews.

Entrees

Today entrees or soup are most often served as the first course at a dinner party — or as an elegant light supper or luncheon dish. Attractively presented, they provide the magic that welcomes guests to the table.

Duck and Mushroom Pate Pots

Duck and Mushroom Pate

4 oz rindless bacon, chopped
4 oz veal, thinly sliced
4 oz duck livers, cleaned and
* drained*
2 oz butter
1 leek, finely chopped
¼ cup port
salt and pepper to taste
¼ teaspoon thyme
1 egg
½ cup cream
6 small button mushrooms

Aspic

1 tablespoon gelatin
1 cup white wine
salt and pepper
½ tablespoon fresh dill, chopped

Serving Suggestion

celery sticks
carrot sticks
toast squares

Time: 12 minutes. Serves

Place bacon, veal, duck livers, butter, leek, port, salt, peppe and thyme in a shallow dish. Cover and cook on medium 1 minutes. Drain keeping 1 tablespoon of juice.

Transfer mixture to food processor bowl, add egg and crea and blend until smooth. Spoon into 6 pate pots. Thinly slic mushrooms and arrange slices on top of pate.

Combine aspic ingredients in small dish. Cook on high minutes. Allow to cool without setting. Pour aspic over eac pate and chill. Serve with toast squares, celery sticks or carro sticks.

Duck and Mushroom Pate Pots

Shrimp and Scallop Brochettes with Saffron Rice

Shrimp and Scallop Brochettes

18 uncooked shrimps, shelled
  and deveined
12 scallops
juice and rind of 1 lemon
6 scallions, chopped
freshly ground black pepper to taste
dash ground ginger
dash ground coriander
½ cup white wine
¼ cup sesame seeds
2 teaspoons oil

Saffron Rice

2 cups long-grain rice
3 cups water
pinch powdered saffron
salt and pepper to taste
1 tablespoon freshly chopped
  parsley

Time: 31 minutes. Serves 6

To make Shrimp and Scallop Brochettes, thread 3 shrimp and 2 scallops alternately on 6 wooden skewers and place into a shallow dish. Combine lemon juice, rind, scallions, pepper, ginger, coriander and white wine. Pour over brochettes, cover and marinate 1 hour. Drain and sprinkle with sesame seeds.

Preheat browning dish on high 5 minutes. Add oil and cook brochettes 4–6 minutes on high, turning once.

To prepare Saffron Rice, place ingredients in a 6 cup casserole. Cover and cook on high 15 minutes, then a further 5 minutes on medium. Allow to stand covered for 5 minutes.

Chilled Borscht

2 pt rich beef stock or 2 cans
  consomme
4 fl oz sour cream or yogurt
1 lb beets
2 tablespoons lemon juice, strained
finely cut chives

Time: 20 minutes. Serves 4–6

Wash beets, remove stalks. Wrap each bulb in plastic wrap. Place in oven and cook on high 15–20 minutes. Turn beets over half way through cooking. Let stand, covered, 5 minutes.

When cooked, remove plastic wrap and peel and cut beets into small dice or grate.

Pour stock into serving bowl. Beat in cream or yogurt until smooth. Add beets, lemon juice and chives. Refrigerate until chilled.

Top each serving with sour cream and garnish with a small piece of watercress or dill.

If preferred this soup may be pureed.

The Main Course

It is usually the style and flavor of the main course which determines what comes before and after. So when designing dinner delights for your guests, always bear in mind, that it is the main meal which is paramount. In this section recipes are given for seafood, poultry, game and meat dishes. Among the traditional dinner recipes, like lobster and leg of lamb, there are some surprise recipes which will display your cooking talents and the range of the microwave oven to your guests.

Whole Baby Lobsters with Lemon Butter Sauce

Lobster

2 medium-sized lobsters, halved
salt and pepper to taste
½ teaspoon thyme
½ teaspoon oregano
2 tablespoons butter, melted
1 lemon, sliced

Lemon Butter

grated rind 1 lemon
7 oz butter
salt and pepper to taste

Time: 15 minutes. Serves 2

Place lobster halves in shallow casserole dish. Season with salt, pepper, thyme, oregano and butter. Top with lemon slices. Cover and cook on medium for 15 minutes. Allow to stand covered.

Blend lemon rind, butter, salt and pepper till smooth. Serve lobster halves with lemon slices and lemon butter dotted on each tail.

Whole Baby Lobsters with Lemon Butter Sauce

Whole Crumbed Whiting with Walnut Sauce

Crumbed Whiting

6 medium-sized whole whiting,
    washed and dried
2 eggs, beaten
2 tablespoons water
½ cup seasoned breadcrumbs
freshly ground black pepper
1 tablespoon freshly chopped
    parsley
½ teaspoon oregano
2 tablespoons oil

Walnut Sauce

½ cup crushed walnuts
¼ cup olive oil
¼ cup cream
salt and pepper to taste
dash nutmeg

Garnish

6 lemon wedges
freshly chopped parsley

Time: 20 minutes. Serves 6

Blend together egg and water. Combine breadcrumbs, pepper, parsley and oregano. Dip fish in egg mix and then coat with crumb mix. Refrigerate fish for 10 minutes.

Preheat browning dish on high 5 minutes. Add oil and cook fish, 3 at a time, 6–7 minutes on high, turning once.

Combine sauce ingredients in a bowl and cook 1 minute on high. Stir.

Serve fish with walnut sauce garnished with lemon wedges and parsley.

Whole Fish with Cashew Nuts

1 × 2 lb silver bream
1 tablespoon lemon juice
2 scallions
2 slices green ginger, finely shredded
2–3 tablespoons peanut oil
2 tablespoons soy sauce
¼ cup finely chopped cashews
lemon slices

Time: 14 minutes. Serves 8–10

Prepare whole fish by trimming fins and tail. Remove or pierce eyes. Place three diagonal cuts on the thickest section of fish to ensure even cooking. Rub inside of fish lightly with salt and lemon juice, place on serving plate and cover with plastic wrap.

Trim and cut scallions into 2 inch sections, cut each section into 2 inch long strips and soak in cold water.

Cook fish on high 8–10 minutes. Place oil in basin. Cook on high 4 minutes.

Remove plastic wrap, pour soy sauce over fish and top with scallion strips and green ginger. Then pour over hot oil and add topping of chopped cashews. Serve hot with lemon garnish.

Stuffed Trout

2 × 8 oz whole trout
1 cup chopped, blanched broccoli
3 scallions, finely chopped
2 tablespoons butter
2 tablespoons roughly chopped
    cashews
2 oz small shelled shrimp
¼ teaspoon salt
¼ teaspoon lemon pepper
1 teaspoon lemon juice, strained

Time: 7 minutes. Serves

Place scallions and butter in a small bowl. Cook on high minute. Add cashews, shrimp, broccoli, salt and pepper.

Place trout in baking dish in single layer with the thicke part of the fish to the outside of the dish. Spoon prepare mixture into cavity of each fish. Arrange remaining mixtu around trout and sprinkle with lemon juice.

Cover and cook on high 6 minutes or until fish flakes.

Stuffed Trout: **Step 1** Mix scallions and butter together

Step 2 Add cashews, shrimp, broccoli and seasonings

Step 3 Spoon stuffing into fish cavity

Fish Cutlets with Creamy Sauce

Fish Cutlets with Creamy Sauce

Time: 19½ minutes. Serves 6

medium fish cutlets
tablespoon butter
oz mushrooms, sliced
oz scallops, poached
scallions, finely chopped

2 tablespoons lemon juice
5 fl oz cream
1 tablespoon cornstarch
1 teaspoon dill
pine nuts to garnish

Arrange fish cutlets in a shallow container in a single layer. Cover and cook on medium 10–15 minutes. Melt butter in a 2 pint casserole on high for 30 seconds. Add mushrooms, scallops, scallions and lemon juice. Cook on medium 2 minutes, stirring once.

Blend together cream, cornstarch and dill. Add to mushroom mixture and stir. Cook on medium high 2 minutes. Stir.

Arrange fish cutlets on serving platter and pour over creamy sauce. Garnish with pine cuts.

Whole Chicken Breasts, Florentine Style

¼ cup shredded carrot
¼ cup pine nuts
8 oz frozen spinach, thawed,
  drained and chopped
2 cloves garlic, crushed
salt and pepper to taste
2 tablespoons freshly chopped
  parsley
4 whole chicken breasts, boned
1 egg, beaten
1 tablespoon water
dash nutmeg
1 cup seasoned breadcrumbs
1 tablespoon oil

Time: 9 minutes. Serves 4

Combine carrot, pine nuts, spinach, garlic, salt, pepper and parsley. Fill center of chicken breasts with small portion of spinach mixture. Fold over and secure with wooden skewer or tie with string.

Blend egg and water. Combine nutmeg and breadcrumbs. Dip chicken breasts in egg mix and coat with breadcrumb mixture. Place on microwave roasting rack and cook on high 9 minutes, turning once during the cooking. Serve hot or cold.

Potted Guinea Fowl with Cherry Sauce

6 small guinea fowl
juice and rind of 2 oranges
2 tablespoons butter, melted

Cherry Sauce

1 × 20 oz can pitted black
  cherries
freshly ground black pepper
½ teaspoon marjoram

Time: 75 minutes. Serves 6

Combine orange juice, rind and butter and brush over guinea fowl. Place 3 guinea fowl on shallow roasting dish and cook on medium high 30 minutes or until tender when pierced with a skewer. Transfer to individual pots, such as ramekins. Repeat for remaining guinea fowl.

Drain cherries, retaining 1 cup juice. Coarsely chop cherries. Combine sauce ingredients including cherry juice in a 3½ pt mixing bowl. Cook on high 5 minutes.

Pour sauce over guinea fowl, cover pots and cook on high, 3 pots at a time 5–10 minutes to heat through. Serve in individual pots.

Florentine Style Chicken Breasts served with pasta and salad

Roasted Rosemary Leg of Lamb

3–4 lb leg of lamb
2 tablespoons butter
2 cloves garlic, peeled and cut
  in slivers
2 sprigs fresh rosemary

Time: 40 minutes. Serves 6–8

Trim excess fat from lamb. Stud lamb with garlic slivers and sprigs of rosemary. Lightly coat with butter and place, fat side down, on a roasting rack in a shallow casserole dish.

Cover and cook for 35–40 minutes on high. Wrap in aluminum foil and allow to stand for 10 minutes before carving.

Roast Venison with Green Peppercorn Sauce

3 lb leg of venison
2 cloves garlic, chopped
1 cup white vinegar
1 cup dry white wine
½ cup oil
1 teaspoon ground cloves
1 teaspoon thyme
1 teaspoon coriander
salt and pepper to taste

Green Peppercorn Sauce

2 tablespoons oil
1 tablespoon cornstarch
4 fl oz sour cream
¼ cup green peppercorns

Time: 76 minutes. Serves 6

Slit surface of meat and insert small pieces of garlic. Combine vinegar, wine, oil, cloves, thyme, coriander, salt and pepper in a large bowl, add meat and marinate 2–3 hours. Drain, retaining 4 fl oz of marinade.

Preheat browning dish on high 5 minutes. Cook venison on medium high 8 minutes, turning after 4 minutes.

Transfer meat to a shallow roasting dish, pour over marinade and cover. Cook on medium 30 minutes, turn and cook a further 20–30 minutes or until fork tender. Stand covered for 10 minutes before carving.

During standing time prepare sauce by combining oil, cornstarch, sour cream and peppercorns. Cook on high 3 minutes. Stir vigorously and serve with venison.

Roasted Rosemary Leg of Lamb

Veal Fillets with Avocado and Hollandaise Sauce

tablespoon oil
veal fillets
large ripe avocado, peeled and sliced

Hollandaise Sauce

½ oz butter
egg yolks
tablespoons lemon juice or
* white wine or tarragon vinegar*
salt and pepper to taste

Time: 17 minutes. Serves 6

To prepare sauce, place butter in bowl and melt on high 1 minute. Beat together egg yolks, lemon juice, salt and pepper and stir into the melted butter. Cook on defrost 4 minutes, stirring every 30–45 seconds. Beat sauce while it cools. Sauce will thicken on cooling.

Preheat browning dish on high 4 minutes. Add oil and cook veal fillets, 3 at a time, on high 4 minutes, turning once. Repeat for remaining fillets.

Serve veal topped with avocado slice and Hollandaise sauce.

Bechamel (White) Sauce

tablespoon butter
tablespoon cornstarch
cup milk
salt and pepper to taste

Time: 5½ minutes. Makes 1 cup

Place butter into glass jug. Cook on high 30 seconds. Blend cornstarch, milk, salt and pepper and cook on high 3–5 minutes. Sauce will become firm, similar to a semi-set jelly. Beat vigorously with wooden spoon or balloon whisk.

For a thicker sauce, cook a further 1–2 minutes on high. To thin sauce, continue beating, gradually adding extra liquid.

Variations

Brandy and Mushroom Sauce

cup bechamel
tablespoon brandy
cup sliced button mushrooms
tablespoon chopped parsley

Place brandy, mushrooms and parsley in glass jug. Cover and cook on high 2 minutes. Combine mushroom mix with white sauce.

Serve with pork, beef or veal.

Veal Fillets with Avocado and Hollandaise Sauce

Hollandaise Sauce: **Step 1** Combine lemon juice, egg yolks, and seasonings

Step 2 Add melted butter and whisk

Step 3 Cook on defrost stirring every 30–45 seconds.

Mustard and Onion Sauce

1 cup bechamel
1 tablespoon wholegrain
* mustard*
1 small onion, finely chopped

Place mustard and onion into glass jug, cover and cook on high 1 minute. Combine mustard and onion mix with bechamel.

Serve with pork, beef, veal or lamb.

Vegetables and Salads

Vegetables and salads are no longer seen as mere accompaniments to meat, fish or poultry dishes. It is not unusual for a main course to consist of only vegetables — or of one or two specially selected, carefully prepared and beautifully presented vegetables. The salad has also undergone change: a variety of fruits or vegetables raw or blanched with a harmonious dressing, served with the main course, or following it, will freshen the palate for the delights to follow.

Celeriac Salad

1 lb celeriac, peeled and sliced
8 fl oz boiling salted water
2 teaspoons vinegar
2 tablespoons sugar
1 onion, finely chopped
freshly ground black pepper
3 tablespoons olive oil
1 tablespoon lemon juice
2 tablespoons chopped walnuts

Time: 7 minutes. Serves 4

Combine celeriac, boiling salted water, vinegar and sugar. Cover. Cook on high 7 minutes. Drain celeriac. Place in serving bowl. Add onion and pepper.
   Combine olive oil, lemon juice and walnuts. Toss through salad. Serve hot or cold.

Celery and Almond Saute

8 stalks celery, cut in diagonal
   slices
⅓ cup chopped scallions
2 tablespoons butter
pinch garlic salt
pinch white pepper
½ teaspoon sugar
toasted almonds

Time: 6 minutes. Serves 6–8

In a 2 pt casserole combine celery, scallions, butter, garlic salt and pepper. Cover and cook on high 6 minutes or until crisp but still tender. After 3 minutes stir in sugar and toasted almonds.

Snow Peas and Onion Salad

8 oz snow peas
1 onion, sliced
1 green pepper, finely chopped

Dressing

¼ cup vinegar
4 tablespoons oil
salt and pepper to taste
½ tablespoon mustard seeds
1 egg, beaten

Time: 3 minutes. Serves

Combine snow peas, onion and green pepper in a shallow dish. Cover and cook on high 3 minutes. Allow to cool. Combine dressing ingredients and toss through vegetables. Serve cold.

Celery and Almond Saute

omatoes with Spinach opping

0 oz frozen, chopped spinach
large ripe tomatoes
 teaspoon salt
 teaspoon pepper
 teaspoon sugar
 teaspoon basil
 cup chopped onion
 cup grated cheese

Time: 10 minutes. Serves 6

ut corner off frozen spinach bag. Cook on high 5–6 min-
tes. Place spinach in a bowl and drain. Cut the tomatoes
 half using a decorative zig-zag cut, and sprinkle with
 lt, pepper, sugar and basil. Combine half the cheese and
 l the onion with spinach. Spoon mixture onto tomato
 alves and cook on high 4 minutes. Top tomatoes with
 maining cheese after cooking for 3 minutes.

omatoes with Spinach Topping

Lemon Butter Asparagus

2 bunches asparagus spears
2 oz butter
juice and rind of 1 lemon
freshly ground black pepper
1 tablespoon freshly chopped
    parsley

Time: 10 minutes. Serves 4

Trim asparagus and place in shallow dish. Dot with butter,
lemon juice, rind and pepper. Cover and cook on high 10
minutes. Drain, keeping juices.

Arrange asparagus spears on plates. Pour over butter
juices and garnish with parsley.

Glazed Orange Sweet Potato

1½ lb orange sweet potato
3 tablespoons butter
2 tablespoons honey
½ teaspoon ground ginger
1 tablespoon finely chopped
    parsley

Time: 13 minutes. Serves 6–8

Peel sweet potatoes and dice into even-sized pieces, about
1 inch. Place in casserole, add 2 tablespoons cold water.
Cover and cook on high 8–12 minutes until fork tender.
Drain.

Mix butter, honey and ginger in small bowl. Cook on
high 1 minute. Pour over potato and toss to coat.

Sprinkle with finely chopped parsley and serve.

Jacket Potatoes

6 medium-sized potatoes
2 bacon slices, diced
2 tablespoons finely cut chives
6 tablespoons sour cream

Time: 20 minutes. Serves 6

Wash and dry potatoes. Prick each one several times with
a skewer. Wrap individually in plastic wrap and arrange
evenly in a dish. Cook on high 14–18 minutes, turning over
halfway through cooking.

Remove plastic and wrap each one in a square of aluminum foil to keep hot and aid presentation.

Place bacon in a basin, cover with a paper towel and
cook on high 2 minutes. Drain well.

Cut potatoes halfway through with sharp knife. Before
serving press potatoes firmly with fingers to force cut edges
to open and puff up. Top with sour cream, bacon slices and
chives.

Pasta

Pasta is possibly one of the most flexible ingredients in any kitchen. It can be simply and easily served in place of potatoes, for example, or dressed-up as a mouth-watering entree or main course.

Fettuccine with Calamari Sauce

Fettuccine

cups boiling water
teaspoon salt
tablespoon oil
oz fettuccine

Calamari Sauce

oz calamari, cleaned and sliced
tablespoon freshly chopped parsley
scallions, chopped
ice 1 lemon
eshly ground black pepper
cup white wine
tablespoons sour cream
armesan cheese, to garnish

Time: 22 minutes. Serves 4

lace boiling water, salt and oil into 3½ pt casserole dish. Add ttuccine, cover and cook on high 15 minutes. Stir and set side.

Combine Sauce ingredients, except for sour cream, in a shal w dish. Cover and cook on high 5–7 minutes. Blend in sour ream.

Drain fettuccine, add sauce and serve garnished with armesan cheese.

Basil-scented Tagliatelle

oz spinach tagliatelle
cups boiling water
teaspoon salt
tablespoons dried basil or 4
  tablespoons finely chopped
  fresh basil
tablespoons butter
clove garlic, crushed
scallions, chopped
tablespoons Parmesan cheese

Time: 15 minutes. Serves 4–6

lace tagliatelle, boiling water and salt into 6 pt casserole dish. over and cook on high 15 minutes. Drain and toss through asil, butter, garlic, scallions and Parmesan cheese. Serve hot.

ettuccine with Calamari Sauce

Fettuccine with Calamari Sauce: **Step 1** Add fettuccine to boiling water

Step 2 Combine sauce ingredients

Step 3 Drain fettuccine, add sauce and garnish with Parmesan cheese

Desserts

delicious dessert to follow the main course — allowing a
[s]uitable pause for conversation and digestion — will bring a
[li]ght to most eyes: even those of guests who loudly proclaim
[th]at they are not 'pudding people'. Choose a recipe you can
[p]repare well in advance or that requires few last minute prep-
[a]rations. Although with a microwave oven, last minute prep-
[a]ration is simply that. In just 2–3 minutes you can reheat
[d]esserts and serve them piping hot.

Hazelnut Pie: **Step 1** Line pie plate with pie dough and chill

Hazelnut Pie

[1] cup roughly chopped roasted
    hazelnuts
[1] × 9 inch raw pie crust
[3] eggs
[½] cup brown sugar
[1] cup corn syrup
[2] tablespoons butter
[1] tablespoon all-purpose flour
[1] teaspoon vanilla extract
[½] teaspoon salt

Pie dough

1 cup flour
½ teaspoon salt
⅓ cup cooking margarine
2 tablespoons butter
3 tablespoons cold water

Time: 18 minutes. Serves 6–8

[T]o make pie dough, combine flour and salt in a medium-sized
[b]owl. Cut in margarine and butter to resemble coarse crumbs.
[Bl]end in water and knead lightly. Let rest in refrigerator 15
[m]inutes. Roll out, line a 9 inch pie plate and chill further 10
[m]inutes.

[B]eat 1 egg yolk lightly and brush evenly over prepared pie
[do]ugh to seal. Cook on high 45 seconds until yolk has set.

[C]ombine in mixing bowl remaining eggs — separated white
[an]d leftover beaten yolk. Add remaining ingredients except
[ha]zelnuts. Blend well. Stir in hazelnuts and cook on high 4
[m]inutes, stirring after 2 minutes.

[P]our into pie dough. Reduce power to medium and cook
[1]0–13 minutes until filling has almost set. Let stand 6 minutes
[be]fore serving. The standing time completes the cooking.
[S]erve hot or cold with whipped cream.

Step 2 Combine filling ingredients

Fruits de Saison

[1] cup frozen berries
[1] cup shredded coconut
[2] tablespoons finely chopped
    pecans
[1¼] cups sour cream
[2] tablespoons fresh cream or
    milk
[a]ssorted fresh fruit wedges
[al]mond macaroons
[pin]k and white marshmallow
    halves
[lem]on juice, strained

Time: 4 minutes. Serves 8–10

Step 3 Pour cooked filling into pie dough

Place frozen berries into bowl. Cook on high 4 minutes. Allow
to cool. Mix in shredded coconut, pecans, sour cream and
fresh cream.

Put berry dip in center of glass platter and arrange selected
fruit, macaroons and marshmallows around bowl. Brush
apple, pear and banana pieces slightly with strained lemon
juice. Refrigerate until chilled.

[Ha]zelnut Pie

239

Strawberry Kahlua Mousse

Mousse

½ cup sugar
3 teaspoons gelatin
2 tablespoons water
1 cup milk
4 egg yolks
1 tablespoon Kahlua
8 oz strawberries, hulled and chopped
10 fl oz thickened cream

Strawberry Kahlua Sauce

¼ cup Kahlua
1 tablespoon sugar
12 strawberries, hulled and chopped finely

Time: 13 minutes. Serves 4–6

Combine sugar, gelatin and water in a small bowl. Cook on high 30–60 seconds. Allow to cool slightly.

Combine milk, egg yolks, Kahlua and strawberries in mixing bowl. Cook on medium 5–7 minutes, stirring occasionally until thickened. Set aside.

Whip cream until stiff. Fold gelatin, strawberry mixture and cream together. Pour into 2 pt mold and chill. When firm, unmold onto serving plate.

Combine sauce ingredients in a bowl and cook on high 5 minutes. Serve with Strawberry Kahlua Mousse.

Step 1 Combine sugar, gelatin and water and cook on high

Step 2 Mix milk, yolks, Kahlua and strawberries

Step 3 Fold together gelatin, strawberry mixture and whipped cream

Strawberry Kahlua Mousse

Strawberries and Kiwi Fruit in Champagne

 sugar cube
 cups champagne
 strawberries, hulled and
   halved
 kiwi fruit, peeled and sliced
 sh nutmeg

Time: 2 minutes. Serves 6

 ace sugar cube, champagne and nutmeg in mixing bowl.
 ook on high 2 minutes. Stir. Divide fruit equally between
 parfait glasses. Pour over champagne. Serve chilled.

Pecan Chocolate Cake

Pecan Chocolate Cake

½ cup butter
⅔ cup brown sugar
⅔ cup coconut
⅔ cup chopped pecan nuts
1½ cups all-purpose flour
1⅓ cups superfine sugar
¼ cup cocoa
1½ teaspoons baking powder
1 level teaspoon salt
1 cup milk
⅔ cup butter
3 eggs
1 teaspoon vanilla extract

Time: 19½ minutes. Serves 8

Line base of 2 × 9-inch souffle dishes with two rounds of wax paper. Place butter in bowl and cook on high 1½ minutes. Stir in brown sugar, coconut and pecans. Spread mixture evenly in each dish and set aside.

Place remaining ingredients in mixing bowl. Blend at low speed. Beat 2 minutes on medium then divide mixture and spread evenly in each dish. Cook one cake at a time on medium for 6 minutes then increase to high and cook 2–3 minutes until cake is light and spongy to touch. Let stand 5 minutes.

Turn onto serving plate. Turn second cake out onto the topping side of first cake. Spread any topping which may cling to paper onto cake top.

Strawberries and Kiwi Fruit in Champagne

241

Coffee Time

offee time treats finish your meal to perfection. With a
icrowave oven, you can create delicious chocolates in
inutes to serve with freshly brewed coffee, Irish coffee or
appuccino.

Mint Slice

oz cooking chocolate
tablespoons butter
cup confectioners' sugar
teaspoon peppermint extract
-5 drops green food coloring
-4 teaspoons milk

Time: 1½ minutes. Makes 25

ut chocolate into small cubes and combine with 2 table-
poons butter in a small bowl. Cook on high 1–1½ minutes or
itil chocolate is soft to touch. Stir until smooth. Spread in an
× 8 inch square dish and chill until set.

In a medium-sized bowl combine confectioners' sugar, 1
blespoon butter, peppermint extract and green food coloring.
eat with electric hand mixer until smooth. Spread over
illed chocolate and refrigerate until firm.

Cut into squares. Store, covered, in refrigerator.

Note: For a thicker base, double the amount of chocolate
itter.

Ginger Nut Chocolate

½ oz dark chocolate
cup ginger in syrup, drained and chopped
cup hazelnuts, crushed

Time: 3 minutes. Makes 24

eak chocolate into pieces and place in mixing bowl. Cook on
h 2–3 minutes. Stir and fold through chopped ginger and
ished hazelnuts. Spread mixture on a greased cookie slide.
hen set, break into bite-sized pieces.

Maraschino Chocolate Clusters

½ oz dark cooking chocolate
oz butter
easpoon maraschino cherry juice
oz maraschino cherries, chopped
oz almond slivers

Time: 3 minutes. Makes 24

eak chocolate into pieces. Place chocolate, butter and mar-
chino juice in mixing bowl and cook on high 2–3 minutes.
r. Fold through chopped cherries and almond slivers. Spoon
o small paper cases and allow to set.

1 Coffee (top); Ginger Nut Chocolate (center); Maraschino
ocolate Clusters and Mint Slice (bottom)

Cappuccino

2–3 teaspoons brown sugar or coffee crystals
2 teaspoons instant coffee
1⅓ cups hot water
¼ cup orange liqueur
whipped cream
cocoa

Time: 4 minutes. Serves 2

In a jug, combine sugar, instant coffee and hot water. Cover
and cook on high 3–4 minutes until boiling. Stir to dissolve
sugar then mix in liqueur. Pour into coffee cups and top with
whipped cream. Sprinkle lightly with cocoa.

Cappuccino

Irish Coffee

¼ cup brown sugar or coffee crystals
9 teaspoons instant coffee
5½ cups water
1½ cups Irish whiskey
whipped cream
cinnamon sugar

Time: 13 minutes. Serves 6–8

In a 3½ pint jug, combine sugar, instant coffee and water and
cook on high 13 minutes or until very hot. Stir in whiskey and
pour into individual cups. Top with cream and sprinkle lightly
with cinnamon sugar.

The Buffet

Buffets are the ultimate in flexible entertaining. They can enhance your barbecue, or alleviate the hunger pangs of a cocktail party, and they're the perfect solution for Christmas entertaining. You can hold a buffet indoors or out, or you can throw open the French windows and have it both ways.

The Art of the Buffet and Barbecue

Popular buffet foods such as a leg of ham, roast chicken, the perennial trio of potato, three bean mix and rice salads enable you to feed a lot of people for minimal cost and you can leave them largely unattended. Fine virtues, but there are many variations on that theme. Curries, stews, pates, terrines, cold roast meats, quiches and indeed anything encased in pie dough fit the same bill. Similarly, the potato variety isn't the only salad impervious to time. Pasta, artichoke, carrot, mushroom, hearts of palm, orange and onion salads all stand up well too.

Serving appetizers as a lead-up to a buffet always says, 'Look, I care; I bothered'. Warning: over-indulgence in 'tidbits' can blunt the effect of the most meticulously prepared dishes. If you offer too many irresistibles, bird-like eaters will fill up on them and overeaters will wolf them down and go on to overeat at table.

The microwave oven is one of the best appliances to use for preparing those short-order run-ups to a buffet meal. Appetizers can be prepared the night or morning before. Good microwave appetizers include meatballs, stuffed mussels, bacon-wrapped oysters or water chestnuts, hot vegetable and cheese dips, herbed scallops and easy pate or seafood canapes.

Pull out all the stops — selectively
One of the main drawcards of buffet entertaining is that you can have the choice of two main dishes, two salads, or a vegetable and a salad, and two desserts. Too many dishes will erode your valuable time and patience. Most of us like a bit of everything, so make sure all the selected recipes blend harmoniously, thus avoiding taste conflict.

Buffet food should always be easy to manage. No matter how delicious the food tastes or how ravenous they are, people are apt to throw in the towel if they have to struggle and juggle. Go for fork food, and keep away from any recipe that demands too much last minute attention. Dishes that can be wholly or partly cooked ahead are the ones to seek out.

In these days of astronomical food prices think in terms of market specials' like chicken, turkey, ground meat, continental sausages, eggs, cheese, less costly meat cuts that can be boned and stuffed, and then look for exciting ways to prepare them. Ethnic cuisines throughout the world offer thousands of dishes that eke out the protein part of the menu with cheaper

French Bean and Zucchini Salad, Green and White Salad, Rice Pilaf and Apricot Brandy Jelly (top, left to right); Pork Satay, Chicken in Spicy Sauce, Ratatouille with Coconut Sauce and Rollmops (bottom, left to right)

Party Cheese Ball

utes to achieve the proper sheen. Zappy pork chops al
benefit from two layer cooking. Simply microwave for 12–
minutes, shift the action to the grilling plate and cook for
further 10 minutes.

Cheese: a fine dessert

No food complements a good meal better than a well-chose
cheese. One of the benefits of concluding a meal with chee
is that it spares the cook having to prepare a more exot
dessert. Orchestrating a cheese platter is like conducting
symphony — harmony is all.

There's no need to offer a vast assortment of cheese, eithe
Two to four compatible cheeses are adequate, and for a lig
buffet luncheon or supper one good cheese — or party chee
ball — is all you need.

For ease and comfort

Whether the party takes place inside or out, an important co
sideration is to always provide adequate sit-down space f
everyone, and put salt and pepper shakers out so they c
season their food to their own taste. The same feeling
largesse should also apply to plates and glasses.

At large gatherings really good wines go unnoticed and u
appreciated. Reasonably cheap and cheerful is the right cour
to steer. Buy up big on the flagons and casks.

ingredients such as beans, pasta, chickpeas, rice, potatoes and
root vegetables. An excellent chili con carne, paella, lasagne,
moussaka or stuffed crepe can be the best of buffet dishes. Big
parties with small price tags needn't be an impossible dream.

Barbecue supreme

One of the greatest pleasures of eating outdoors is that almost
any kind of food goes. In the relaxed atmosphere of the garden
or backyard, you can allow yourself great freedom of choice
in the type and range of food you serve. Virtually every type
of meat and seafood is a candidate for barbecuing — pork,
beef, lamb, chicken, fish, scampi and lobster. But what really
makes modern barbecues so deliciously different is the widespread use of marinades.

The imaginative use of spices, herbs, fresh vegetables,
wines, yoghurt, citrus juices and vinegar can elevate a plain
steak or chop into something special. There are two types of
marinade — cooked and uncooked. Cooked marinades are
often used for larger cuts of meat, such as leg and shoulder of
lamb, loin of pork, rolled beef roast and whole chickens.
Uncooked marinades are the number one choice for small cuts
of meat, such as chops, steaks, poultry pieces and seafood.
There are also two types of barbecue sauce — the basting
sauces and the accompaniment sauces. Both can add im-
measurably to the occasion.

Quicker barbecuing

Speed up the cooking time of barbecued food by using the
microwave oven. Or, use the microwave oven to reheat leftover charcoaled foods. By grilling extras over the coals, you
can have a barbecue meal stored away for another occasion
without heating the grilling plate.

For example, pre-cook barbecued spare ribs in the microwave for 20 minutes, then transfer to the barbecue for a finishing off period of 15 minutes. Marinated chicken can be micro-
cooked for 18 minutes, then grilled over the coals for 10 min-

Menu Number 3

Luncheon Buffet for 6-8

Rollmops
Pork Satay
Chicken in Spicy Sauce
Ratatouille with Coconut Sauce
French Bean and Courgette Salad
Green and White Salad
Rice Pilaf
Cheese Damper
Apricot Brandy Jelly

This menu provides a delicious luncheon buffet with
clean, cool salad tastes and textures contrasting with t
spicy hot dishes.

246

Preparation Timetable

Week ahead: Prepare Rollmops. Place in shallow dish and cover with lid or a layer of plastic wrap then aluminum foil. Refrigerate

Day ahead: Prepare Apricot Brandy Jelly. Set into bowl or individual dishes. Refrigerate.

Prepare Pork Satay. Marinate pork pieces in a shallow dish covered with plastic wrap. Refrigerate.

Prepare Chicken in Spicy Sauce. Place chicken into a shallow dish, coat with oil and sauce, sprinkle with paprika, celery salt and pepper. Cover with plastic wrap and refrigerate.

Prepare Rice Pilaf. Cook rice but do not add ham, peas, peppers, seasonings and toasted almonds. Place rice covered with plastic wrap in refrigerator. Dice ham and peppers, placing in separate containers covered with plastic wrap. Refrigerate.

Place wine, beer and cold drinks into refrigerator to chill. Check tablecloth, napkins, glassware, dinnerware and cutlery. Ensure that all are clean and polished, ready to use.

3 hours before: Set table with tablecloth, napkins, glassware, dinnerware and cutlery. Arrange table decoration. Prepare drinks tray and appetizers.

2 hours before: Prepare Ratatouille with Coconut Sauce. Cook Ratatouille and set aside covered with plastic wrap. Prepare Coconut Sauce, set aside covered. Ensure that plastic wrap rests on surface of sauce to prevent skin from forming.

Prepare Cheese Damper (pie dough) but do not cook. Set aside covered with plastic wrap.

Prepare salads. For Green and White Salad, cook cauliflower florets and drain. Combine remaining ingredients in serving bowl. Refrigerate until serving time. Prepare garlic, salt, oil and vinegar for dressing. Keep in airtight container. Refrigerate

1 hour before: Cook Cheese Damper. When cooked, place on cake rack to cool. Cover with tea towel till serving time.

Cook Chicken in Spicy Sauce for 20 minutes. Remove dish from microwave and set aside. Cook Pork Satay for 5 minutes, cover with plastic wrap and set aside.

30 minutes before: Remove Rollmops from refrigerator. Drain and serve on one large platter, garnished with onions and capers from mixture. Add lemon quarters and parsley. Set aside in refrigerator. Uncork red wine and allow to breathe.

15 minutes before: Whip cream for Apricot Brandy Jelly. Add to cream 1 teaspoon gelatin dissolved in ½ tablespoon water. Cook on high 30 seconds. Fold through whipped cream. Pipe cream rosettes onto jelly to decorate. Return to refrigerator until serving time.

Toss ham, peppers, peas, seasonings and toasted almonds through rice, place on serving dish and set aside.

Buffet time: Serve Rollmops. Cook Chicken in Spicy Sauce for remaining 10 minutes. Heat Ratatouille on high for 3 minutes. Heat Pork Satay uncovered on high for 5 minutes. Pour vinegar and garlic dressing over Green and White Salad. Pour Coconut Sauce over Ratatouille.

Serve Pork Satay, Chicken in Spicy Sauce, Ratatouille with Coconut Sauce, Salads, Rice Pilaf, Cheese Damper on buffet table.

Serve Apricot Brandy Jelly.

Rollmops

pt cold water
salt herrings, cleaned and
    filleted
onion, thinly sliced
cup water
tablespoon peppercorns
bay leaf
tablespoon capers
tablespoon dried dill
arsley sprigs

Time: 5 minutes. Serves 10–12

lace herring fillets into cold water. Allow to soak 3 hours. rain. Place herring and onion rings in layers in a shallow ish.

Combine water, peppercorns, bay leaf, capers and dill. our over herrings. Cover and cook on medium 5 minutes.

Allow to chill overnight in refrigerator. Drain off liquid. emove bay leaf. Serve herring, onions and capers garished with parsley sprigs.

Pork Satay

1½ lb pork meat, cut into ¾
    inch cubes
2 teaspoons turmeric
2 teaspoons ground cumin
rind ½ lemon
1 teaspoon salt
1 tablespoon sugar
4 tablespoons coconut cream
1 tablespoon water

Time: 10 minutes. Serves 6

Thread pork meat onto wooden skewers. Blend turmeric, cumin, lemon rind, salt, sugar, coconut cream and water and coat satay. Marinate 1 hour. Drain and place into shallow dish and cook on high 5 minutes. Turn and cook further 5 minutes or finish cooking on barbecue.

Chicken in Spicy Sauce

2 × 3 lb whole roasting
    chickens
1 tablespoon oil
1 teaspoon chili sauce
1 tablespoon paprika
1 teaspoon celery salt
freshly ground black pepper

Time: 30 minutes. Serves 6-8

Cut chicken into quarters. Combine oil and chili sauce and coat chicken quarters. Place chicken portions in shallow dish.

Combine paprika, celery salt and pepper. Sprinkle over chicken.

Cover and cook on medium high 20 minutes.

Uncover and cook further 10 minutes. Stand 5 minutes. Alternatively, barbecue 10 minutes to complete cooking.

Cold Ratatouille

1 lb white onions, peeled and
    quartered
1 lb green and red pepper, cut
    into 1 inch pieces
1 lb eggplant, chopped
4 tomatoes, skinned and
    quartered
1 lb zucchini, sliced
1 teaspoon dried thyme
1 bay leaf
2 tablespoons basil
freshly ground black pepper
2 cloves garlic, crushed

Time: 15 minutes. Serves 6-8

Combine all ingredients in a shallow dish. Cover and cook on high 10-15 minutes. Serve with Coconut Sauce (see recipe).

Coconut Sauce

½ small coconut
1 teaspoon oil
1 clove garlic, crushed
salt to taste
½ teaspoon sugar
½ teaspoon cayenne pepper
½ cup white wine
juice ½ lime

Time: 1 minute. Makes 1¼ cups

Combine all ingredients. Cook on high 1 minute. Serve with Cold Ratatouille or other vegetable dishes.

French Bean and Zucchini Salad

¾ lb green beans
¾ lb small zucchini
1 bay leaf
1 clove garlic, peeled
½ teaspoon salt
1 onion, sliced
1 red pepper, shredded
iced water

Dressing

1 clove garlic, chopped
½ teaspoon salt
½ teaspoon white pepper
¼ cup olive oil
¼ cup tarragon vinegar
2 teaspoons sesame oil

Time: 6 minutes. Serves 8-1

String beans and cut into ¾ inch lengths. Trim zucchini cut into ½ inch rings. Place vegetables into casserole dis and add bay leaf, garlic, salt and 3 tablespoons cold wate Cover and cook on high 6 minutes. Drain, chill in ice water and drain again.

Combine all dressing ingredients in a jar and shake wel

To serve, arrange vegetables in salad bowl and toss wit dressing.

Green and White Salad

½ small head cauliflower
1 head fresh green lettuce
½ bunch curly endive
8 oz artichoke hearts, drained
12 black olives
¼ cup salad oil
2 tablespoons tarragon or white
    vinegar
½ teaspoon salt
1 clove chopped garlic

Time: 7 minutes. Serves 8-1

Cut cauliflower into small florets each with a portion stalk. Wash in cold water. Place into casserole dish and ad 1-2 tablespoons cold water. Cover and cook on high 6- minutes until crispy tender. Rinse cauliflower in iced wate to prevent overcooking.

Wash lettuce and endive and separate leaves from stall Refrigerate until crisp. Tear greens into bite-size pieces an dry by shaking in a clean tea towel. Place into glass sala bowl, cut artichokes into quarters and add to bowl wit olives and cauliflower. Refrigerate until serving time.

Sprinkle garlic with salt and puree using side of knif Add to oil and vinegar. Blend well. Just before serving, ad to salad and toss until vegetables are well coated.

Rice Pilaf

tablespoon butter
small onion, finely chopped
love garlic, finely chopped
cup washed long grain rice
¾ cups boiling chicken stock
  or canned beef consomme
 cup ham, diced
 cup cooked peas
 red pepper, diced
 green pepper, diced
tablespoons toasted flaked almonds
alt to taste
round pepper

Time: 12 minutes. Serves 8

lace butter, onion and garlic into a deep casserole dish.
Cover and cook on high 3 minutes. Add rice and cook 1
minute. Add boiling stock. Cover and cook on high 8 min-
tes. Let stand 4 minutes.
  Lightly fork in ham, peas, peppers and seasonings and
prinkle with toasted almonds.

Rice Pilaf: **Step 1** Combine rice, butter, onion and garlic

Step 2 Add boiling stock

Step 3 Lightly fork through ham, peas, peppers and seasoning

Rice Pilaf

Cheese Damper Scones

3 cups self-rising flour
1 teaspoon salt
3 tablespoons butter
½ cup milk
¾ cup water
2 tablespoons grated Parmesan cheese (optional)
paprika

Time: 13 minutes. Serves 10–12

Sift flour and salt into a bowl, rub in butter until mixture resembles breadcrumbs. Make well in center and add milk and water. Mix lightly in a cutting motion with a table knife, adding one tablespoon of grated Parmesan cheese. Turn onto floured board. Knead lightly and shape into a ball.

Shape into circle. Brush top of damper with extra milk. Sprinkle with remaining Parmesan cheese and paprika.

Heat browning dish on high 5 minutes. Sprinkle with a little plain flour and place damper carefully on top. Cook uncovered on high 7–8 minutes.

Cheese Damper: **Step 1** Sift flour and salt and rub in butter

Step 2 Add milk and water

Step 3 Lightly knead and shape into ball

Apricot Brandy Jelly: **Step 1** Combine apricots, pears, cherries and water

Step 2 Mix brandy, gelatin and water

Step 3 Gently stir gelatin mixture into fruit

Apricot Brandy Jelly

4 oz dried apricots
4 oz dried pears, chopped
2 oz glace cherries
20 fl oz water
¼ cup brandy
2 tablespoons gelatin
extra 4 tablespoons water
whipped cream

Time: 16 minutes. Serves 6–

Combine apricots, pears, cherries and water in a 3½ pir casserole. Cover and cook on high 10 minutes, then further 5 minutes on medium.

Combine brandy, gelatin and water. Cook on high 1 minute. Stir gelatin mix into fruit. Pour into a wet flan dish Allow to set in refrigerator. Before serving, invert ont platter and garnish with whipped cream.

Cheese and Bacon Ruffs (top) and Liver Canapes (Bottor

Buffet Appetizers

These irresistible hors d'oeuvres will whet appetites and enhance appreciation of the cook's culinary skills.

Shrimp and Bacon Rolls

12 uncooked shrimps or scallops,
    prepared
4 slices bacon, rindless
12 cubes canned pineapple,
    drained
12 glace cherries
12 cocktail sticks

Time: 9 minutes. Serves 12

Cut each bacon slice into thirds. Wrap one strip of bacon around each shrimp. Place a cherry, a cube of pineapple and one wrapped shrimp on each cocktail stick.

Heat browning dish on high for 6 minutes. Arrange shrimp rolls around outer edge. Cook on high 1½ minutes on each side.

Bacon and Cheese Ruffs

8 slices white bread, toasted
2 tablespoons melted butter
1 cup grated tasty cheese
2 egg whites
⅔ cup finely chopped peppers
1 teaspoon chopped parsley
½ teaspoon salt
dash pepper
3 bacon slices, finely chopped
    and cooked

Time: 6 minutes. Makes 32

Using a cookie cutter, cut four rounds out of each slice of bread. Brush one side with melted butter. Beat egg whites until stiff. Fold in cheese, peppers, parsley, salt and pepper. Spoon mixture onto unbuttered side of bread and sprinkle with bacon.

Heat browning dish on high 4 minutes. Arrange 16 rounds, butter side down, in dish. Cook on high about 1 minute until cheese melts. Repeat with remaining rounds.

Liver Canapes

2 tablespoons butter
1 onion, finely chopped
3 slices rindless bacon, chopped
2 oz mushrooms, chopped
½ teaspoon dried thyme
4 oz chicken livers, washed and drained
salt and pepper to taste
1 tablespoon sherry
1 tablespoon brandy
½ cup cream
¼ cup crushed walnuts

Time: 7 minutes. Makes 2 cups

Place all ingredients except cream and walnuts into shallow dish. Cover and cook on medium high 7 minutes.

Blend mixture till smooth. Fold through cream and walnuts. Place in bowl and chill. Spread over crackers or toast squares and serve.

Stuffed Mussels

30 mussels in shells
1 tablespoon oil

Rice Stuffing

4 oz long grain rice
2 onions, finely chopped
2 tablespoons olive oil
2 oz pine nuts
2 oz currants
1 oz sugar
1 tablespoon chopped parsley
salt and pepper to taste
10 fl oz fish stock

Time: 25–35 minutes. Serves 4–

Place half the mussels into shallow dish, add oil and cook o high 5–10 minutes. Remove mussels from oven as shells ope Continue cooking until all shells open. Set aside.

Place ingredients for rice stuffing into 3½ pt casserole disl Cover and cook on high 10 minutes, then a further 5 minute on medium. To serve whole stuffed mussels, follow Step 3. T serve as below, remove mussel and half of shell. Place sma portion stuffing on base of shell and top with mussel. Serv cold.

Stuffed Mussels

ed Mussels: **Step 1** Arrange half mussels in shallow dish, add oil
cook

p **2** Combine rice stuffing ingredients

Party Cheese Ball

¼ cup finely cut green peppers
¼ cup finely chopped scallions
1 teaspoon butter
8 oz cream cheese
2 cups grated Cheddar cheese
4 oz blue vein cheese, crumbled
1 tablespoon canned pimiento
   or red peppers, chopped
2 teaspoons prepared horseradish
2 teaspoons Worcestershire sauce
1 clove garlic, chopped very finely
1 cup chopped pecans, cashews or almond flakes

               Time: 2–3 minutes. Serves 12–14

In a bowl combine green peppers, scallions and butter.
Cover and cook on high 45 seconds. Place cream cheese in
a large bowl. Cook on medium 1–1½ minutes or until
softened. Stir in vegetables and remaining ingredients
except nuts.

   Shape into ball. Wrap in plastic wrap and chill 2–3
hours. Unwrap, roll in chopped nuts and serve with
assorted crackers and celery sticks.

Party Cheese Ball

p **3** Place small portion rice stuffing into shell

Soup Starters

chilled soup makes a wonderful starter for buffet
ntertaining: it can be prepared well in advance, kept in the
frigerator and simply garnished and served. No last minute
reparations. And while your guests enjoy the soup, you can
e putting the finishing touches to the main buffet meal or
rning the meat on the barbecue.

Chilled Avocado Bisque

large ripe avocado or 2
  medium-sized avocados, mashed
small onion, finely chopped
tablespoon butter
tablespoons all-purpose flour
fl oz rich chicken stock
fl oz fresh cream or natural yogurt
sh dill
mon slices
lt and pepper to taste

Time: 23 minutes. Serves 4–6

ace onion and butter into casserole dish and cook on high
minutes.
Blend in flour and cook a further minute. Warm chicken
ock in a jug by heating on high for 5 minutes. Stir stock into
ion mixture. Add avocado. Cook on medium 12 minutes or
til boiling, stirring every 3 minutes. Chill soup before fold-
g in cream or yogurt. Correct seasonings. Garnish with
sh dill and lemon slices.

Gazpacho

oz ripe tomatoes
oz bread, crusts removed
tablespoons olive oil
fl oz chicken stock
clove garlic, peeled
tablespoon vinegar
lt and pepper to taste
easpoon sugar

Garnish

oz ripe tomatoes, diced
oz green peppers, diced
oz cucumber, peeled, deseeded
  and diced
oz croutons

Time: 1 minute. Serves 4–6

move core from tomatoes and place in oven. Cook on high
minute. Peel tomatoes and chop roughly. Place tomatoes and
ead into food processor or blender. Add oil and one cup of
ock and puree.
Cut garlic clove in half and rub the inside of serving bowl.
ur in remaining stock and vinegar. Blend in tomato puree
d refrigerate until chilled. Chill diced tomato, pepper and
cumber. Serve garnishes along with soup in separate bowls.

Chilled Cherry Soup

Chilled Cherry Soup

1 × 16 oz can cherries, pitted
2 tablespoons brown sugar
1 tablespoon cornstarch
1/8 teaspoon cinnamon
1/2 cup orange juice or red wine
sour cream for garnish

Time: 6 minutes. Serves 4–6

Dice six cherries for garnish. Place remaining cherries and
juice into 2 pint casserole. Mix in sugar, cornstarch, cinnamon
and orange juice (or red wine). Cook on high 5–6 minutes until
boiling. Stir twice during cooking. Cool mixture and puree in
food processor or blender.
Refrigerate until chilled. Top each serving with sour cream,
sprinkle with reserved cherry pieces.

Main Buffet Meals

uffet food should be easy to manage. Kebabs and fork dishes
re ideal. Our selection includes a wide range of easy-to-eat
ods ideal on their own for just a few guests or combined
ith other dishes for a crowd. When catering for quantity plan
varied menu — watch for clashes — of dishes that can be
repared ahead of time so the cook isn't trapped in the kitchen
ar from the fun of the party. This section also includes
arinades and accompaniment sauces for barbecue buffets.

Marinated Beef

-4 lb whole fillet beef
tablespoon wholegrain mustard
tablespoon oil
ice and rind 1 lemon
tablespoon honey
teaspoon soy sauce

Time: 30–35 minutes. Serves 8–10

ombine mustard, oil, lemon juice and rind, honey and soy
uce. Coat fillet with mixture. Cook fillet on roasting rack on
edium high 30–35 minutes. Turn once about halfway
rough cooking. Stand covered with foil 15 minutes. Slice
ef thinly to serve.

Barbecued Whole Leg of Lamb

lb leg lamb, boned
tablespoons honey
tablespoon soy sauce
eshly ground black pepper
ash cayenne pepper
tablespoon sesame oil
ice 1 lemon
tablespoons dried rosemary

Time: 40 minutes. Serves 6–8

ombine honey, soy sauce, pepper, cayenne pepper, sesame
l and lemon juice. Cook on high 30 seconds. Spread lamb flat
d coat both sides with mixture. Sprinkle with rosemary.
ook lamb on roasting rack on medium high 40 minutes.
lternatively barbecue last 10 minutes to complete cooking.

arinated Beef and Home-made Mustard

Home-made Mustard

1 cup mustard seeds
1 tablespoon whole black
   peppercorns
1 cup olive oil
¼ cup vermouth
¾ cup white wine vinegar
½ tablespoon salt
½ teaspoon dried tarragon leaves
½ teaspoon dried dill

Time: 2 minutes. Makes 1½ cups

Place mustard seeds and peppercorns into blender. Blend 1
minute. Combine with remaining ingredients in a 2 pint
casserole dish. Cover and cook on high 2 minutes.

Pour mustard mixture into 2 jars. Seal. Allow to stand at
least 24 hours before using.

Home-made Mustard: **Step 1** Pound together mustard seeds
and peppercorns

Step 2 Combine remaining ingredients

Step 3 Spoon into jars and set aside

Marinades and Sauces

Orange-Sherry Marinade

1 cup orange juice
⅔ cup sweet sherry
¼ cup vinegar
¼ cup orange marmalade
2 tablespoons parsley, chopped
1 teaspoon basil
¾ teaspoon salt

Makes 2 cups

Combine all ingredients. Coat meat or poultry and leave to marinate 1–2 hours.

Red Wine Marinade

1 cup dry red wine
⅔ cup salad oil
2 cloves garlic, crushed
½ lemon, sliced
2 teaspoons parsley, chopped
1 teaspoon dried thyme
1 teaspoon dried basil
½ teaspoon salt
freshly ground black pepper

Makes 1⅔ cups

Combine all ingredients. Coat beef or lamb and leave to marinate 1–2 hours.

Steak Marinade

1 cup tarragon vinegar
⅔ cup salad oil
½ onion, thinly sliced
1 teaspoon salt
3 cloves garlic, sliced
8 peppercorns
1 teaspoon dried basil
1 teaspoon dried thyme
1 teaspoon dried oregano

Makes 1¾ cup

Combine all ingredients. Coat and marinate beef or lamb for 1–2 hours.

Tangy Barbecue Sauce

½ cup celery, chopped
3 tablespoons onion, finely
   chopped
2 tablespoons butter
1 cup ketchup
1 teaspoon chili sauce
¼ cup lemon juice
2 tablespoons vinegar
2 tablespoons brown sugar
1 tablespoon Worcestershire sauce
1 teaspoon dry mustard
¼ teaspoon salt
freshly ground black pepper

Time: 12 minutes. Makes 1½ cup

Place celery, onion and butter in 2 pint casserole dish. Cook on high 2 minutes. Add remaining ingredients. Cover and cook on high 5 minutes. Turn down and cook a further minutes on medium. Allow to cool before serving.

Marinades (left to right): Orange Sherry Marinade, Red Wine Marinade and Steak Marinade

Whole Silver Bream with Chili Ginger Sauce

× 2 lb silver bream or snapper
tablespoons lemon juice
½ teaspoon salt

Sauce

tablespoons oil
red chilies, deseeded, finely chopped
slices green ginger, finely chopped
cloves garlic, finely chopped
tablespoons onion, finely chopped
½ tablespoons dry sherry
tablespoons ketchup
tablespoons sugar
tablespoons white vinegar
scallions, shredded, for garnish

Time: 20 minutes. Serves 8–10

Place oil into basin, add chilies, ginger, garlic and onion. Cook on high 4 minutes stirring every minute. Add sherry, ketchup, sugar and vinegar. Cook on medium 5–6 minutes stirring every 2 minutes. Sauce can be made in advance and stored in refrigerator. Reheat just before serving.

Trim fins and tail of fish. Remove eyes using a melon baller or prick eyes to prevent them from bursting. Cut the thickest section of the fish three times on each side to enable the fish to cook evenly. Place fish onto serving plate. Rub inside of fish with salt. Squeeze lemon juice over fish. Cover with plastic wrap. Cook on high 8–10 minutes. Test with fork for doneness. The flesh should flake easily.

Drain any juice from platter. Mask fish with chili ginger sauce and top with shredded scallions. Serve hot.

Seafood Kebabs

Whole Fish with Cashew Nuts (top) and Whole Silver Bream with Chili Ginger Sauce (bottom)

Seafood Kebabs

4 oz uncooked shrimps
2 oz prepared scallops
2 oz thick fish fillet, jewfish
2 firm tomatoes, quartered then
    halved
6 stuffed olives
2 tablespoons lemon or lime juice
1 tablespoon butter
2 tablespoons cut parsley
12 pineapple wedges
12 green pepper wedges, diced
6 bamboo satay sticks

Time: 7½ minutes. Serves 6–8

Devein and wash shrimp. Cut fish fillet into ¾ inch cubes. Place one piece pepper onto each stick followed by a piece of pineapple. Alternate shrimp, scallops, fish fillet and tomato. Finish with one piece pineapple, peppers and one stuffed olive.

Place butter in basin and cook on high 30 seconds. Add strained lemon or lime juice. Brush over kebabs. Arrange kebabs in an oblong pyrex roasting dish or serving platter. Cook on high 4 minutes. Turn kebabs over and brush with butter. Continue cooking 2–3 minutes. Sprinkle with cut parsley before serving.

259

Chicken and Avocado Salad

8 chicken fillets
1 tablespoon oil
1 teaspoon paprika
1 tablespoon chopped parsley
1 teaspoon oregano
1 × 13 oz can seedless grapes
2 medium-sized avocados
6 scallions, chopped
2 radishes, sliced
¼ cup sour cream
dash Tabasco sauce

Time: 10 minutes. Serves 6–8

Place chicken fillets in shallow dish. Coat with oil and sprinkle with paprika, parsley and oregano. Cover with plastic wrap and cook on medium high 10 minutes. Stand 5 minutes then cut chicken into strips.

Drain grapes and add to chicken pieces. Peel and roughly chop avocado. Add avocado, scallions and radish to chicken mix. Toss salad together.

Blend together sour cream and Tabasco sauce. Serve sauce on chicken and avocado salad or separately.

Chicken and Avocado Salad

Rice

ce-based dishes are popular for buffet meals. They contribute to the visual appeal of the table, are ideal to eat hot or cold ith a wide variety of main dishes and, thanks to the chef's agination, can add interesting and piquant flavors to the eal. And with microwave cooking you can be guaranteed rfect, fluffy rice every time.

Saffron Brown Rice

cup washed brown rice
small onion, chopped
tablespoon butter
chicken cube, crumbled
teaspoon salt
teaspoon saffron powder
ound pepper
¼ cups water
cup dry white wine

Time: 31 minutes. Serves 8

ace rice, onion, butter, chicken cube, salt, saffron and pepper to deep casserole dish. Combine water and wine in a bowl d cook on high 5 minutes until boiling. Pour over rice, cover d cook on high 26 minutes. Let stand covered 10 minutes complete cooking.

Spicy Rice with Peas

tablespoons butter
teaspoon cumin seeds
teaspoon dry crushed chili or ⅛ teaspoon chili powder

½ teaspoon ground pepper
1 cup washed rice
½ teaspoon turmeric
1 teaspoon salt
1 cup peas
1¾ cups boiling water or stock

Time: 15 minutes. Serves 8

Place butter into large casserole dish. Cook on high 1 minute. Add cumin seeds, chili and pepper and cook 1 minute more. Add washed rice, turmeric and salt and cook on high 1 minute. Add peas and boiling water or stock. Cover.

Place casserole on large plate to collect any spillovers. Cook on high 12 minutes. Stand 4 minutes then fork rice up lightly. Serve hot.

Vegetable Rice Ring

1 cup washed long grain rice
1½ cups water
1 teaspoon butter
⅛ teaspoon salt
1 firm tomato, diced, seeds removed
2 scallions, finely cut
1 tablespoon green peppers, finely chopped
1 teaspoon oil
2 tablespoons cut parsley

Time: 16 minutes. Serves 8

Place water and butter in deep casserole. Cook on high 4 minutes. Add rice and salt. Cover and cook on high 8 minutes. Stand 4 minutes.

Place oil, tomato, scallions, peppers in small basin. Cook on high 1 minute then add parsley. Fork mixture through cooked rice.

Spoon into a greased ring mold, pressing down gently. Cook on high 2–3 minutes to reheat. Invert onto round serving plate and serve hot.

icy Rice with Peas

Salads

alads look lovely and are delightful to eat. Crisp and crunchy
r lightly blanched they are an invaluable part of any buffet.

To give a lift to a green salad add any or all of the following
s the mood and the season take you: avocado, artichoke
earts, carrot, cauliflower or broccoli florets, cucumber, ham,
ushrooms, radishes, onions, or zucchini. Avoid bruised vege-
ables and fruit, and keep greens crisp.

Arrange your salad ingredients attractively in a bowl or on
platter that's big enough to avoid spilling. Add as much or
s little dressing as taste requires, toss and serve.

Salad Nicoise

oz French beans
tablespoons water
oz tomatoes
oz stuffed olives
medium-sized potatoes, peeled
   and diced
oz anchovy fillets
teaspoon capers
tablespoons vinaigrette dressing

Time: 9 minutes. Serves 6–8

ut beans into 1 inch pieces. Blanch for 2 minutes on high in
small casserole with two tablespoons water. Place the
otatoes in a bowl, cover with plastic wrap and cook on high
minutes. Set beans and potatoes aside to cool.

Toss potatoes, beans, tomatoes and olives together in serv-
g bowl. Combine anchovy fillets, capers and vinaigrette
ressing. Pour over the vegetables and toss. Serve chilled.

Vinaigrette Dressing

tablespoons salad oil
teaspoon French mustard
tablespoon white or tarragon
   vinegar
lt and ground pepper to taste

ombine all ingredients in a jar. Replace lid and shake well.
tore in airtight jar.

Variations

nglish mustard (in place of French mustard)
hopped chives or parsley
hopped hard-boiled egg
rained lemon juice (in place of vinegar)

Pasta and Broccoli Salad

8 oz pasta
4 cups boiling water
1 teaspoon salt
8 oz broccoli spears, cut in half
1 tomato, chopped
¼ cup olive oil
freshly ground black pepper
½ teaspoon dried basil
2 tablespoons Parmesan cheese,
   grated

Time: 20 minutes. Serves 8–10

Place pasta, boiling water and salt in 6 pint casserole dish.
Cover and cook on high 15 minutes. Set aside. Place broccoli
in shallow dish. Cover and cook on high 5 minutes. Combine
broccoli spears with tomato, olive oil, pepper and basil.

Drain pasta. Toss broccoli and pasta together. Serve
sprinkled with Parmesan cheese.

Pasta and Broccoli Salad with Italian Herb Loaf

Gado Gado Salad

1 lb bean or soy bean sprouts
8 oz finely-shredded cabbage
8 oz green beans, cut in ¾ inch lengths
4 lb carrots, cut matchstick size

Sauce

1 onion, sliced
2 cloves garlic, chopped
2 teaspoons oil
¼ teaspoon salt
2 teaspoons brown sugar
1 teaspoon lemon juice
1 teaspoon soy sauce
1 teaspoon chili sauce
4 oz crunchy peanut butter
½ cup Coconut Milk (see recipe)

Garnish

sliced cucumber
sliced radish
sliced hard-boiled egg
parsley sprigs

Time: 11½ minutes. Serves 10

Place bean sprouts, cabbage, beans and carrots into individual plastic bags with 1 tablespoon water for each bag. Fold in open edge. Place bags in oven and cook on high 3–4 minutes until vegetables are crispy tender. Rinse vegetables in cold water and drain.

Place onion, garlic and oil in bowl. Cook on high 5 minutes. Add remaining sauce ingredients and blend well.

Place peanut sauce in center of flat salad platter. Arrange blanched vegetables. Garnish with cucumber, radish, egg and parsley. Chill and serve.

Coconut Milk

¾ cup cold water
3–4 tablespoons desiccated
 coconut

Place water and coconut in basin. Cook on high 2½ minutes. Allow to cool, strain and squeeze through white cloth.

Gado Gado Salad: **Step 1** Place sprouts, cabbage, beans and carrots in plastic bags

Step 2 Combine onion, garlic and oil for sauce

Step 3 Add remaining sauce ingredients, mix and serve with salad

Peanut and Cabbage Salad

½ head cabbage, shredded
tablespoons all-purpose flour
¼ cup sugar
¼ teaspoon salt
⅛ teaspoon pepper
eggs, beaten
1½ cups cold water
½ cup white vinegar
tablespoons prepared mustard
½ cup chopped peanuts

Time: 10 minutes. Serves 8–10

Wash shredded cabbage and shake dry in clean tea towel. Place in bowl and cover. Sift flour, sugar, salt and pepper into casserole dish. Combine eggs, water, vinegar and mustard then blend into dry ingredients. Cook on medium 10 minutes stirring every 2 minutes until mixture thickens and forms a sauce. Allow to cool then pour over cabbage, add peanuts, toss well. Chill and serve.

Potato Salad with Bacon

medium-sized potatoes, peeled and sliced
stalk of celery, chopped
½ teaspoon dried basil
½ cup meat stock
fl oz olive oil
tablespoons white vinegar
freshly ground black pepper
oz smoked bacon, diced

Time: 17 minutes. Serves 6

Place sliced potatoes in a shallow dish. Cover and cook on high 10–12 minutes. Set aside. Combine celery, basil, stock, olive oil, vinegar and pepper in a 4 cup measure. Cook on high 5 minutes then add bacon. Pour over potatoes to serve.

Potato Salad with Bacon

Potato Salad with Bacon: **Step 1** Layer sliced potatoes in shallow dish

Step 2 Combine celery, basil, stock, olive oil, vinegar and pepper

Step 3 Pour sauce over potatoes and serve

Breads for Buffets

ost yeast breads can be proven and baked in a microwave
en. To give the loaf a crust, the clever cook sprinkles the
eased loaf dish with oatmeal, crumbed crisp savory cookies
cracked wheat.
Dried or fresh yeast when mixed with warm water and
gar will prove only on warm setting — defrost will kill the
ast. Fresh and tasty home-made breads, speedily baked in
e microwave oven are greatly appreciated by one and all in
e age of sliced bread.

Whole Wheat Bread

packet dry yeast
fl oz tepid water
fl oz tepid milk
egg
tablespoons sugar
tablespoon salt
cup butter or margarine, melted
-10 drops yellow food coloring (optional)
2–4 cups whole wheat flour

Time: About 28 minutes.

ften yeast in tepid water and milk. Stir to help dissolve
stantly. In large bowl combine yeast mixture with remaining
gredients, except for flour, and beat well. Add flour gradu-
ly to form a very stiff dough, beating well. Knead dough on
lightly-floured board and place in a greased bowl large
ough to hold it when doubled. Cover with plastic wrap.
Prove on warm 3 minutes and then allow to stand 15 min-
es. Turn dough over in bowl carefully if surface appears to
 drying. Repeat cycle 2 or 3 times, proving in microwave
d standing, until dough is light and doubled in size. Punch
wn and shape as required.
Place in loaf dish, cover and allow to double in size. Un-
ver and cook on medium 15 minutes. Increase to high and
ok a further 1–4 minutes. Bread is cooked when it 'sounds'
llow when tapped

Variations
Caraway and Sesame Seed Bread

cup caraway seeds
cup sesame seeds
g yolk, beaten

dd caraway seeds and sesame seeds to whole wheat flour.
rm proven dough into loaf shape and place in 6 cup ring
old. Brush with beaten egg yolk and sprinkle with extra
raway and sesame seeds. Cover and allow to double in size.
ncover and cook following method for Whole Wheat Bread.

hole Wheat Bread (left); Caraway and Sesame Seed Rolls (top right)
d Braided Herb Loaf (bottom right)

Herb Loaf

½ tablespoon oregano
½ tablespoon ground black pepper
½ tablespoon thyme
½ tablespoon dill
egg yolk, beaten

Add herbs and pepper to whole wheat flour. Form proven
dough into French loaf shape, cut into 3 lengths and braid
Place on microwave baking sheet and brush with beaten egg
yolk. Sprinkle with poppy seeds or extra herbs. Cover and
allow to double in size. Uncover and cook following method
for Whole Wheat Bread.

Whole Wheat Bread: **Step 1** Soften yeast in tepid water and milk

Step 2 Combine sifted flour with remaining ingredients

Step 3 Knead on a lightly floured board

Cornmeal Bread

1 cup all-purpose flour
1 cup cornmeal
1 tablespoon baking powder
2 tablespoons sugar
dash mustard powder
salt and pepper to taste

1 × 13 oz can creamed corn
3 eggs, beaten
2 tablespoons oil
¼ cup grated Cheddar cheese
dash paprika

Time: 13 minutes. Makes 1 loaf

Sift flour, cornmeal, baking powder, sugar, mustard, salt and pepper. Fold in creamed corn, beaten eggs and oil.

Grease 4 cup mold. Coat with grated cheese and paprika. Pour in bread mix. Cook on medium 12 minutes, then a further 1 minute on high. Stand 5 minutes before inverting.

Cornmeal Bread

Cornmeal Bread Step 1 Sift flour, cornmeal, baking powder, sugar, mustard and seasonings

Step 2 Fold in creamed corn, beaten eggs and oil

Step 3 Coat dish with grated cheese and paprika

Garlic Bread Rolls

6 whole wheat or white bread rolls
5 oz butter
¼ cup thinly sliced scallions
1–2 cloves garlic, crushed

Time: 2½ minutes. Serves

Cut each bread roll three times from the top two-third through the roll. Combine butter, scallions and garlic i basin. Cook on medium low 30–60 seconds until butte softens. Spread butter mixture between each cut in brea rolls. Place roll in large brown paper bag or wrap in wa paper. Cook on high 1½ minutes.

Italian Herb Loaf

1 loaf Italian bread
4 oz butter
2 teaspoons cut parsley
¼ teaspoon dried oregano,
  crumbled
¼ teaspoon dried drill
1 clove garlic, finely chopped
½ cup Parmesan cheese, grated

Time: 2½ minutes. Serves

Cut bread diagonally into ¾ inch slices two-thirds throug the loaf. Place butter and garlic into bowl, soften medium low 30–60 seconds. Blend in herbs and chees Spread butter mixture on each slice bread. Wrap bread a sheet of wax paper and cook on high 1½ minutes.

If the bread should be too long for oven, cut in half an wrap each piece in waxproof paper. Place side by side oven and cook as above.

Desserts

hen dessert is the crowning glory of your meal, the micro-
ave will enable you to prepare an almost endless variety.
etter yet, many of them can be made in advance, which
akes entertaining so much easier.

With a microwave oven you can thaw prebaked flan cases,
ok fruit pies, defrost frozen desserts and whip up superlative
uces — all in an instant.

nnamon Pear Upside Down Tart: **Step 1** Sprinkle sugar and cinnamon
er pear halves

ep 2 Add red wine

ep 3 Roll out dough to make pie lid

Cinnamon Pear Upside Down Tart

4 firm pears, halved, peeled and
  cored
3 oz sugar
½ teaspoon cinnamon
20 fl oz red wine

Pie Dough

1 lb all-purpose flour, sifted
2 teaspoons salt
8 oz butter
3–4 tablespoons iced water

Time: 35 minutes. Serves 4–6

Rub butter into flour and salt. Cut water through to form a soft
dough. Knead lightly on floured board. Wrap in plastic wrap
and refrigerate.

Arrange pear halves, cut-side up, in a 12 inch baking dish.
Sprinkle over sugar and cinnamon. Pour over red wine to
cover. Cover and cook on high 5 minutes, then reduce to medium and cook 10 minutes. Drain liquid into jug. Cook on high
10 minutes.

Pour sauce over pears. Roll out dough, cover dish, seal and
trim edges. Cook on medium high 10 minutes. Cool 5 minutes
then unmold on serving plate. Serve with whipped cream.

Peaches Italian Style

12 large canned peach halves
12 macaroons, crumbled
2 tablespoons Grand Marnier
4 tablespoons toasted almond slivers
10 fl oz whipped cream

Time: 4 minutes. Serves 12

Place peach halves in microwave roasting dish. Combine macaroons and Grand Marnier, divide mixture and fill center of each peach. Cook on medium 4 minutes or until hot. Before serving top with whipped cream or ice cream and sprinkle with almond slivers.

Strawberry Brandy Cream

1 × 27 oz can strawberries
⅓ cup cherry brandy
6 teaspoons gelatin
2 cups cream
¼ cup sugar
4 fresh strawberries for garnish,
  hulled and chopped

Time: 3 minutes. Serves 6–8

Drain canned strawberries and reserve syrup. Combine ¼ cup syrup, brandy and gelatin in a bowl and stir. Cook on high 1 minute. Set aside to cool.

Whip cream and sugar till stiff. Fold in strawberries with cream. Gradually fold in gelatin mix and extra ¼ cup syrup. Pour mixture into wet 4 cup mold. Chill.

Place remaining syrup and strawberries in glass jug. Cook on high 1–2 minutes.

To serve, unmold Strawberry Cream. Pour syrup over and garnish with chopped fresh strawberries.

Fruit Salad Kebabs

1 red-skinned apple, cubed
8 oz fresh pineapple wedges
1 can mandarin segments, drained
8 oz assorted melon balls or cubes
1 firm banana, sliced in ¾ inch pieces
8 strawberries

Glaze

1 tablespoon cornstarch or arrowroot
⅛ teaspoon cinnamon
¼ cup strained lemon juice
¼ cup strained orange juice
3 tablespoons honey

Time: 6 minutes. Serves 6–8

Combine glaze ingredients in bowl. Place in oven and cook on high 2–3 minutes or until thick, stirring twice. One teaspoon freshly chopped mint may be added.

Select a range of seasonal and canned fruits to make a colorful kebab.

Thread fruit on wooden satay sticks and brush with glaze. Arrange in shallow dish. Heat on high 2–3 minutes or until hot. Serve.

Fruit Salad Kebabs

Buffet Beverages

Fruit punches make entertaining easy. These tasty beverages look attractive, can be prepared in large quantities and are so simple to serve. Punch was originally a drink based on rum and flavored with lemon and cinnamon. Today it can be alcoholic or not and enlivened with fruit juices, fresh fruits and carbonated drinks for extra sparkle.

Champagne Punch

1 teaspoon sugar
1 teaspoon water
3 slices orange
3 slices lemon
rind 1 lemon
1 teaspoon Angostura Bitters
2 fl oz brandy
2 fl oz maraschino
2 fl oz curacao
4 fl oz sherry
25 fl oz chilled champagne
25 fl oz soda water

Time: 2 minutes. Serves 6–8

Combine sugar, water, orange and lemon slices in shallow dish. Cook on high 2 minutes. Place in punch bowl. Add remaining ingredients and stir gently.

White Wine and Vermouth Punch

1 cup sugar
1 cup orange juice
1 teaspoon cinnamon
2 cups hulled strawberries
1 lemon, sliced
4 mint leaves, bruised
2 cups vermouth
2 × 25 fl oz bottles sweet white
    wine
25 fl oz bottle soda water
ice cubes

Time: 5 minutes. Serves 12–

Place sugar and orange juice in jug. Cook on high 5 minute Pour into punch bowl. Add strawberries, lemon slices, mi leaves and vermouth. Stand covered 1 hour.

Before serving add white wine, soda water and ice cube

Cherry Punch

2 cups sugar
2 cups water
2 oranges, thinly sliced
8 oz maraschino cherries,
    drained
8 fl oz cherry brandy
2 × 25 fl oz bottles soda water
crushed ice

Time: 10 minutes. Serves 8–1

Place sugar and water in 3½ pint casserole dish. Cook on hig 6 minutes. Stir twice. Add orange slices. Cook on high 4 mi utes. Add maraschino cherries and cherry brandy. Cover ar chill.

To serve, pour cherry brandy mixture into punch bowl, ac soda water and crushed ice.

Pineapple Punch

1 fl oz pineapple juice
1 fl oz grenadine
3 fl oz maraschino
2 fl oz dry gin
juice 3 lemons
2 teaspoons Angostura Bitters
3 pts moselle
25 fl oz soda water
1 pineapple, cut into cubes

Serves 1

Combine all ingredients in a punch bowl. Add ice just befo serving.

Champagne Punch

Parties for Young People

The young from 12–21 are all still growing — their capacity to consume will amaze you. Turned loose, they are quite capable of gorging on sweet and junk food, making themselves ill in the process. Afterwards, they may want to know why you let them do it! So make the main meal delicious, nutritious and filling, and titillate their palates with the 'befores' and 'afters'.

Food for Thought

Adolescence used to be a phase, then it became a rite of passage, now it is a profession. Like all professions it exacts a toll from its associates, nowhere more so than in the realm of entertainment.

What sort of party do you give someone aged between 12 and 20? At 12 you still have a dependent youngster: at 20 that 'youngster' is standing on the threshold of adult life. They all seem to enjoy a party whether to celebrate a birthday, congratulate the winning team or simply a get-together with friends — old and new. Parents always remember the seemingly simpler pleasures of their youthful parties. But times have changed and tastes have changed along with them. These days, a theme seems to help the party along.

Chocolate Flake Cheesecake

Entertaining 12–14-year-olds

Let's start with the 12–14-year-olds, the teenyboppers. Nine times out of ten they are in the thrall of some pop idol. Get the boys to dress like their heroes; the girls can have all the fun they want as glitz and glitter of the current number one hit. The nearest one to approximate a garage sale takes the prize. The music, is of course, a foregone conclusion.

Now that you have a theme, your next task is to feed them. Not extravagantly (in the sense of your time and money), just well. Incipient teenagers outside of French novels aren't noted for their sophisticated palates. A good idea is to serve up home-made fast foods like burgers, pizzas and hot dogs, preferably in an outdoors or barbecue setting. Simply lay on the buns, the meat patties and all the additions — tomatoes, beets, lettuce, onions and pickles. Point them towards the broiling plate and let them serve themselves.

Pizza is always popular. To make it easy on yourself on the day — make the pizzas in advance on a pie dough base and simply reheat in the microwave as required. Or, still on the microwave note, offer hot dogs. Spread a home-made ketchup over frankfurters, heat them through and slip them into the waiting buns.

Count on the partygoers downing one burger, one hot dog and a wedge of pizza each. Let them wash it all down with the usual array of 'in' soft drinks. For dessert, indulge in rich, rich chocolate nut ice cream cake or chocolate flake cheesecake.

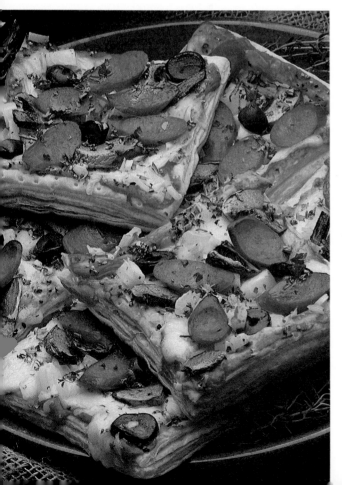

Pie Dough Pizzas

The mid-teens

Fifteen to seventeen-year-olds are hard core video kids —
given a chance — so have a VCR party. Again, go for a dress-
up theme, anyone from 8 to 80 loves the challenge. How about
a horror night? Hire horror movie videos. Let them think up
the best of their worst, and offer an 'Oscar' for the most imaginative get-up.

The food should be in keeping with the mood. For example,
make up really hot and spicy microwave frankfurters to send
tingles down the spine. A recipe of 2 lb cocktail frankfurters,
1 cup chili sauce, 3 tablespoons dry sherry, 1 finely chopped
clove of garlic and the grated rind of half a lemon takes only
5 minutes to cook on high. Just layer the frankfurters in a
shallow baking dish, pour over the chili mix, cover and cook.
You can serve it straight away, but it's best if made in advance
and left to marinate for an hour or two then reheated for 2
minutes. Accompany with tacos, shredded lettuce and grated
cheese.

Rare roast beef is another option. Microwave a 3–4 lb beef
roast. Carve off thin slices, and make roast beef sandwiches
with accompaniments such as beets, tabouli, coleslaw and dill

Spicy Frankfurters

Mexican Tacos

pickles. Follow up with a Halloween-type pumpkin pie. A
the drinks should be red such as Bloody Marys (without t
vodka) or a non-alcoholic punch colored with grenadine.

Not children anymore: The 18–20-year-olds

You can hardly call 18–20-year-olds children anymore.
most cases they dwarf you, look like men and women and fe
they are adult — though you may not always agree. Thinki
up a special theme for this age group is fraught with dange
A milestone, such as passing an exam, is an obvious candida
but avoid anything that sounds too cutesy. Most probably th
will come up with their own theme.

The good thing about the late teen years is that most no
just want their close friends around them. The stimulation
good company is usually enough. The excitement of the eve
ing should lie with the food.

The cardinal rule for entertaining in quantity with ease
not to plan a menu that traps anyone in the kitchen. No la
minute souffles, no fried foods, not too many choices. Instea
prepare everything that you possibly can ahead of time.

The question of drink is a thorny issue in this age grou
With today's health conscious society, drinking is look
down upon in adult groups but not necessarily by your
people. But, drinking while driving has become such
dangerous and widespread problem that it's a good idea
avoid alcohol altogether at a party. So, offer fruit juic
soft drinks or mineral water.

Punches are always popular. Try this Aloha Punch
combine ⅓ cup sugar, ⅓ cup water, 8 cloves and 1 cinn
mon stick over heat and allow to simmer for 5 minute
Leave to cool and then strain into 3 cups of pineapple juic
3 cups orange juice and ⅓ cup lemon juice. Ch
thoroughly. Serve with 2 pints ginger ale and ice cub
Makes 5 pints. One caveat should be entered he
punchbowls can all too easily be spiked, particularly
those who are still wallowing in 'cool'. If you think this
a possibility, don't serve punch.

As for the music — relax. They will look after that. Y
won't have to do a thing.

Hiring

So you have decided to have a party! You have the occasion, the date and the friends and family — but where do you go from here? The most important point is to have a plan of action. No party will be a success unless it is meticulously planned. Give yourself lots of time. No one needs the hassle of a last minute panic.

When it comes to the food, decorations and the music, you can always choose to do all the work yourself — and have the party in your lounge room. But for an occasional thing, or a special occasion like a 21st birthday, the increasingly popular alternative is to hire.

Why hire?

These days the options are incredible. You can hire anything from cups to camels! The advantages of hiring are obvious. Firstly, because of the range of food, music, decorations available for hire, you can give the kind of party you'd never be able to arrange all by yourself.

Most importantly, hiring can save you enormous amounts of time and trouble. There are hundreds of experienced caterers who will look after your every whim. Some just supply the food. Others bring the crockery and cutlery too. At the top of the scale, there are caterers who will organize everything for your party — from the food and decorations, to the entertainment and the cleaning up. Once again, it depends on the budget.

You can hire staff to act as waiters and cleaners, leaving you free to enjoy the party. You can hire instant entertainment and wonderful decorations, creating a terrific atmosphere and ensuring that everyone has a good time.

Few homes have enough glassware, cutlery or crockery for lots of guests. Hiring quickly solves that problem. Hiring also solves the problem of location. If your house won't do, why not erect a marquee in the back garden?

If you want to do all the cooking yourself, hiring can make the task easier. You can hire microwave ovens or pie warmers to help out. The same applies to the barbecue. If you can't fit enough meat on your own, you can always hire a spit or rotisserie.

What you can hire

A quick check through your telephone book will reveal the full extent of the wonderful world of hiring. To start with, you can hire glasses, often from your local hotel. There is usually an extensive range including beer glasses, wine glasses, champagne flutes and liqueur glasses. If you search around you may also find a company which hires the best quality crystal glassware. A variety of cutlery is available too, from ordinary stainless steel to ornate silver. The same range of styles applies to crockery. You can hire simple, plain dinner plates or a complete English china dinner service with gold trim.

Marquees now come in a variety of sizes, shapes and colors. Almost gone forever are the pieces of green tarpaulin that used to pass for a marquee. Hire a simple, old-fashioned marquee or choose a magnificent, white, silk-lined one.

To furnish the marquee, tables are available in many sizes and shapes — round, square, oblong, trestle-style, high or low. You will even be able to hire crisp white cloths and flounces to dress up the tables. Naturally there are chairs for the tables too.

You can either hire an expert caterer to do the cooking for you — usually in your own home with their equipment — or you can hire the equipment and do the cooking yourself. Popular are rotisseries, or spit roasts which you can hire with or without meat and with or without a chef. You can also choose electric or gas barbecues, pie ovens, hot water urns and microwave ovens.

Hired staff, including experienced bar staff, will enhance the atmosphere as well as making the party more enjoyable for everyone. Waiters and waitresses in black and white look very smart, or they will dress in national costumes or novelty outfits such as jockey silks.

Entertaining the party

Entertainment is a vital ingredient in any good party. Discos are very popular, especially for young people. You can either hire a full disco complete with disc jockey, light show, dance floor and professional sound system, or just the sound system and/or dance floor. Live bands are also popular — and during the breaks you can play music videos on a giant, hired video screen. For small children there are clowns, magicians, puppeteers and gangsters for hire.

The party mood or atmosphere can also be helped along by hiring — especially with a theme party. A children's choir or string quartet will set the scene for a delightful Viennese afternoon tea, or a jazz band for a 'twenties' party. If you decide to go Arabian, why not hire a camel? It is bound to impress your guests! Children will be delighted with a mini farm including ducks, sheep and rabbits. If you have something special to announce at a party, why not call on the services of a costumed town crier.

Decorations set the scene. Hire plants such as palms and orchids, or helium balloons, flags and kites. Some caterers offer a design service where they organise the entire party, including the decorations, and can offer intriguing novelties such as elaborate ice carvings for the tables. To record the fun for posterity, why not video it all? And, for a quick getaway, you can arrange for a helicopter to come and collect you!

A word about breakages: In virtually every instance, the hirer is responsible for damages and breakages. And, while all companies will have some form of public liability insurance (if, for example, someone trips over a marquee rope and hurts themselves) you may also like to insure yourself.

All companies will deliver and most expect cash on delivery. If you employ a catering company, they will expect a substantial deposit some time before the date of the party.

Menu Number 4

Supper Party for 8-10 Hungry Young

Crudites with Curry Dip
Mexican Nachos
Crunchy Tuna Pie
Veal Scaloppine
Baby Buttered Potatoes
Green Salad
Chocolate Flake Cheesecake

This party starts with two spicy entrees, combining the smooth and crunchy textures of dips with the heat of curry and chili. There are two main dishes — don't count on your young eating from only one of them. The simple salad and potato dishes can be easily prepared in large quantities, and are sure to please everyone. There's no need to keep them *only* for the young. The dessert is a rich creamy cheesecake, chocolate-flavored, the high note of the meal, as your young guests are sure to tell you.

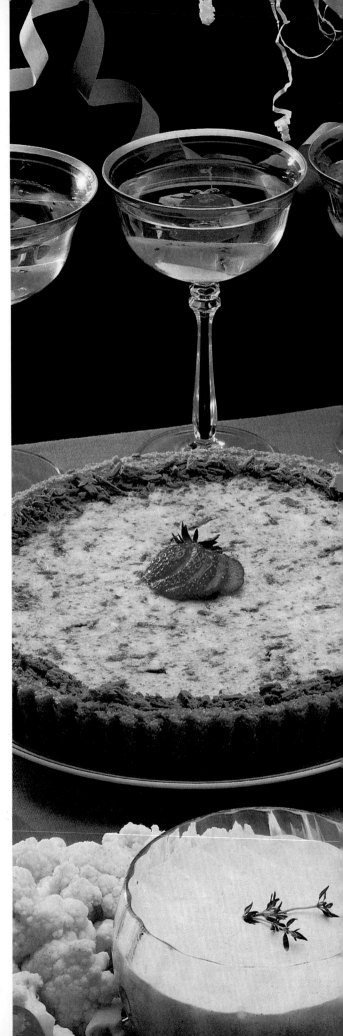

Baby Buttered Potatoes and Green Salad (top); Chocolate Flake Cheesecake, Veal Scaloppine and Mexican Nachos (center); Crudites with Curry Dip and Crunchy Tuna Pie (bottom)

Preparation Timetable

Week ahead: Buy party fare: hats, balloons, paper napkins, tablecloths etc.

Day ahead: Prepare Mexican Bean Dip. Set aside covered in refrigerator.

Prepare Guacamole. Set aside covered in refrigerator.

Cut vegetables for crudites. Place into bowl. Cover with water and plastic wrap. Refrigerate.

Prepare and cook Crunchy Tuna Pie. Do not add potato straws. Cover pie and refrigerate.

Prepare Veal Scaloppine. Do not complete last 10 minutes of cooking. Cover and refrigerate.

Prepare Chocolate Flake Cheesecake. Decorate with extra flakes and refrigerate.

Place cold drinks into refrigerator to chill. Check tablecloth, napkins, glassware, dinnerware and cutlery. Make sure that all are clean and polished, ready to use. Prepare any after-dinner chocolates and store in an airtight container.

3 hours before: Set table with tablecloth, napkins, glassware, dinnerware and cutlery and arrange decorations. Prepare tray for pre-dinner drinks and party starters.

2 hours before: Prepare Curry Dip. Place into serving bowl, cover and refrigerate.

1 hour before: Remove Crunchy Tuna Pie and Veal Scaloppine from refrigerator. Set aside on bench uncovered.

Peel potatoes for Baby Buttered Potatoes. Place in dish and cover. Cook and set aside. Grate cheese for Nachos and set aside.

30 minutes before: Prepare Green Salad, arrange in serving bowl but do not add dressing. Cover and refrigerate.

Cook Baby Buttered Potatoes. Leave covered. Set aside.

15 minutes before: Cut cheesecake into portions.

Cook Veal Scaloppine on medium high 10 minutes. Top Crunchy Tuna Pie with potato straws. Cook on medium 10 minutes.

Suppertime: Drain vegetables and place around Curry Dip ready to serve.

Place Mexican Bean Dip in serving bowl. Top with corn chips and cheese and cook on high 3 minutes per bowl. Add 2 tablespoons Guacamole and 1 tablespoon sour cream in each bowl. Serve hot with corn chips.

Place Crunchy Tuna Pie, Veal Scaloppine, Baby Buttered Potatoes and Green Salad on table and let the young people serve themselves.

Serve Chocolate Flake Cheesecake.

Crudites with Curry Dip

8 oz cream cheese
2 tablespoons milk
1 teaspoon curry paste
¼ teaspoon onion salt
1 cup sour cream

Crudites

green beans, blanched
broccoli and cauliflower florets, blanched
carrot matchsticks
button mushrooms
celery slices
green and red peppers, finely sliced

Time: 1½ minutes. Serves 6–

Cut cream cheese into cubes and place in a bowl. Cook on high 30–40 seconds.

Blend in milk, curry paste and onion salt and cook on high 1 minute. Stir to blend.

Mix in sour cream and serve with crudites.

Mexican Nachos

10 oz corn chips
2 cups grated Cheddar cheese
10 fl oz sour cream

Mexican Bean Dip

1 × 13 oz can red kidney beans, drained
2 teaspoons chili sauce
freshly ground black pepper
1 green chili, chopped
1 small onion, finely chopped

Guacamole

1 tomato
1 large ripe avocado, halved and seeded
1 tablespoon finely chopped onion
1 teaspoon olive oil
1 teaspoon lemon juice
½ teaspoon salt
freshly ground black pepper
1 clove garlic, crushed

Time: 10½ minutes. Serves 10–1

Place all ingredients for Mexican Bean Dip in blender bowl. Chop roughly. Set aside.

For Guacamole, slit skin around outside of tomato and place in oven. Cook on high 30 seconds. Peel tomato and chop finely.

Scoop out flesh of avocado and mash. Combine tomato pulp, avocado, onion, olive oil, lemon juice, salt, pepper and garlic. Blend till smooth.

In each of 4 shallow serving bowls, place 2 tablespoons Mexican Bean Dip. Top with half the corn chips and all the grated Cheddar cheese. Cook 2 bowls at a time on high 4– minutes. Spoon over 2 tablespoons Guacamole and top with 1 tablespoon sour cream. Serve hot, with rest of corn chips.

Crunchy Tuna Pie

oz noodles
cups boiling water
 teaspoon salt
oz grated Cheddar cheese
 cup sour cream
hard-boiled eggs, shelled and chopped
teaspoon tomato paste
cups drained and flaked tuna
lt and pepper to taste
oz packet potato straws

Time: 20 minutes. Serves 8–10

ace noodles, water and salt into 3½ pint casserole dish.
over and cook on high 10 minutes. Stand in hot water for
 minutes. Drain noodles. Combine with Cheddar cheese,
ur cream, hard-boiled eggs, tomato paste, tuna, salt and
epper.
 Place mixture in shallow baking dish. Top with potato
raws. Cook uncovered on medium 10 minutes. Serve hot.

Veal Scaloppine: **Step 1** Coat veal with breadcrumbs, Parmesan
cheese, parsley and seasonings

unchy Tuna Pie: **Step 1** Combine cooked noodles with cheese,
ur cream, eggs, tomato paste, tuna and seasonings.

Step 2 Arrange veal in shallow dish and add tomato mixture and
mozzarella cheese

ep 2 Top with potato chips

Veal Scaloppine

8 veal steaks
¼ cup seasoned breadcrumbs
⅓ cup Parmesan cheese
1 tablespoon chopped parsley
salt and pepper to taste
1 teaspoon basil
1 egg, beaten
1 × 27 oz can whole peeled tomatoes
4 oz mozzarella cheese, grated

Time: 22 minutes. Serves 8–10

Pound veal steaks and slice in half. Combine seasoned
breadcrumbs, tablespoon Parmesan cheese, parsley, salt,
pepper and basil. Dip veal in egg and coat with crumb
mixture. Place veal on microwave roasting rack. Cook on
medium high uncovered 10–12 minutes turning once.

Chop whole tomatoes. Layer veal steaks, tomato mixture
and mozzarella cheese in shallow dish. Sprinkle surface
with rest of Parmesan cheese. Cook on medium high 10
minutes. Serve hot with a green salad garnished with
orange segments.

Baby Buttered Potatoes

1 lb baby potatoes
2 oz butter
2 tablespoons chopped parsley
celery salt

Time: 12 minutes. Serves 8–10

Place potatoes, butter and parsley in shallow dish. Cover with plastic wrap. Cook on high 12 minutes. Stand covered 5 minutes. Serve hot, sprinkled with celery salt.

Chocolate Flake Cheesecake

1½ cups semi-sweet cookie
    crumbs
2 tablespoons sugar
½ teaspoon cinnamon
½ teaspoon nutmeg
6 tablespoons butter, melted
4 cups cream-style cottage cheese
1 cup sour cream
6 eggs, beaten
1½ cups sugar
½ cup flour
pinch salt
3 chocolate flake candy bars,
    crumbled
1 teaspoon rum extract

Time: 23 minutes. Serves 8–10

Combine semi-sweet cookie crumbs, sugar, cinnamon, nut meg and butter. Press mixture into base and sides of 10 inch cake dish. Cook on high 3 minutes. Chill till set.

Combine cottage cheese, sour cream, eggs and sugar. Beat thoroughly. Fold in sifted flour and salt. Fold in 2 flake candy bars and rum extract. Pour mixture into cookie crust. Cook on medium 15–20 minutes. Stand 10 minutes. Decorate with extra flake candy bar. Serve cold.

Party Starters

Nibbles are very popular with the young. Not only are they tasty, but you can use them to break the ice by giving a platt to someone a bit shy. Offering the nibbly bits around encourages them to move from one group to another, while finding their feet.

Pork Balls with Dipping Sauce

2 oz pork, ground
1 cup seasoned breadcrumbs
¼ cup Parmesan cheese
1 tablespoon finely chopped
    parsley
⅛ teaspoon cayenne pepper
2 eggs

Time: 10 minutes. Makes

Crumble pork into a bowl and cook on high 4 minutes, stirri after 2 minutes. Drain well. Blend in remaining ingredien

Using a teaspoon, shape mixture into small balls. Chill 15 minutes. Put a toothpick into each ball.

Line a 12 inch plate with paper towel and place 24 ba evenly around the edge. Cook on high for 3 minutes or ur firm and heated through. Repeat with remaining balls.

Dipping Sauce

1 tablespoon French mustard
½ cup bechamel sauce (see recipe)

Blend mustard into the sauce. Serve in a small bowl.

Prune and Bacon Rolls

12 pitted prunes
12 blanched almonds
4 bacon slices
12 cocktail sticks

Time: 9 minutes. Makes

Place one almond in each pitted prune. Cut bacon slices in thirds and wrap one strip around each prune. Fasten with cocktail stick.

Heat browning dish on high 6 minutes. Cook bacon rolls high 1½ minutes, turn and cook a further 1½ minutes. Ser hot.

Pork Balls with Dipping Sauce (top
Chinese Ravioli (center) and Salami Whirls (botto

280

Salami Whirls

2 sheets ready-rolled frozen pie
  dough, thawed
1 egg yolk, beaten
1 tablespoon chopped parsley
1 tablespoon sesame seeds
8 slices salami
extra sesame seeds

Time: 30 minutes. Makes 36

Lightly brush one side of pie dough with egg yolk and sprinkle with parsley and sesame seeds. Arrange the salami slices on pie dough then carefully roll up into a log shape. Brush with egg and sprinkle with sesame seeds.

Slice log into 2 inch wide pieces and place flat on wax proof paper on 2 or 3 microwave-safe platters. Cook each platter on high 8–10 minutes. When cooked, allow to cool on a cake rack and serve cold.

Salami Whirls: **Step 1** Sprinkle parsley and sesame seeds over pie dough

Step 2 Spread salami over pie dough

Step 3 Roll up pie dough and slice into 2 inch wide pieces

Chinese Ravioli

8 oz pork, ground
4 oz uncooked shrimp meat, ground
4 dried mushrooms, soaked in
  warm water for 20 minutes
  and finely chopped
1 scallion, finely chopped
1 tablespoon soy sauce
½ teaspoon salt
½ teaspoon sesame oil
1 beaten egg yolk
30 dim sim (Chinese) pie dough sheets
1 egg white
6–8 cups boiling water
¼ cup oil

Time: 20 or 35 minutes. Makes 3

Combine pork and shrimp meat, mushrooms and scallion together in a small bowl. Mix in the soy sauce, salt and sesame oil and stir in the beaten egg yolk so that the mixture resembles a thick paste.

Place 1 teaspoon of filling into center of each dim sim sheet. Brush edges with egg white. Fold over sheet to form a triangle or fold opposite corners together. Press edges to seal.

Steamed method: Pour boiling water into a large casserole. Add half the triangles, cover and cook on medium 1 minutes. Drain and repeat with remaining triangles.

Fried method: Preheat browning dish on high 5 minutes. Add oil and cook in batches of 6 on high for 4–6 minutes turning once while each batch is cooking.

Serve with Pork Balls Dipping Sauce (*see recipe*) or ready made chili sauce.

Pie Dough Pizzas

2 sheets ready-rolled frozen pie
  dough, thawed
½ cup tomato paste
1 onion, finely chopped
1 teaspoon oregano
salt to taste
freshly ground black pepper
2 oz mushrooms, sliced
¼ cup black olives
16 slices salami
1 tablespoon chopped parsley
8 oz mozzarella cheese, grated
paprika

Time: 36 minutes. Serves

Cut pie dough into quarters. Combine tomato paste, onion, oregano, salt and pepper. Spread a small amount of topping over each square and top with mushrooms, olives and salami. Sprinkle with mozzarella, parsley and paprika.

Preheat browning dish on high 6 minutes. Cook squares 4 at a time, on high 15 minutes a batch. Stand 1 minute before serving.

Cheese and Liverwurst Ro

Cheese and Liverwurst Roll

oz cream cheese
oz liverwurst
finely chopped scallions
teaspoon Worcestershire sauce
cup finely chopped parsley

Time: 1½ minutes. Serves 6–8

ut cream cheese into eighths. Place into bowl. Cook on
edium 1½ minutes to soften. Add liverwurst, scallions
nd Worcestershire sauce and blend together.

Turn out onto a piece of plastic wrap 8 × 14 inch. Form
to a log shape 1½ inch thick by rolling in plastic wrap.
hill until set and remove plastic wrap.

Spread parsley onto pie dough board, place cheese roll
to board and roll to coat evenly with parsley.

Serve garnished with Melba toast, assorted crackers and
elery sticks.

Cheese and Liverwurst Roll: **Step 1** Combine softened cheese, scallions, liverwurst and sauce

Melba Toast

slices day-old sliced white
bread

Time: 13 minutes. Makes 48

emove crusts from day-old sliced bread. Cut each slice
to 4 rounds using round 2 inch cutter and then carefully
ut each through the middle producing very thin rounds.

Heat browning dish on high 5 minutes. Cook 12 rounds
t a time on high 1 minute on each side or until crisp.

Step 2 Coat rolled cheese with chopped parsley

The Party Platter

The main course for a party needs to look good but more importantly there must be plenty of it. Depending on the number of guests, you will need two or three main dishes. Choose those that can be prepared in advance as much as possible, and take care to provide variety with taste and color and texture. Ethnic dishes add a touch of the exotic and are popular with the 12–20 age group these days. Our international selection of party platters combines the taste of tangy herbs and spices with the unbeatable flavor of home cooking.

Mexican Tacos

1 lb ground beef
1 onion, finely chopped
2 tablespoons oil
¼ cup tomato paste
1 teaspoon mixed herbs
½ teaspoon chili powder
1 green chili, finely chopped
salt and pepper to taste
dash tabasco sauce
dash cayenne pepper
8–10 taco shells
1 lettuce, shredded
2 tomatoes, chopped
½ cup grated Cheddar cheese
10 fl oz sour cream

Time: 20½ minutes. Serves 8–

Place beef, onion, oil, tomato paste, mixed herbs, chili powde green chili, salt, pepper, tabasco sauce and cayenne pepp into shallow dish. Cover and cook on high 10 minutes, stirri twice.

Uncover and cook on medium 10 minutes. Set aside.

Place 8–10 taco shells upside down on baking sheet. Coc on high 30 seconds. Serve taco shells filled with lettuce, tor ato, meat mixture, sprinkled with cheese and a spoonful sour cream.

Cannelloni Crepes

Crepes

1¼ cups all-purpose flour
pinch salt
1 egg, beaten
10 fl oz milk
1 tablespoon butter

Mexican Tacos

Filling

lb veal, ground
onion, finely chopped
tablespoon finely chopped parsley
lt and pepper to taste
clove garlic, crushed
tablespoon oil
× 27 oz can whole peeled tomatoes
teaspoon basil
oz mozzarella cheese, grated
cup Parmesan cheese

Time: 35 minutes. Serves 6–8

ft flour and salt, gradually beat in egg and milk to form
atter. Cover and stand 30 minutes. Grease crepe pan with
mall portion of butter. Drop spoonfuls of mixture onto hot
an. Tilt pan to allow batter to cover base. Cook till mixture
ts. Turn. Cook for an extra few seconds. Remove and cool.
ayer wax paper between crepes.

Combine veal, onion, parsley, salt, pepper, garlic and oil in
rge casserole dish. Cover and cook in microwave on high
-10 minutes. Stir twice during cooking.

Add tomatoes and basil. Combine evenly. Cook uncovered
high 5 minutes then reduce to medium and cook a further
minutes. Allow to cool slightly.

Place 2 tablespoons of meat mixture on center of each crepe.
oll up. Place, roll side down, in shallow dish. Continue cover-
g base of dish with crepe cannelloni. Top with half the
ated mozzarella cheese and half the Parmesan cheese. Add
econd layer of crepe cannelloni and top with remaining
ozzarella and Parmesan cheeses.

Cook on high 5 minutes then reduce to medium and cook
further 10 minutes. Allow to stand 5 minutes. Serve hot.

Cannelloni Crepes: **Step 1** Make crepes in the conventional way

Step 2 Combine ingredients for filling

nnelloni Crepes

Step 3 Fill and roll up crepes

285

Pork and Mushroom Stroganoff

1 lb pork fillet, sliced thinly
1 medium onion, peeled and
*   sliced*
½ teaspoon basil
3 tablespoons oil
4 oz button mushrooms

2 tablespoons cornstarch
salt and pepper to taste
1 cup chicken stock
10 fl oz sour cream
1 tablespoon chopped parsley

Time: 30 minutes. Serves 6–8

Place pork, onion, basil and 1 tablespoon oil in shallo[w]
dish. Cover and cook on medium high 10 minutes stirri[ng]
once. Add mushrooms and cook a further 5 minutes [on]
medium. Set aside.

Combine rest of oil, cornstarch, salt, pepper and stock [in]
glass jug. Cook on high 3–5 minutes. Stir vigorously whe[n]
cooked. Fold through pork mixture. Cover and cook [on]
medium 5 minutes. Add sour cream and parsley. S[tir]
through evenly. Cook uncovered on high 5 minutes. Ser[ve]
hot with rice or noodles.

Step 1 Combine pork, onion, basil and oil

Step 2 Add mushrooms

Step 3 Add oil, cornflour, stock and seasonings

Pork and Mushroom Stroganoff served with pasta

Drum Favorites

chicken or 6 turkey
drumsticks

Poppy Seed Coating

cup cornmeal (polenta)
tablespoons poppy seeds
teaspoons paprika
Dip: 2 beaten eggs
tablespoons melted butter

Basil Coating

½ cups seasoned stuffing mix
teaspoon basil
teaspoon garlic powder
Dip: 1 beaten egg
tablespoons milk or 1
additional beaten egg
tablespoons melted butter

Time: 25 minutes. Serves 6–8

Spicy Rice Salad and Turkey Drumsticks with Tangy Barbecue Coating

Remove skin from drumsticks. Combine coating ingredients in a shallow dish. Cool melted butter and beat into eggs. Combine dip ingredients and brush over drumsticks. Dredge in coating, pressing into each drumstick.

Place drumsticks on microwave roasting rack with the thick end near the outer edge. Cook on high 10 minutes. Turn and cook further 8–15 minutes or until juice runs clear.

Tangy Barbecue Baste

juice and rind 1 orange
1 tablespoon honey
½ teaspoon chili sauce
1 tablespoon barbecue sauce
freshly ground black pepper
1 tablespoon oil
1 teaspoon dried thyme

Combine orange juice and rind, honey, chili sauce, barbecue sauce, pepper, oil and thyme in glass jug. Cook on high 1 minute.

Coat drumsticks with baste. Place in shallow dish with thick end near the edge of dish. Cook on medium high 15 minutes, turn and cook further 10 minutes or until juice runs clear.

Satay Chicken Teriyaki

1 lb chicken fillets
6 scallions

Marinade

½ cup soy sauce
¼ cup honey
1 clove garlic, crushed
½ teaspoon ground ginger
2–3 tablespoons oil

Time: 28 minutes. Serves 6–8

Cut fillets into ¾ inch cubes. Combine marinade ingredients with 2 tablespoons oil in bowl. Add chicken and toss to coat. Marinate 30 minutes.

Trim scallions and cut into ¾ inch lengths. Place 5 chicken cubes onto each satay stick with a piece of scallion in between. Brush chicken with oil. Heat browning dish on high 8 minutes. Place 6 satays on dish and cook on high 10 minutes turning sticks every 3 minutes. Brush with remaining marinade and oil. Cook remaining satays and serve arranged on rice platter.

Savory Lasagne

Savory Lasagne

8 sheets short lasagne
2 cups boiling water
½ teaspoon salt
1 × 27 oz can whole peeled
    tomatoes, chopped
½ teaspoon basil
8 oz peperoni sausage, sliced
1 onion, finely chopped
1 clove garlic, crushed
freshly ground black pepper
8 oz ricotta cheese
2 eggs, beaten
½ cup cream
8 oz mozzarella cheese, grated
¼ cup Parmesan cheese

Time: 31 minutes. Serves 8–10

Place 4 sheets short lasagne in a shallow dish, add boiling water and salt. Cover with plastic wrap and cook on high 4 minutes. Carefully lift out pasta and allow to drain. Cook remaining lasagne on high 4 minutes and drain.

Mix together tomatoes, basil, peperoni sausage, onion, garlic and black pepper and set aside. Combine ricotta cheese, eggs and cream in glass jug. Cook on high 3 minutes, stirring twice.

Starting with lasagne sheets, arrange lasagne, tomato and sausage mixture and ricotta sauce in layers in a greased shallow dish. Sprinkle ricotta layer with grated mozzarella and Parmesan cheeses. Top with ricotta mix and Parmesan cheese.

Cook on medium high 10 minutes, then reduce power and cook on medium 10 minutes. Stand 5 minutes uncovered. Serve hot.

Sweet and Sour Meat Kebabs

3 lb leg lamb, deboned
12 bacon slices, rind removed

Marinade

½ cup raisins
1 cup ketchup
1 cup dry white wine
¼ cup brown sugar
2 teaspoons Worcestershire
    sauce
½ teaspoon ground ginger
salt and pepper to taste

Time: 30 minutes. Makes 30 keba

Cut lamb meat into 1 inch cubes and thread alternate onto wooden satay sticks with bacon rolls. Place kebabs shallow dish.

Combine raisins, ketchup, white wine, sugar, Worceste shire sauce, ginger, salt and pepper. Baste kebabs wi marinade. Cover with plastic wrap and marinate 1 hours. Drain

Arrange 15 kebabs in a circular pattern on microwav safe platter. Cook on medium high 15 minutes. Repe cooking remaining kebabs. Reheat all kebabs (arrange t cooler ones on top) on high 2 minutes. Serve immediatel

Salad Time

alads are the perfect party food. They are easy on the eye, ontributing to the festive air. They are simple to make and asy to eat single-handed: fork food. With fresh fruit and vegables available all year round, the salad is a popular party hoice. Here we have included cooked salads, using the microwave, to extend your salad vocabulary.

Sour Cream Potato Salad

large potatoes
tablespoons vinaigrette (see recipe)
cup peeled and seeded
  cucumber or dill cucumber,
  cut into ¾ inch dice
cup celery, in ¾ inch dice
scallions, in ¾ inch dice
hard-boiled eggs in ¾ inch dice
cup Microwave Mayonnaise (see recipe)
cup sour cream
tablespoon horseradish
lt and ground pepper to taste
slices rindless bacon
ely cut chives

Time: 22 minutes. Serves 10–12

ace bacon slices between 2 sheets of white paper towel. ook on high 3 minutes. Cut into cubes.
  Prick each potato several times with skewer. Wrap potatoes plastic wrap. Space out evenly in oven. Cook 15 minutes or ntil tender, turning over halfway through cooking. Remove astic wrap.
  Peel potatoes, cut into ¾ inch cubes, place in bowl and pour ver vinaigrette. When cool add cucumber, celery, scallions d eggs.
  Blend mayonnaise, sour cream and horseradish together. ur over salad and toss lightly. Garnish with bacon and ives.

Microwave Mayonnaise

egg yolks, beaten
fl oz cream
cup dry white wine
teaspoons prepared French mustard
tablespoon lemon juice
eshly ground black pepper
tablespoon finely chopped parsley

Time: 7 minutes. Makes 1½ cups

ace all ingredients in glass jug. Cook on medium 5–7 min-es, stirring every minute, to thicken. Serve over vegetables salad.

Broccoli Salad

1¼ lb fresh broccoli
3 hard-boiled eggs, chopped
3 oz dried red pimiento or
    pepper, finely diced
10 black olives, stoned and chopped

Time: 6 minutes. Serves 6–8

Prepare broccoli by cutting into florets. Place into plastic bag with 1 tablespoon water and fold in open edge. Cook on high 5–6 minutes. Plunge broccoli in chilled water and drain well.
  Arrange broccoli on flat salad platter. Moisten with Italian dressing (see recipe). Garnish with chopped eggs, pimiento or peppers and olives.

Italian Dressing

¼ cup olive oil
2 tablespoons strained lemon juice
1 teaspoon grated lemon zest
salt to taste
½ teaspoon oregano
1 clove garlic, finely chopped
1 tablespoon grated Parmesan cheese
½ teaspoon freshly ground pepper

Combine all ingredients, mix well and chill. Store in an airtight container. Mix again before using.

Broccoli Salad

Spicy Rice Salad

8 oz long grain rice
2 cups water
1 inch piece green ginger
salt and pepper to taste
dash nutmeg
½ teaspoon powdered
    coriander seed
1 tablespoon lemon juice
1 scallion, finely chopped
5 tablespoons olive oil
2 oz raisins
2 oz currants
4 dried apricots, chopped
1 oz toasted almonds (see recipe)

Time: 19 minutes. Serves 4–6

Combine all ingredients, except almonds. Place in 3½ pt casserole dish. Cover and cook on high 10 minutes, then a further 5 minutes on medium. Allow to stand 5 minutes before serving. Serve hot or cold.

Toasting Almonds

Place 3 tablespoons butter and almonds into small bowl. Microwave on high 3–4 minutes until golden, stirring every minute.

Use almond flavored butter for basting vegetable and chicken kebabs.

Spicy Rice Salad: **Step 1** Combine rice and vegetables

Step 2 Add 2 cups water, then cover and cook on high

Avocado Jelly Salad

1 tablespoon gelatin
2 tablespoons cold water
1 × 4 oz packet lime jelly
2 cups hot water
1 cup mashed ripe avocado
½ cup ready-made mayonnaise
½ cup sour cream
fresh dill or mint sprigs for garnish

Time: 6 minutes. Serves 1

Place water and gelatin in small bowl. Stir to dissolve. Th gelatin will absorb the water. Place in oven and cook o medium 30–60 seconds until dissolved.

Place 2 cups water in large bowl. Cook on high 5 min utes. Blend in jelly crystals and gelatin, stir to dissolve Chill until partially set. Fold in avocado, mayonnaise an cream. Pour into a ring or jelly mold greased with extr mayonnaise. Chill until firm.

Unmold onto a bed of crisp salad greens. Garnish wit fresh fruit or seafood, sprigs of fresh dill or mint. Serv chilled.

Pineapple and Vegetable Kebabs

1 × 16 oz can pineapple pieces
1 large red pepper, cut into ¾
    inch pieces
1 large green pepper, cut into
    ¾ inch pieces
1 large onion, cut into ¾ inch
    pieces
6–8 bamboo satay sticks

Glaze

½ cup honey
1 tablespoon French mustard

Time: 15 minutes. Serves 6

Combine honey and mustard in small basin. Heat o medium 3–4 minutes then set aside. Place pieces of pin apple, onion, red pepper, pineapple, green pepper alte nately on satay sticks. Repeat if sticks are long.

Heat browning dish on high 5 minutes. Place one tab spoon of oil in dish. Using a piece of white paper tow spread oil over dish. Brush kebabs with honey glaze a cook 6 minutes on high turning and basting after 3 mi utes. Pour remaining glaze over kebabs before serving.

The Staff of Life

n essential nutrient, bread is often the life and soul of a party
o — or at least of the eating side of it. Bread is easy 'finger'
od, and an excellent basis for the most exotic topping you
n think of, or the simplest. After you try these recipes, you
ay not want to 'dress' the bread at all.

Whole Wheat Bread Sticks

Vitamin C tablet
tablespoons brown sugar
tablespoons compressed yeast
½ cups lukewarm water
cup whole wheat flour
oz butter

Time: Microwave 60 minutes. Makes 4
Conventional 25 minutes

ace all ingredients in a bowl. Blend together and cook on
arm 15–20 minutes or until mixture doubles in bulk.

cup vegetable oil
cups whole wheat flour
cup cracked wheat
cup gluten flour
teaspoons warm salted water
cup rolled oats

lend oil and dry ingredients in a large bowl. Stir in yeast
ixture and mix with table knife to form a dough. Knead 5
inutes on lightly-floured board. Return dough to basin and
ess out onto the sides of the basin until 1 inch thick. Cover
ith plastic wrap. Cook on warm 20 minutes or until doubled
bulk.
  Punch down dough to release the carbon dioxide gas. Knead
r 5 minutes. Cut dough into quarters and shape into four
read sticks. Place on large tray and cover lightly with plastic
rap. Cook on warm 20 minutes or until doubled in bulk.
  Transfer to a greased tray. Brush each stick with warm
ater and sprinkle with rolled oats. Bake in conventional oven
400°F for 20–25 minutes until bread is well risen and crisp
d sounds hollow when tapped. Cool before serving.

Whole Wheat Bread Sticks

Pumpkin Biscuit Ring

2 tablespoons butter
2 tablespoons sugar
1 cup cooked pumpkin, mashed
1 small onion, finely chopped
2 tablespoons finely chopped parsley
1 egg, beaten
½ cup milk
2½ cups self-rising flour, sifted
½ teaspoon salt
assorted vegetable and cheese
    sticks: carrot, celery, red and
    green pepper, cucumber

Time: 8 minutes. Makes 1 ring

Grease and line a ring mold. Cream butter and sugar. Add pumpkin, onion and parsley. Blend in beaten egg and milk. Add flour and salt. Mix with a table knife to form a dough. Place in ring mold. Cook on high 7–8 minutes. Let stand 3–4 minutes before turning out to cool.

Fill center of biscuit ring with assorted vegetable and cheese sticks.

Note: For 1 cup of pumpkin you will require 12 oz raw pumpkin. Peel and seed pumpkin, prick with skewer. Wrap in plastic wrap. Cook on high 4–5 minutes until tender then mash and leave to cool.

Cheese and Bacon Ring

½ oz dried yeast
5 fl oz warm milk
4 fl oz warm water
1 tablespoon oil
1 egg, beaten
3½ cups whole wheat flour
1 teaspoon salt
1 tablespoon brown sugar
¼ cup bacon, diced
¼ cup Cheddar cheese, diced
½ teaspoon mustard powder
4 slices Swiss cheese
paprika
1 tablespoon finely chopped parsley

Time: 9 minutes. Makes 1 loaf

Combine yeast, milk and water. Blend till smooth. Add oil and beaten egg. Combine 3 cups whole wheat flour, salt and sugar. Add bacon, cheese and mustard powder. Mix together.

Pour in milk and yeast mixture. Sprinkle over remaining ½ cup flour. Cover with plastic wrap. Allow to stand in a warm place till mixture 'bubbles'. Uncover and combine ingredients to form a soft dough ball.

Place mixture into greased ring mold. Cover with plastic wrap. Stand 30 minutes in a warm place until doubled in size.

Cook on medium 7 minutes, then top with Swiss cheese and sprinkle with paprika and parsley. Cook a further 1–2 minutes on high. Allow to cool slightly in mold 10 minutes. Turn out onto cake rack. Serve warm.

Cheese and Ham Loaf

1 stick French bread
8–10 slices Swiss cheese
8–10 slices ham

Time: 2 minutes. Serves 8–1

Slice French bread into 8–10 portions. Between each slic place 1 slice cheese and 1 slice ham. Place loaf into servin basket. Cook on high 1–2 minutes. Cheese will melt. Serv slices with melted cheese and ham.

Cheese and Bacon Ring: **Step 1** Combine cheese, bacon and dry ingredients

Step 2 Add dissolved yeast, oil, and egg, milk and water

Cheese and Ham Loaf (top); Cheese and Bacon Ring (bottom

The Sweet Tooth

ome of these rich desserts are designed to tempt and delight
he younger teens, some are better offered to the older teens.
hey are visually the center of attention and the 'point' of the
arty with a purpose, such as birthdays or victory feasts.

Pavlova

ase

egg white
cup confectioners' sugar

Marshmallow Pavlova

egg whites
cup superfine sugar
teaspoon cream of tartar
0 fl oz whipped cream
cup chopped strawberries
cup almond flakes
orange, halved and thinly sliced
ark chocolate, melted

Time: 3 minutes. Serves 8–10

ombine egg white and confectioners' sugar to form a soft
ough. Roll out to fit 10–12 inch microwave-safe platter and
et aside.

Whisk egg whites for marshmallow pavlova till stiff. Beat in
uperfine sugar and cream of tartar. Ensure that mixture is
ery stiff. Pipe pavlova mixture around edge of base to form
est shape. Spoon remaining mixture into center of base.
mooth with knife.

Cook on high 3 minutes. Stand in oven for 5 minutes.
emove and decorate with whipped cream, strawberries,
lmond flakes, orange slices and piped chocolate. Crushed
alnuts and passionfruit also make an attractive garnish.

Chocolate Truffles

oz butter
0 fl oz milk cooking chocolate
tablespoon rum
cup sour cream
xtra 2 oz chocolate, grated

Time: 4 minutes. Makes 18–22 balls

reak up chocolate. Place butter, chocolate and rum into 3½
int mixing bowl. Cook on high 3–4 minutes. Stir to melt
hocolate. Fold in sour cream. Pour mixture into shallow dish.
llow to chill for 1 hour in refrigerator.

Quickly spoon 1 teaspoon of mixture onto grated chocolate,
orking to form a ball. Coat with extra grated chocolate. Chill
ll set.

Pineapple Fruit Salad Meringue

1 firm ripe pineapple
1 can fruit salad or two fruits,
    drained
4 tablespoons Cointreau or
    Grand Marnier

Meringue

3 egg whites
½ cup superfine sugar
¼ cup toasted almond slivers
12 glace cherries

Time: 3 minutes. Serves 12

Cut pineapple in half lengthwise through top. Remove flesh
from each pineapple half. Cut out core, dice pineapple into ¾
inch pieces and combine with fruit salad and Cointreau. Marinate 15 minutes. Return mixture to pineapple cases.

Beat egg whites until stiff peaks form. Gradually beat in
sugar, spread meringue over fruit and top with cherries and
almonds. Cook on high 2–3 minutes until set.

Chocolate Truffles

Chocolate Nut Ice Cream Cake

Cake

8 oz almond flakes
1 packet chocolate cake mix
2 oz butter, melted
2 eggs
½ cup milk
1 tablespoon rum

Ice Cream

6 egg yolks, beaten
2 cups sugar
3 oz milk chocolate
1¾ cups confectioners' sugar
1 tablespoon drinking
  chocolate
4 × 10 fl oz cream, whipped

Garnish (optional)

4 strawberries
1 kiwi fruit, peeled and sliced
2 tablespoons cherry brandy

Time: 25 minutes. Serves 10–12

Combine almond flakes, chocolate cake mix, butter, 2 eggs and milk. Blend together till smooth. Pour batter into a 9 inch cake dish. Cook on medium 15 minutes. Stand 10 minutes, uncovered.

Crumble cake, add rum to crumbs. Set aside.

Combine egg yolks and sugar in 3½ pint casserole dish. Cook on medium 5–7 minutes. Stir twice. Set aside. Break up chocolate into glass jug. Cook on high 2–3 minutes. Stir.

Sift together confectioners' sugar and drinking chocolate. Fold together egg yolk mixture, melted chocolate, confectioners' sugar, drinking chocolate and cream. Blend evenly.

Press 1 cup cake crumble into 9 inch spring-form cake tin then pour over 2 cups ice cream mix. Repeat layering ¾ cup crumble and 2 cups ice cream finishing with ice cream. Freeze for 6–8 hours.

One hour before serving, carefully release spring-form tin. Mark surface of cake into slices. Decorate with strawberries and kiwi fruit. Freeze for 1 hour.

Pour over cherry brandy and serve immediately.

Step 1 Combine almonds, chocolate cake mix, butter, eggs and milk

Step 2 Fold together egg yolks, melted chocolate, confectioners' sugar, drinking chocolate and cream

Step 3 Layer cake and ice cream mixtures in spring-form tin

Cinnamon Shortbread

2 cups all-purpose flour
½ cup confectioners' sugar
½ teaspoon cream of tartar
½ teaspoon bicarbonate of soda
1 teaspoon ground cinnamon
½ cup melted butter
1 egg
milk to mix if required
¼ cup superfine sugar
¼ cup crushed hazelnuts

Time: 17½ minutes. Makes about 48

Combine flour, confectioners' sugar, cream of tartar, bicarbonate of soda and cinnamon in mixing bowl. Blend in butter and egg to form soft cookie dough. If dough is too dry, add small quantity of milk and knead into dough.

Divide dough into 5 portions. Shape each portion into 9 inch roll on wax paper. Place wax paper and dough on microwave baking sheet. Press down dough. Sprinkle with crushed hazelnuts and sugar.

Cook each roll on medium for 3–3½ minutes. Remove from oven. When cool, slice each portion into 1 inch wide strips. Cool completely and store in airtight container between layers of waxed paper.

Cinnamon Shortbread: **Step 1** Mix together melted butter and dry ingredients

Step 2 Shape dough into 9 inch long rolls

Rocky Road

12 oz cooking chocolate
1 tablespoon butter
2 eggs
1¼ cups sifted confectioners'
    sugar
1½ teaspoons vanilla extract
1½ cups roasted peanuts
1 cup coconut
2 cups marshmallows

Time: 3 minutes

Cook chocolate and butter on high 2–3 minutes or until soft. Beat eggs, sugar and vanilla until sugar dissolves. Blend in peanuts, coconut and chocolate mixture. Fold in marshmallows. Pour into oblong dish to set. Cut into serving pieces.

Step 3 Sprinkle with crushed hazelnuts and sugar before cooking.

Hot Mocha Chocolate

½ cup cocoa
¼ cup instant coffee
4–6 teaspoons coffee sugar
4 cups hot water
whipped cream
chocolate curls

Time: 6–8 minutes. Serves

Combine coffee, cocoa and coffee sugar. Heat water jug on high for 6–8 minutes until almost boiling. Stir coffee mixture.

Pour into serving cups, top with whipped cream a chocolate curls and serve.

Chocolate Thick Shake

3 scoops chocolate ice cream
3 tablespoons milk
2 tablespoons chocolate syrup
4 whole marshmallows
2 tablespoons whipped cream

Time: 1 minute. Serves 2

Place all ingredients into a large glass or jug. Cook on medium 1 minute, stirring twice during cooking. Top with whipped cream.

Hot Mocha Chocolate with Cinnamon Shortbrec

298

Index

(1) Indicates recipe for one.